Contents

TRANSITIONS AND THE LIFECOURSE

Challenging the constructions of 'growing old'

Amanda Grenier

**LEARNING
RESOURCES
CENTRE**

First published in Great Britain in 2012 by

The Policy Press
University of Bristol
Fourth Floor
Beacon House
Queen's Road
Bristol BS8 1QU
UK
t: +44 (0)117 331 4054
f: +44 (0)117 331 4093
tpp-info@bristol.ac.uk
www.policypress.co.uk

North American office:
The Policy Press
c/o The University of Chicago Press
1427 East 60th Street
Chicago, IL 60637, USA
t: +1 773 702 7700
f: +1 773-702-9756
sales@press.uchicago.edu
www.press.uchicago.edu

© The Policy Press 2012

British Library Cataloguing in Publication Data
A catalogue record for this book is available from the British Library.

Library of Congress Cataloging-in-Publication Data
A catalog record for this book has been requested.

ISBN 978 1 84742 691 8 paperback
ISBN 978 1 84742 692 5 hardcover

Cover design by The Policy Press.
Front cover: image kindly supplied by Getty images.
Printed and bound in Great Britain by Hobbs, Southampton.
The Policy Press uses environmentally responsible print partners.

To James

About the author

Amanda Grenier is Associate Professor in the Department of Health, Aging, and Society at McMaster University, Canada. She holds the Gilbrea Chair on Aging and Mental Health, and is Director of the Gilbrea Centre for Studies in Aging. She is also affiliated with the Centre for Research and Expertise in Social Gerontology at the Centre de santé et de services sociaux (CSSS) Cavendish, Montreal, Canada and with McGill University School of Social Work, and is Honorary Research Fellow at the Institute for Life Course Studies at Keele University, UK. Her research focuses on the intersections of policy, organisational practice and lived experience in relation to ageing, frailty and care.

Acknowledgements

This book is based on findings from a Social Sciences and Humanities Research Council Standard Grant on Late Life Transitions. Additional support was received from the Leverhulme Foundation (UK), the International Opportunities Fund of the Social Sciences and Humanities Research Council (Canada), and the Centre de recherche et d'expertise en gérontologie sociale (CREGES).

I am thankful for the support and feedback of my colleagues and students, and grateful for the stories older people have shared with me and my research team. Thank you to everyone at the Centre for Social Gerontology at Keele University for providing me with a place to think and write during my sabbatical, and to my past and present colleagues who have guided me since my doctoral and post-doc days. A special thank you to Chris Phillipson and Simon Biggs for their comments on earlier chapters and for ongoing discussions. Any errors or omissions are clearly mine. Thank you to my doctoral students, Emilie Raymond, Marjorie Silverman, Ilyan Ferrer and Victoria Burns for their critical questions and feedback on an earlier draft; my research team, Lee Airton, Megan Harvey, Lisa Trimble and Ilyan Ferrer, for their commitment to collecting and understanding the stories (and a bit of fun squeezed between); my research assistants Elham Bidgoli, Sarina Isenberg and Markie Ryckman for their assistance in the preparation of the manuscript; my new colleagues at McMaster for the much-needed time to complete the final revisions; and my furry writing companions Olive and Lewis. I am indebted to Judith Phillips, Emily Watt, Laura Greaves and the staff at The Policy Press for their encouragement and editorial support. Finally, I am grateful to my family and friends who have supported me throughout the writing process. James, I could not have completed this project without your love and support. Thank you.

Foreword

Judith Phillips

This book captures the essence of the 'Ageing and the Lifecourse' series, based on critical gerontology and lifecourse perspectives. Drawing on US and European literature it provides a refreshing, topical and challenging approach to the dominant models of later life, and by highlighting the increasing diversity in experience and changing social context it gives an opportunity to rethink the notion of transitions in later life. It sets out a framework for looking at the changing understandings and concepts of later life and has considerable relevance for appropriate policy and practice responses.

Transitions are fundamental to our experiences across the lifecourse, particularly in later life. As the book highlights, there are various underlying tensions in arriving at a common interdisciplinary definition of 'transition': whether it has fixed stages or is a fluid process, is about continuity or change, and the tension inherent when viewing transitions within normative age- and stage-based assumptions.

For many, a fixed view of change into decline in older age is a one-way street of service provision; but Grenier challenges this, putting forward fresh models for rethinking transitions in later life that call for a more flexible approach, and one that does not stigmatise those who do not fall within the concept of successful or healthy ageing. Her analysis is based on a review of theory, policy and practice and centrally incorporates older people's voices. The contemporary context in which ageing occurs and the increasing diversity of the ageing experience along with the attention to subjectivity has challenged our notions of transitions and can enable policy and practice to move forward with more flexible arrangements.

Students and academic scholars in gerontology, professionals in social work and social care practice and policy makers who base their actions on their understandings of change and transition in later life will be attracted to this text.

Part One
The context of growing old

ONE

The study of transition in late life

This book is about reconsidering how we understand and approach late life transitions as scholars, members of society and individuals. Transitions between events and experiences are threaded throughout the lifecourse and into late life. But the pathways through them are not always as straightforward or predictable as depicted in standard models. Some transitions are achieved with ease; others are more difficult, with the meanings of each varying according to context, expectations and circumstances. The models by which we understand and make sense of our lifecourse and our ageing exist and are enacted through socio-cultural, relational and personal processes. Yet, these models and the various ideals about ageing and the lifecourse are themselves shifting. What it means to age has changed in the contemporary context, with scholars and older people alike questioning and challenging the constructions of 'growing old'.

This book takes a critical approach to reconsidering transitions in late life. It calls into question the assumptions about ageing and late life, including the models put forward by institutional and organisational practices. It focuses on the interface between academic understandings, socio-cultural discourses, public policy frameworks and lived experiences. Setting the narratives of older people against dominant understandings, it details the discrepancies that can exist between larger models and lived experience. It draws attention to how older people incorporate accepted notions of ageing into their experience, as well as develop innovative strategies to address late life concerns. As such, it points to extending understandings of transition from existing normative concepts of age and stage, into models that account for diverse and varied experiences that take place within and across socio-cultural contexts.

Ageing societies: changing contexts and transitions

In a contemporary context characterised by movement towards 'ageing societies', questions related to late-life transitions are key. The contemporary challenge of planning for 'ageing societies' has often been attributed to the shifting global demographic profile, with responses interpreted accordingly. The combined trends of declining fertility and mortality rates and increased migration have resulted in higher percentages of older people throughout most of the world, as well as greater diversity within the older population (United Nations, 2002a). However, the socio-cultural meanings and experiences of growing old that exist within and between these accounts often receive less attention, at least in public discourse. Yet, planning for ageing societies will require an assessment not only of the larger statistical trends, but also of the ways in which these changes alter the fabric of societies, social and interpersonal relations, and the meanings of the everyday experiences of growing old. Addressing this current imbalance is the work of critical scholars. Five intersecting issues may be considered in relation to transitions in late life. They include, but are not limited to, the following:

- the changing context of growing old characterised by demographic change and cultural transformations in medicine and technology;
- the increased importance and acknowledgement of subjective interpretations of ageing;
- the collapse of standard age or stage-based categories, based on experiences that differ from normative age-based expectations or particular timing of events;
- the growing tendency to emphasise lifestyle possibilities with less attention to the inherent socioeconomic bias of such approaches;
- the altered policy and service context of the mixed economy, whereby ongoing efforts are reducing the breadth of public programs based on economic rationale and biomedical and functional health criteria.

Together, these five factors form a complex backdrop from which to consider the question of transition in late life. As governments, social planners and policymakers reflect on contemporary realities and reconsider approaches to ageing and late life, models for late life and criteria for eligibility will continue to shift. For example, policies are currently changing the age of eligibility for social programmes such as retirement, as well as grappling with how best to address modern forms of labour force involvement including contract work, early or late retirement, and so forth. The implications of altered conceptualisations of age can greatly affect experience. While changes based on the rationale of healthier older people may seem positive, they may simultaneously overlook the specific needs of older people at marginalised locations. Further, lack of attention to the diversity that characterises contemporary experiences of ageing may fail to account for the differential impacts of locations such as advanced age, disability, gender, 'race' or ethnicity, socioeconomic status and sexual orientation. The contemporary context thus requires academics and policymakers alike to understand and address the transformations that are happening at social, cultural and experiential levels. It is in this context that the study of transition can provide a pathway toward new understandings of late life.

This chapter provides a brief context for the study of transition in relation to ageing and late life. It begins by sketching out the issues to be explored in detail throughout the book. It outlines the definition of transition, underlying assumptions, key issues and debates, and differentiates between terminology used in the field. It then situates the critical perspective, and sets the stage for a reconsideration of transition in relation to late life. Finally, it outlines the structure and content of the chapters of the book.

Underlying tensions in the study of transition

Transition became a central social science concept in the late 1970s and early 1980s, where attention turned to explaining the relationship between continuity and change across the lifecourse (Elder, 1975, 1978; Hareven, 1978a,b; Hareven and Adams, 1982). Used to delineate social categories, analyse social relations and mark social differences, the study of transition gained momentum and greatly influenced approaches to the lifecourse, ageing and late life. The study of transition in the social sciences covers a large body of scholarship and as a result contains several inherent tensions relevant to an analysis of late life. The popularity of the concept of transition, and in particular its explanatory power, was not, however, limited to academic circles. Transition and the lifecourse were also used in policy domain and organisational practices. As such, transition can be considered a meaningful concept that shapes understandings of ageing and late life on a discursive and practice level. Yet, the understandings and applications of transition vary across discipline and context, characterised by the following tensions: conceptualisations based on movement across fixed stages or fluid processes; multi- or interdisciplinary studies; a focus on macro-level social change or individual-level social processes; explanations based on continuity or change; and varying attempts to set age- and stage-based criteria. Together, these perspectives shape the study of transition providing a complex site for approaches to ageing and the interpretations of late life.

Fixed stages and fluid processes

Definitions of transitions contain an inherent tension between fixed stages and fluid processes. The literal definition of transition highlights underlying associations that are relevant to the study of ageing and the lifecourse. The Oxford English Dictionary (1989) provides several definitions of transition (n). At the broadest level, transition is 'A passing or passage from one condition, action, or (rarely) place, to another; change'. The definition also includes understandings of transition as a change 'from one quantized state to another' (Physics), to 'passage in thought, speech, or writing'; 'passage from one key to another, modulation' (Music) and 'the passage from an earlier to a later stage of development or formation' (Oxford English Dictionary, 1989). These definitions denote the centrality of passage and change, suggesting interpretations that range from movement between well-defined stages of development, to processes involving interval or intermediate stages. While the emphasis in the literal definition is one of change, there is an inherent tension in how change is understood. Change is depicted as both movement through fixed stages or conditions, and a fluid, more temporal reference to the process involved. Such subtle variations are perceptible in the social study of transition as it relates to ageing and the lifecourse. It is this tension between the fixed and the fluid that requires further attention in relation to what we know, understand and expect of late-life transitions – in particular, the extent to which fixedness or fluidity are assumed in dominant approaches to transitions in ageing and late life.

Multi- and interdisciplinary perspectives

The study of transitions across the lifecourse and in late life has been tackled through various disciplines, including anthropology, sociology and psychology, with unique aspects developed in relation to culture, society and individual development. In anthropology, the study of transition draws attention to the processes and cultural meanings of change, with transition most often conceptualised as a passage between status groups, roles or stages in Western and non-Western societies. In sociology, transition is conceptualised as a study of social change, focusing on trends and movement between norms, roles, or status groups in society. In psychology, the study of transition centres on adult development across the life span, including models for 'normal' development throughout life. Together, the contributions from each discipline have created a solid foundation for the study of transition in the social sciences, albeit from varying perspectives. Yet, although the differences between the strands have become increasingly blurred over time in applied contexts such as social policy or social gerontology, interpretations of transitions contain several differing perspectives on continuity and change. The study of transition is indeed multidisciplinary – comprised of many disciplines – rather than interdisciplinary, which refers to a process of collaboration between disciplines. With little collaboration between disciplinary approaches, shortcomings can be identified in each of the perspectives. A review of the emphasis and development of the study of transition in each of these three fields, as explored in Chapter Three, provides a useful starting point from which to link existing approaches and creates the space from which to consider transition as it relates to late life.

Individual experiences and social change

Studies of transition in multidisciplinary studies have taken place at the individual and social levels of experience. In most cases, the approaches taken maintain a binary division between studies of macro-level social change and micro-level or individual change. In the field of ageing studies, for example, transition is either used to refer to the shifting demographic composition of societies or the individual experiences of particular types of transition (retirement, widowhood). Although the distinction between the level of study reflects the multidisciplinary differences mentioned above, it also replicates a long-standing division within disciplines such as sociology, where scholars focus on either macro or micro levels of change. Intriguing, however, is that both the macro- and micro-level studies have resulted in standard fixed models of change that occur according to roles or norms at the social level, and stages at the individual level, rather than the fluid processes that are nuanced in the definition of transition. At the practical level, the dominant approaches to the social and individual have influenced assumptions about ageing and late life, and given precedence to standard models of change that occur over the lifecourse. With these models widely used, the unspoken assumptions, debates and tensions that result in applied fields such as policy or gerontology are rarely brought to light. Further consideration, however, can link understandings of the social with individual experiences in ways that move beyond fixed interpretations.

Continuity and change

Regardless of the level of study, however, is the inherent tension between continuity and change. The study of transitions and the lifecourse, and their application in gerontology and social policy, reveal an ongoing struggle between continuity and change. The study of transition is rooted in this tension, and, regardless of discipline, attempts to explain the extent to which societal or individual experiences can be characterised by consistency (continuity) or difference (change). Explanations tend not to focus on how experiences of transition may be considered in relation to both continuity and change. In this regards, late life presents a further challenge: whether experiences of continuity and change are seen to occur across the lifecourse or are segmented into the period of late life. Where concepts such as the lifecourse are intended to take account of ageing as a lifelong process, the practical studies of the lifecourse often fail to incorporate ageing and late life into their analysis. Similarly, studies of ageing and late life tend to isolate the roles, experiences or events that occur in a particular portion of the lifecourse. The majority of studies of the lifecourse (Elder, 1975, 1978; Hareven, 1978b; Hareven and Adams, 1982) tend to operate separately from the works of scholars interested in social gerontology and the transitions experienced in late life (see Walker, 1980; Townsend, 1981; Ferraro, 1984; Martin-Matthews, 1991; Chambers, 2000; Phillipson, 2002, 2004). There is thus, little consistency with regard to the study of transitions, late life and the lifecourse. This book attempts to correct this imbalance by exploring the fundamental relationship between continuity and change that exists in relations to transitions, ageing and late life.

Age- and stage-based criteria

Despite tensions between continuity and change in scholarly work, the idea that late life is characterised by change is firmly embedded in socio-cultural and organisational practices of policy, programming and service. Transition is often used to delineate the boundaries of experience according to age- or stage-based expectations across the lifecourse. Scholars and policymakers alike employ the concept of transition as a framework around which to organise population groups and target service needs. As a result, the notion of transition as change underlies most policies and services in late life. For example, at the root of retirement policies and health and social care services is the idea that advanced age brings about a change related to productivity or health status that can affect involvement in the labour force, and thus requires alternate means of financial compensation or specialised services. On a practical level, transitions are primarily demarcated by ages or stages of eligibility for social programmes. Take, for example, the Quebec homecare tax credit where age-based eligibility is 70, or the classic example of eligibility for federal pensions that occurs at age 65. Yet, although deeply embedded in socio-cultural contexts and practices, the impact that understandings of transition as change has on the expectations of ageing and late life is seldom critically appraised. Grounded in critical gerontology and the lifecourse perspective, this book explores how marking late life according to expected periods of change and subsequently establishing social and practical responses based on these corresponding categorisations is problematic.

Transitional terms: lifecycle, life span, lifecourse and late life

Moving forward with a reconsideration of transition in relation to late life requires that the differences used to speak of ageing and late life be clarified. Three notions connected to the study of transition as it relates to age are the lifecycle, the life span and the lifecourse. Developed primarily in social and developmental psychology, the first term, the lifecycle (see Erikson, 1959; Levinson and Darrow, 1978; Levinson, 1986), refers to models that depict stages of maturation and development. Somewhat confusing is that the concept is also used to denote the cyclical nature of life and rebirth, although this definition is less commonly used in Western scholarship (see Spencer, 1990). Second, the concept of the life span, used predominantly in psychology, and specifically the sub-discipline of life-span psychology (see Baltes, 1987a, 1987b), outlines the nature and timing of developmental tasks. Third, the popular term 'the lifecourse' is used to refer to an overall trajectory across the entire period of one's life (Clausen, 1986; Elder et al, 2003). Rooted in the sociological perspective, the lifecourse is intended to capture the fluid and changing aspects of experience.

The differences between these concepts point to the debates that exist in the study of transition with regard to ageing and late life. The life span is a specific term used primarily to refer to psychological development, and is therefore limited where interdisciplinary discussions of transition are concerned. The lifecycle implies continuity and regeneration, and has been applied in social and developmental models. However, as in the case of the life span, the lifecycle tends to denote boundaries according to stages. Of the three, the lifecourse is the broadest, and can be used to denote a fluid path with opportunities for change and development. Although this term has shortcomings relating to its association with a specific development in sociology, its overtones of an inherent linear structure and a dominant scholarship that has tended to overlook the specificities of late life is the most familiar concept in the field of ageing. It is also a concept that, at least in principle, can be used to situate older people's experiences over the duration of a lifetime. In this book, the terms lifecycle, life span and lifecourse are used according to these traditions, with preference given to the notion of the lifecourse as a means to link the trajectory of life. In this sense, the 'lifecourse' provides the context and frame required to understand continuity and change. Chapter Two explores the approaches to the study of the lifecourse in more detail in order to highlight the benefits and drawbacks in relation to transition and ageing.

The term late life is a more recent development in the discussions of ageing and transition. Rooted in the lifecourse perspective, 'late life' draws attention to the later parts of the lifecourse that tend to be overlooked in research on transitions and the lifecourse. In general, it references a large relatively unspecified period of life that may be comparable to that implied by the process-based statement 'growing old'. Utilising late life is intended to avoid specific age- or stage-based generalisations. However, while the strength of the term 'late life' is its inclusiveness, its weakness is that it can be unspecific. To date, it has been used in a variety of ways, including to refer to persons aged 50 overlooked by models of adult development; older people as defined by eligibility for social benefits at 65+; and those in the 'fourth age', with its connotation of decline. A further complication is that the term late life does not permit the population-based focus that is often required in a policy context. As such, in order to situate the group of older people including those in the fourth age, and to avoid the pitfalls of being overly vague, the concept of 'late life' is interchanged with older persons throughout the book.

This book suggests using the terminology of transition and late life in a new and distinct way. For specificity, the use of transition will be accompanied by the qualifying terms of 'as it applies to ageing' or 'in late life'. As such, it places emphasis on the socially constructed nature of transitions, ageing and late life. In doing so, an explicit attempt is made to move the discussions of transition as they relate to age and late life away from normative age- and stage-based assumptions into more fluid understandings of experience over time. Yet, while called into question, notions of age are not abandoned entirely because, as socially and culturally constructed concepts, they structure relationships and influence socio-cultural expectations and responses (Hendricks and Hendricks, 1977; Gubrium and Holstein, 1998, 2000; Hendricks, 2004). Consider for example, retirement, changes in the body and loss, which all tend to be associated with late life. The position taken throughout the book is that structured locations, socially constructed concepts and socio-cultural responses, affect and influence meanings and interpretations of transitions in late life. Reconsidering the definition, uses and applications of transition has much to offer an understanding of ageing and late life.

Contemporary challenges: key concepts and debates in gerontology

Shifting boundaries and expectations

The boundaries and expectations of transitions throughout the lifecourse and in late life are changing. In gerontology and policy, transitions tend to be understood in relation to relatively fixed social roles, age-based or social stages, or marked types of experiences. Typical understandings of transitions across the lifecourse are derived from the stages of development, with childhood, middle age and late life marking expected stages, and roles defined in relation to family, work and society. In most cases, the accepted models of transition are assumed to be generic and fixed across the lifecourse (Schlossberg et al, 1995), with late life rarely taken into account (Hendricks, 2003). Models that do address adult ageing, however, tend to focus on specific types of transition that occur between well-defined stages such as retirement, grandparenthood or widowhood (see Levinson and Darrow, 1978; Erikson, 1982; Levinson, 1986). In social gerontology, late-life transitions have historically been explained in a variety of ways, such as movements between roles (Burgess, 1960); being active (Havinghurst, 1963) and disengaged (Cumming and Henry, 1961); or simply 'becoming' an older person. Whether in the broad study of transitions or that of social gerontology, dominant approaches to transition assume that movement takes place across a stable backdrop, of age- and stage-based expectations (Danish et al, 1980; Atchley, 1999). There is little flexibility between set points, and dominant models tend to assume a discrete point of entry and exit. It is these predominantly fixed frameworks for understanding late-life transitions that are translated into policies and programmes for older persons, and sketch the boundaries within which transitions are expected to occur.

Altered contemporary conditions

However, shifting contemporary conditions and new theoretical perspectives mean that generic models of transitions can be challenged on several fronts. At present, the timing of standard expectations of transitions that take place in relation to labour and the family are increasingly blurred. For example, entry and exit to and from the labour force can vary as a result of 'delayed' entry into the workforce, or early exit, as in the case of early retirement. Similarly, the time at which one enters and exits 'typical' family roles is not easily standardised across situations, contexts and families. This variability may affect the types of transition experienced, the success of moving through transitions, and the meaning derived from them. Drawing on the critical literature in gerontology, these shifting contemporary conditions mean that standard norm-based transitions can be questioned in relation to age (Featherstone and Hepworth, 1989; Featherstone and Wernick, 1995; Blaikie, 1999; Gilleard and Higgs, 2000); diversity (Dannefer, 1989, 1996, 2003; Blakemore and Boneham, 1994); the complex relationships between body, psychological, social and cultural aspects of ageing over time (Cole, 1992; Dannefer, 1996; Estes et al, 2003; Katz, 2005); and the geographical context within which the transitions occur.

Growing attention to subjectivity

Increased attention to subjective interpretations of late life and the negotiation of experience also call proposed models of ageing and the lifecourse into question.

In several domains, accounts from older people highlight how lived experiences can vary from, or clash with, dominant understandings of ageing and late life. These include challenges to standard concepts of age (Kerner Furman, 1997; Bytheway, 2005; Twigg, 2006), dependency (Walker, 1980; Phillipson, 1982) and models based on either success or vulnerability. Likewise, a focus on subjective experiences of particular transitions such as widowhood has demonstrated that experiences may differ from expectations, with some women feeling liberation rather than depression, for example (Chambers, 2000). Attention to the subjective interpretation of experience has underscored the role of perception in subjective wellbeing and quality of life (see Diener, 2009). More recently, emphasis has been placed on the ways that older people may negotiate or perform ageing and late life through identities or lifestyle choices (Jones, 2006) – a tendency that also seems to be visible in policy and practice. In a similar line of thinking, drawing on subjective insights can call into question knowledge and practice related to transitions, and in doing so, challenge dominant models and expectations.

Age, diversity and disadvantage

Ongoing challenges related to the study of transition and late life include accounting for age, diversity and cumulative disadvantage in relation to continuity and change. Issues of variation in the frameworks and expectations related to transitions and advanced age require attention. While authors have focused on the differentiation between the third and fourth age (Laslett, 1989), as well as questions of frailty and decline (Gullette, 1997, 2004; Grenier, 2007b), the majority of this work fails to connect these questions with more general understandings of transitions. With policies and practices reflecting an increasing polarisation of health and illness in late life, questions about advanced age as a major transition that shapes expectations and experiences must be asked. Further to this is the increased recognition of diversity, and the impact social locations may have on transitions and the experiences of late life. For example, scholars in social gerontology should begin to more carefully consider how social locations can affect the type, timing and experience of transitions, including whether those proposed are indeed relevant to varying locations. Finally, the issue of cumulative disadvantage also requires more detailed attention in relation to transitions and late life. For example, how does disadvantage across the lifecourse, and in late life, affect the experience of continuity and change? Together, the breakdown of fixed and accepted forms of transition, accompanied by the greater recognition of diversity, and the acceptance of late life as negotiated terrain, represent significant contemporary challenges to be addressed in order to better respond to the needs of older people in ageing societies.

A critical perspective on ageing and late life

This book is rooted in a critical perspective concerned with the conceptual debates and practical approaches to transition and the lifecourse. A major aim is to combine an analysis of socio–cultural models and policy frameworks on ageing with lived experience (Gubrium, 1975; Cole and Gadow, 1986; Moody, 1995; Katz, 1996, 2005; Minkler and Estes, 1997; Phillipson, 1998; Gilleard and Higgs, 2000; Andersson, 2002; Estes et al, 2003; Victor, 2005; Bernard and Scharf, 2007). Critical perspectives on the study of ageing and late life view ageing as a process influenced by social, cultural and relational dimensions. A range of interconnected elements can be explored from this perspective: the dominant frameworks of transition in policy and public services; the impact of major social divisions and cumulative disadvantage on the experience of ageing; the social and cultural construction of the process of ageing and transition; discrepancies between structured and lived experience; and the perceptions of older people, as revealed in the narratives of the subjects themselves. Exploring these from a critical perspective aims to better understand the relationship between expected frameworks and interpretations of late life. This includes the types of transitions experienced, the 'fit' with current models and debates, and alternate pathways taken across the lifecourse and in late life. Approaching the study of transition from this perspective intends to develop a fresh understanding that takes late-life experience into account.

The approach taken throughout the book takes place at the interface of socio-cultural frameworks, public policies and the experiences of older people. It explores dominant interpretations of transitions and macro-level notions of ageing that may contribute to, or alter, expectations and experiences in relation to late life. Critical perspectives have long focused on the study of structures, experience and social change (Moody, 1995; Minkler and Estes, 1997; Phillipson, 1998; Estes et al, 2003); subjective experiences, meanings and cultural notions related to ageing in society (Gubrium, 1975; Cole and Gadow, 1986; Katz, 1996, 2005; Gilleard and Higgs, 2000); and considered the impacts of diverse social locations (Dannefer, 1988; Calasanti, 1996, 2009; McMullin, 2000, 2004; Torres, 2006b). This book draws on these strengths in order to question taken-for-granted practices and expectations related to transitions and late life. It makes explicit the dominant models of transition and underlying assumptions that operate in research and practice, comparing these with the experiences of older people from various social locations. The relationship between social policies, suggested models for growing old, and lived experiences at varying social locations is thus central to this reflection on transition in relation to late life.

An underlying premise of this book is that expectations about late-life transitions form models that influence socio-cultural constructs and lived experiences of older people. As such, changes in policy are important, not only because they are connected to the release of social expenditures, but that they also provide frameworks within which to 'grow old', and thus speak to the legitimacy of older people's experiences in the public domain (Biggs, 2001, 2004b; Hendricks, 2004).

Policy is both a response to, and an attempt to engineer, 'the problem of ageing', and a bridge between macro-social discourses and everyday experience (Leonard, 1997; Gubrium and Holstein, 2000). Understanding the relationship between suggested and experienced models becomes more important in a context where views of ageing and late life are rapidly transforming, and where governments are increasingly invested in reshaping expectations and approaches to ageing. A combined focus on the macro-level discourses and micro level narratives can thus help to explore how transitions experienced by older people may or may not correspond with the emerging policy picture. The accounts of older people may be consistent in some cases, but challenge or conflict with dominant understandings in others. For example, consider the questions of experiential 'fit' that take place at the crossroads of traditional dependency models for adult ageing and those based on new notions of productive ageing (see Katz and Green, 2002). The intersections between policy, institutional practices and lived experiences are thus central to a reconsideration of transition in late life.

Reconsidering transitions in late life

This book argues for a reconsideration of transition in relation to ageing and late life. Using the notion of transition as a point of departure, it draws together the concepts, frameworks and discourses used to understand and approach the lifecourse. In doing so, it highlights the contradictions, tensions and challenges that exist within current conceptualisations of late life. This includes attention to the ways in which suggested models available in policy and social planning efforts and older people's experiences may differ. It engages with the fixed and fluid notions of ageing and transition; the international and national discourses related to ageing; and the lived experiences of older people at varying social locations. Challenges taken up include: questioning fixed age and stage-based understandings of transitions; juxtaposing taken-for-granted assumptions with contemporary conditions and older people's experiences; and rethinking long-standing issues related to intersections of age, diversity and disadvantage. As such, the experiences of transitions in late life come to represent a contested terrain that is no longer adequately explained by dominant age- and stage-based models. Instead, a more flexible interpretation of late-life transitions is suggested, where older people's experiences can include both continuity and change, that may correspond with, or deviate from, expected models. Contrasting broad-level conceptualisation of ageing with local levels creates the space for a more realistic assessment of whether larger expectations surrounding healthy, successful and productive ageing are possible, and for whom. Flexible interpretations of experience that depict transition as a process rather than an achievement of fixed and normative stages reveals how more fluid interpretations of transitions may more closely align with the pathways experienced by older people.

Material is drawn from multidisciplinary academic sources in psychology, sociology, anthropology and the social sciences more broadly, and informed by research on social policy and narrative experiences in the domains of social gerontology and social care. In the case of policy and experience, research findings are used to inform conceptual interpretations of transitions in relation to ageing and the lifecourse. Examples discussed throughout the book originate from studies conducted on late-life transitions, and supplemented by research on public home care services in Quebec, the reform of health and social care services in Quebec and the UK, older women's narratives on frailty, and social networks. The illustrative cases discussed in the second part of the book are drawn from a research project entitled Late Life Transitions: Exploring the Fit Between Policy and Personal Experience,[1] which explored the various shapes of ageing promoted within policy frameworks and the narrative accounts of 60 older people in Montreal, Quebec, Canada. The project focused on identifying available models for ageing, and the degree of fit between proposed models and lived experiences, considering contemporary issues such as diverse social locations and advanced age – for example, how variations in social locations such as age, 'ability', gender, class, ethnicity, 'race' and socioeconomic status can inform or alter the continuous and discontinuous experiences across the lifecourse and into late life.

The debates and issues addressed are intended to inform approaches to ageing and late life in various international contexts. Set within the context of 'ageing societies', the conceptual and contemporary themes discussed in this book transcend international borders. Although based on experience in Canada and the UK, the debates resonate with discussions in gerontology and care that are taking place elsewhere. Although the details of the policies alluded to, such as retirement or healthcare, are often specific to country and region, there are increasing similarities in conceptual and practical approaches. The illustrations used serve to highlight larger conceptual issues, structured planning efforts and lived experience. As such, the book is aimed at academic scholars and graduate students in critical gerontology, policy studies in health and social care, and social work, who have some existing knowledge of gerontology and policy debates. Discussions are geared to those with an interest in the conceptual issues of transitions, social planning and social gerontology. It is hoped that readers will find that this book challenges their understandings of transitions as depicted in policies and practices, and raises questions about the extent to which objective representations match with subjective interpretations of age – in particular, the challenges to standard normative expectations that are raised by variations in diverse social locations including advanced age, divergent lifecourse patterns and geographic contexts.

Guiding questions

Questions addressed throughout the book include:

- How are transitions and the lifecourse understood in anthropological, sociological and psychological and social science literature? What models are available for ageing, transitions and late life? What are the key debates? How have these shifted across time?

- How do policy frameworks and socio-cultural discourses represent or construe late-life transitions? What policy frameworks are available? How have these shifted over time?
- How do older people frame transitions and the movement across the lifecourse? How do they define and understand their lifecourse transitions? What strategies, trends and innovations exist?
- What tensions, contradictions and points of resonance exist between suggested models and lived experience? To what extent do academic concepts and policy frameworks correspond with older people's lived experiences?
- How is diversity accommodated in the dominant understandings of transition and the lifecourse? What role do diverse social locations play across the lifecourse?
- Can existing theoretical and practical models adequately address the contemporary issues and challenges raised in this analysis? What insights may be gleaned from older people's diverse experiences?

Structure and chapter outline

The book is divided into two sections that reflect the distinction between what is known about transitions and the challenges to this knowledge. Part One sets the context for the study of transition in relation to ageing and the lifecourse. Part Two discusses the contemporary challenges of transition and the lifecourse. The book begins with an overview of the conceptual contributions to late life from the broad academic literatures of anthropology, sociology, psychology and the social sciences. It then moves on to consider public and social discourses as sources that shape knowledge and practice in relation to late life, highlighting how national and global policy frameworks present and construe ageing. In the second part, the analysis moves to a more local site of knowledge, drawing attention to strategies that older people use to make sense of transition and the lifecourse. Building on these issues, the second part of the book focuses on specific themes and contemporary challenges, in particular, rethinking transition in relation to key issues of diversity, the intersections of age and impairment and the challenges each raises to the accepted models of transition in late life.

Chapter Two outlines the theoretical underpinnings of the critical approach taken throughout the book. It discusses the premise for a perspective concerned with the intersections of theory, research, policy and experience at the macro and micro levels. It discusses the strengths and shortcomings of two approaches relevant to the study of transitions and ageing: the lifecourse perspective and critical gerontology. In doing so, it demonstrates how understanding transitions in late life requires attention to complex interactions of structures, constructs and experience. Drawing on the strengths of these perspectives, it suggests a pathway to a more complex understanding of transitions in late life.

Chapter Three provides a socio-historical context of the study of transition. It tracks prominent academic approaches in the social sciences, and outlines the key contributions of each. Reviewing multidisciplinary literature from anthropology, sociology, psychology and social gerontology, it renders visible the dominant and lesser known strands of thinking that have become deeply ingrained in understandings of late life, and that form a foundation for the knowledge and expertise on late life. It demonstrates how in drawing primarily on standard age- and stage-based concepts, social gerontology has overlooked important insights for understanding transitions in late life as more fluid or process-based experiences.

Chapter Four argues for an approach that considers the intersections of policy, practice and lived experience. It outlines a methodological perspective that draws on language and discourse in order to understand the interplay between policy frameworks, social cultural responses and older people's experiences. This includes breaking away from a consideration of standard rigid notions of age and stage, and into subjective pathways, the accumulation of structured experience, and diversity. For example, it provides space for the ways that older people may accept, negotiate and disrupt the dominant models of late life.

Turning from accepted academic understandings to cultural representations, Chapter Five explores key social and cultural strands that form suggested models for growing older in contemporary societies. It identifies dominant strands and competing influences in contemporary public policies on ageing as they relate to transition. Themes addressed within this chapter include the tension between success-based models and those focused on decline. While the immediate context is Western, illustrations from international, national and local policy frameworks highlight how such models are located within time, place and space. The chapter outlines how the shapes of ageing are relatively fixed into particular typologies that shape expectations of ageing and late life.

As mentioned earlier, Part Two focuses on contested models of transition that emerge from subjective experience. Chapters Six to Ten discuss insights and issues related to the contemporary challenges of ageing and the lifecourse, most importantly, how fixed concepts of transition fail to address the multifaceted ways people move in and out of transitions, as well as the fluid ways in which they exist within and between points in aging and late life. Older people may live in a cultural space where they may not abruptly move into defined periods, but rather take trajectories that represent both continuous and new pathways of experience. Here, the notion of liminality is used to shed light on current approaches.

Chapter Six outlines case illustrations that depict older people's interpretations of transition and late life. Organised according to typologies that correspond with dominant models of success or decline, and diverse social locations, illustrations provide insight into the complexities that transcend suggested models. The cases presented clearly illustrate a range of pathways through lifecourse transitions and demonstrate the extent to which older people's experiences may correspond or clash with fixed understandings. These include key turning points and difficult moments; the types of experiences recognised as transitions; themes of continuity and change; diversity; and age. As such, their experiences exemplify the ways in which older people may challenge the constructed models for transitions and growing old.

Chapter Seven identifies and discusses alternate and flexible interpretations of transition in relation to late life. Drawing on connections between the accounts of nine older people, this chapter reconsiders the forms of transition that have become commonplace in social science approaches to late-life transitions. Material is presented according to five intersecting themes that allow for a reconsideration of late life transitions: passage and liminality; multiple and intersecting forms of transition; events, social locations and identity; linked lives and relational notions of transition; and continuity, adaptation and cumulative disadvantage. Together, these interpretations provide evidence of just how the lifecourse may be more fluid or subjective than previously understood, and suggest fresh models of rethinking transition in late life.

Chapter Eight explores how difference rooted in social locations can affect the lives and accounts of older people across the lifecourse, and in particular in relation to late life. This chapter focuses on the unresolved issue of diversity. Drawing on illustrations presented in Chapter Six, this chapter highlights the extent to which accounts from diverse social locations correspond and conflict with the knowledge and expectations of transition and late life. It links the accounts from older people to the conceptual and theoretical debates on age and diversity, and draws on post-colonial interpretations of 'otherness' and 'liminality' to offer alternate interpretations. Together, the lessons learned move the analysis into a more complex reconsideration of diversity, transitions and the relations of age.

Chapter Nine explores how impairment in late life can affect the lives and experiences of older people, arguing that the intersections of impairment and advanced age represent a major challenge for the study of transitions as they relate to late life. This chapter problematises the assumptions and practices related to ageing and decline, including the polarisation of health and illness in age. It draws attention to the socio-cultural and emotional significance of this change, specifically, the significance of achieving continuity amid change, the liminality of 'being between', and the structured and interpretive nature of vulnerability across the lifecourse. Through these issues, the reader can begin to witness how older people with impairments in late life are located within and between dominant and alternative models of late-life transitions.

Finally, Chapter Ten draws together the arguments made in relation to the study of transition with the contested models of growing old. It explores the critical questions raised throughout the book and points to future directions that have emerged. Chapter Ten argues that transitions, as they are currently defined as fixed age- and stage- based categories, fail to address several contemporary issues of ageing, including the tension between structured and lived experience, balanced accounts of continuity and change across the lifecourse, diverse social locations of older people, and issues of advanced age.

Overall, this book suggests that a fresh understanding of transitions as turning points and moments characterised by a greater sense of liminality, rather than fixed age- and stage-based periods, may help to bring suggested models closer to lived experiences of ageing, and work toward addressing contemporary challenges such as diversity and advanced age. In sum, the chapters in this book comprise a critical reflection on the academic, social and cultural conceptions of age; personal and social understandings of lifecourse transitions; and the ways in which these understandings may guide and reflect public, social and personal responses to ageing. It is hoped that this reflection will inform current debates and provide a pathway towards new considerations and approaches to late life.

Note
[1] Grenier, A., Biggs, S., Manthorpe, J., Leonard, P. (2005–08) Late Life Transitions: Exploring the Fit Between Policy and Personal Experience, standard research grant of the Social Sciences and Humanities Research Council of Canada (SSHRC), Project no 410 2005 1928.

TWO

Critical perspectives on ageing and the lifecourse

The notions of transitions and the lifecourse are overdue for a critical analysis with regard to the study of ageing and late life. While the study of transitions and the lifecourse have made considerable contributions to social gerontology (Elder, 1974, 1982; Hareven, 1978a, 1978b; Rossi, 1980; Hareven and Adams, 1982; Cohen, 1987; Antonucci et al, 1996; Phillipson, 2004), the perspectives taken have resulted in a relatively defined approach to the study of the lifecourse that tends to remain unquestioned. This is particularly the case where fixed cohorts, age- and stage- based assumptions, and accompanying normative expectations are concerned. Reconsidering what has become taken for granted in relation to the lifecourse requires theoretical and methodological schemes capable of integrating varying interpretations and practices. An approach that draws attention to socio-cultural relations and constructions of ageing, combined with subjective interpretations from diverse social locations, can provide a fresh perspective from which to reconsider transitions as they relate to ageing and late life. Drawing on a critical perspective as such highlights the constructed nature of the lifecourse, and the models and expectations within which people age, as well as the strategies used to negotiate transition and life in general.

This chapter outlines the theoretical underpinnings and the analytic foundations of the critical approach taken throughout this book. To do so, it explores critical approaches to the study of ageing and the lifecourse perspective, reviewing each separately in order to highlight strengths and shortcomings. First, it provides an overview of critical gerontology and critical perspectives to the study of ageing and late life that anchor the analysis. It discusses relevant insights and pitfalls from the field, and details how critical gerontology may be used to explore transitions in late life. Second, it outlines prevalent approaches to the study of the lifecourse, and in particular, the lifecourse perspective. Reviewing this, it delineates the contributions and limitations of this approach and draws attention to the less prominent constructivist interpretations of the lifecourse. Third, it suggests a critical perspective on the study of ageing and the lifecourse that can guide a reconsideration of transitions in relation to ageing and late life.

Critical perspectives and the lifecourse

Many approaches to the study of transitions and ageing claim to be anchored in the lifecourse – a concept that has become fundamental to the study of continuity, change and transition. Three converging issues explain this tendency. First, the concept of transition is anchored conceptually in the lifecourse, resulting in a coupling of the terms transitions and the lifecourse. Second, the study of transition and the lifecourse has become a prominent approach to understanding social change over time, particularly in the disciplines of sociology and social psychology. Third, a view emerged in the social gerontology of the 1980s and 1990s that ageing should be conceptualised as a process across the span of a lifetime rather than as a separate or distinct period. While embedding late life in the context of an entire life represents a more complex understanding of older people's lives, this idea has become deeply entrenched in social gerontology without acknowledging the inherent challenges. Taking a lifecourse perspective can mean that the extent to which approaches sustain age- and stage-based interpretations or ignore late life is overlooked. An important quandary that takes place at the intersections of research, policy, expectations and experience thus remains unaddressed.

In research and practice, there is an ongoing tension between late life as a part of an entire lifecourse, and age as a separate period characterised by distinct biological, psychological, social and cultural issues. The strain between views of a lifecourse process and a distinct period are in part structured through practices whereby chronological age, or the construct of 'being old', is central to eligibility criteria. For example, one must reach retirement age in order to receive pension benefits. In these cases, the age- and stage-based criteria are central to the constructions of experience and expectations. At the same time, the process of accumulated experience across a lifecourse is also integral to understanding late life. Yet, the consideration of ageing as a lifelong process and a separate period are differently constructed depending on the issue, with circumstances such as material disadvantage often understood to occur across a lifecourse (Walker 2005a, 2006a, 2006b; Baars et al, 2006), and others such as decline seen to occur in late life (Laslett, 1989). This tension between age as a continuation of the lifecourse and a separate or different period of life is central to rethinking approaches to transition in late life. The transitions related to ageing exist in these complex locations between lifelong processes and the specificities of late life.

A critical perspective was chosen for this analysis in order to link understandings of ageing in society with social relations, cultural contexts, and, more important, the relationships between structures, constructs, expectations and experiences. Critical perspectives have played a vital role in outlining the lifelong effects that accrue in late life. Yet, the meaning and practice of contextualising ageing in the context of the lifecourse must be questioned, and distinguished from what has become a prominent method in social studies, especially in the United States – the lifecourse perspective. Although a great deal of the work in social gerontology claims to ground analysis in the lifecourse, contextualising an individual's experiences in the context of their life differs from what has come to be known as 'the lifecourse perspective' (see Elder, 1985, 1994). The uncoupling of these terms and practices can provide a greater specificity of what is meant by the lifecourse, and create the space to bridge understandings of structural inequalities, socio–cultural constructs and the subjective interpretations that alter everyday experiences of late life.

The lifecourse is a general concept used to refer to a holistic view of life, with studies of the lifecourse the domain of varying multi- and interdisciplinary efforts (see Clausen, 1986). The lifecourse perspective, while certainly linked to the lifecourse, denotes a specific methodological approach developed by authors such as Elder (1994), and George (1993). The plethora of studies from a lifecourse perspective means that approaches highlighting the constructed nature of the lifecourse (Holstein and Gubrium, 2000) or negotiated identities across the lifecourse (Hockey and James, 2003), for example, represent less prominent strands in the study of the lifecourse. This includes approaches taken in Europe that integrate structural features into lifecourse research (see Dannefer and Settersen, 2010). However, critical gerontological and constructivist interpretations of the lifecourse and the lifecourse perspective each provide insights that are important to the reconsideration of transition as it relates to ageing and late life. Yet, in order to better understand the suggestions being put forward, the frame of reference must be made more explicit. In this analysis, drawing on a critical perspective on ageing provides the conceptual groundwork for the analysis. The concept of the lifecourse is used to refer to a fluid and interpretive process that occurs throughout the period of one's life that ultimately forms the context for lived experience.

A critical perspective on ageing and the lifecourse offers a pathway to reconsider the study of transitions in late life. However, while both critical gerontology and the study of the lifecourse are relevant to the study of transitions, their focal points have differed. Critical gerontology has concentrated on the study of structural and lived experiences of ageing, questioning taken-for-granted assumptions and practices and the inequities that exist within society (Estes, 1979; Guillemard, 1980; Walker 1980, 1981, 1982; Phillipson, 1982). Lifecourse studies, and the lifecourse perspective, have detailed various types of transitions, often drawing on trends and comparisons of groups and cohorts. Yet, the study of age-related transitions is not always contextualised in the lifecourse, or approached via lifecourse research. Further, the study of transition from a lifecourse perspective often overlooks late life, the structured issues of ageing, and, most important, the intersections that occur between policy, practice and lived experience. Insights from a critical perspective on ageing and the lifecourse, in particular when considered from a constructivist perspective, can take account of macro and micro elements, including the complex interactions of socio-cultural and psychological change. As such, the analysis put forward in this book is concerned with two conceptual tensions relevant to the examination of transition in late life: integrating the macro and micro levels in ways that account for the interplay between the two, and balancing a view of life as a whole with the specificities of socio-cultural relations and expectations that are associated with old age.

Critical perspectives on ageing and late life

Drawn together from various disciplines and across different geographic spaces, there exist several interpretations of critical perspectives to the study of ageing. These critical perspectives encompass approaches known as critical gerontology, and humanistic and cultural gerontology. Although grounded in differing theoretical traditions, critical perspectives are linked through a series of approaches concerned with research, policy and practice; a balancing of socio-cultural issues and individual experiences; and, in many cases, a desire for social change (Moody, 1992, 1995; Minkler and Estes, 1997; Phillipson, 1998; Estes, 2001; Biggs et al, 2003; Estes et al, 2003; Bernard and Scharf, 2007). In general, critical perspectives view ageing as a process influenced by social, cultural and relational dimensions, inequalities in relation to ageing, and questioning taken-for-granted assumptions. Scholars working from critical perspectives are particularly concerned with the ways in which research and social policies affect the lives of older people, focusing on both the societies within which ageing occurs, as well as how societies affect individual experiences of ageing (Sheets et al, 2005).

Brief historical development of critical perspectives on ageing

Critical perspectives in ageing are historically connected to an analysis of social policy and experience. Critical gerontology emerged in the 1980s as a challenge to the theories and approaches being applied to ageing and practice, namely normative approaches rooted in structural functionalism (Estes, 1979; Guillemard, 1980; Walker, 1981, 1982; Phillipson, 1982). Dating back 30 years, scholars in the United Kingdom and the United States turned their efforts towards the ways in which social policies structured the experiences of old age through key works on family and poverty in late life (Townsend, 1981), structured dependency (Walker, 1982; Phillipson and Walker, 1987) and the biomedicalisation of ageing (Estes and Binney, 1989). According to Estes and colleagues (2003, p 2), five major concerns relating to the study of old age led to the formation of critical gerontology as a field in the 1980s and 1990s: the need for a clearer understanding of the 'social construction of dependency' in old age made necessary by the development of welfare state services; the financial impoverishment of a large section of the elderly; ageism, or the systematic stereotyping of older people; the dominance of a biomedical model that construes age with decline and illness; and the individual focus of the field of gerontology that paid insufficient attention to social stratification and other aspects of socioeconomic structures. As critical gerontology developed, two differing strands of thought and analysis became evident, one leaning more towards an analysis of structural components and the other towards more humanistic dimensions (Bengston et al, 1997; Moody, 1988, 1993). In many cases, these may be distinguished conceptually, with the former referred to as the political economy perspective or critical gerontology, and the latter as humanistic, cultural or moral gerontology. Although there remains an

—

inclination in some scholarship to differentiate between the two traditions, there is a growing tendency to combine insights on structured conditions with lived experience in order to better understand the complexities of ageing. It is this tendency that is developed in this book. The following sections will review the strengths of each strand before bringing them together to guide the analysis.

Political economy

Critical perspectives rooted in the political economy perspective offer a robust critique of structured relations and economic disadvantage that can be experienced in late life. Scholarship based on the political economy perspective (see Estes, 1979; Guillemard, 1980; Walker, 1981, 1982; Phillipson, 1982) focuses on the political and economic roots of social structures, power arrangements and inequalities (Estes et al, 2003). In particular, it looks at the structural constraints on the freedom and agency of older people within society. This strand continues to centre on structured inequalities that are created and sustained through social relations and practices related to late life. The following quote from Walker (2005c) highlights the role political economy has, and continues to play, in advancing knowledge of social issues in ageing:

> Political economy theory pointed to the structural constraints on agency, including the role of social policies in opening up or closing down opportunities for older people. It continues to emphasize the central role of the lifecourse, both in structuring these opportunities and in analyses of their outcomes in old age. (p 816)

As a whole, political economy has made major contributions to uncovering the inequalities that occur in late life, in particular those that result from a lifetime of cumulative disadvantage. As such, approaches influenced by political economy can be used to highlight that while disadvantage can be understood to occur across the lifecourse, these differences may become more pronounced in late life, thereby influencing the type and experiences of transitions.

Humanistic perspectives

Approaches drawing on humanistic and cultural traditions question taken-for-granted assumptions and offer insight into the interpretive and cultural aspects of ageing and growing old. Occasionally referred to as the moral economy perspective, culture, experience and interpretation are central to the approaches taken in this line of thinking. According to Estes and colleagues (2003), cultural and humanistic approaches move beyond economics as the 'sole determinant in explaining social institutions such as the state and old age policy' and into social and cultural representations of age, including subjective interpretations of experience (p 21). Humanistic and cultural gerontology are concerned with the ways in which cultural understandings of age and the ageing process affect the meanings, interpretations, experiences and identities of older people (Cole, 1992; Cole et al, 1993; Featherstone and Wernick, 1995; Katz, 1996, 2005; Gullette, 1997, 2004; Blaikie, 1999; Woodard, 1999, 2003; Gilleard and Higgs, 2000; Andersson, 2002; Gubrium and Holstein, 2003; Baars et al, 2006). In particular, this approach focuses on subjectively constructed experience within a wider context, as approached through questions such as the now classic 'What does it mean to grow old in Western society?' (Cole and Gadow, 1986). In this strand, attention has been devoted to the development of gerontology as a discipline (Achenbaum, 1995; Katz, 1996); institutional and organisational practices (Gubrium, 1975; Hendricks, 2004; Grenier, 2005; 2007a); youth culture, consumption and lifestyle (Gullette, 1997; Woodward 1999; 2003; Gilleard and Higgs, 2000; Katz, 2005); and identity and biographical experience (Biggs, 1997, 1999; Chamberlayne et al, 2000; R. Ray, 2000, 2007; Bornat, 2001). In this line of thinking, cultural or humanistic gerontology joins individual or micro-level understandings with socio-cultural perspectives in order to better understand ageing and late life, drawing specific attention to the subjective or interpretive aspects of experience. Such perspectives can provide insight into the meanings and socio-cultural expectations that accompany transitions in late life.

Stable and shifting dimensions of critical perspectives

Critical perspectives have enhanced understandings of ageing from a social perspective and built a strong tradition of scholarship around the conceptual and theoretical issues related to age and growing old (Moody, 1995; Phillipson, 1998; Estes et al, 2003; Bernard and Scharf, 2007). Despite differences among the approaches, insights gleaned over time demonstrate that critical perspectives on ageing have held three stable commitments. First, the approaches taken represent a project that is committed to understanding and questioning social, cultural and personal relations and experiences of ageing. Second, the focus on power relations exposes and challenges inequality and social conflict. Third, in many cases, critical perspectives focus on drawing attention to socio-cultural challenges, and advocating for altered conditions and change. As Phillipson and Walker (1987) outlined in their early work, critical gerontology holds 'a commitment not to just understand the social construction of aging, but to change it' (p 12). Developed as a progressive perspective, it has drawn attention to power and powerlessness, as well as cast an eye towards the study of ageing itself in order to build theoretical scholarship. To this day, critical perspectives offer a reflexive base from which to analyse transitions as they relate to ageing and late life.

At the same time, critical approaches face a number of theoretical and practical challenges, some of which originate from the aforementioned theoretical roots of the approaches taken. Early work in the critical tradition was subjected to criticism for its overemphasis on class, which tended to overlook gender, ethnicity and 'race'. Further, critical gerontologists working in the humanistic stream claimed that structural perspectives such as the political economy of ageing deprive older people of their agency, leaving no possibility for resistance against an oppressive social system (Walker, 2005b). Likewise, approaches focused on social, cultural or individual interpretations have been criticised for their neglect of social structures and inequality. The field, however, has started to shift and attempts to bridge perspectives are surfacing. Similar to theoretical trends in the social sciences, critical gerontology has initiated an increased recognition of diversity (for example, Arber and Ginn, 1995; Yu, 2000; Ginn, 2003; Nazroo et al, 2004; Estes, 2005, 2006; Torres, 2006a) and a changing social and cultural context. The integration of micro-level insights from cultural and humanistic gerontology have also helped to address the issue of agency (see Cole et al, 1993; Featherstone and Wernick, 1995; Katz, 1996, 2005; Gullette, 1997, 2004; Blaikie, 1999; Woodward, 1999, 2003; Gilleard and Higgs, 2000; Andersson, 2002; Gubrium and Holstein, 2003; Twigg, 2006, 2010), as have attention to narrative interpretation and subjective experience (R. Ray, 2000, 2007; Bornat, 2001). However, concerns related to diversity, subjects and structures, linking micro and macro perspectives, and inequalities remain (Grenier et al, 2010).

At present, critical scholars in the field of ageing are focused on questions of how to better understand the link between social issues, contemporary policies and practices, and the experiences of diverse groups of older people. While an applied element has always been central to critical perspectives, there are ongoing attempts to move closer to the everyday practices of professions, communities, and groups of older people, particularly in the context of the UK (see Bernard and Scharf, 2007). In practice, critical perspectives have exposed challenges relating to care and assessment practices (Gubrium, 1975; Kaufman and Becker, 1996; Means et al, 2003; Grenier, 2005, 2007a, 2007b; Phillips, 2006, 2007; Grenier and Hanley, 2007). Yet, the project of linking an analysis of policy, practice and experiences continues to represent a significant challenge. Boundaries are shifting, however, through examining how older people participate in their communities (M. Ray, 2007; Blair and Minkler, 2009); identifying the role of technology and the arts in relation to ageing and late life (Woodward, 1999); exploring ageing on local and international levels (Kreager and Schroder-Butterfill, 2004); and developing innovative methodologies for understanding late life experience (Baker and Wang, 2006; M. Ray, 2007) – all of which represent attempts to move understandings and practices closer to older people's lived realities. Rethinking transitions in relation to ageing and late life is one such location that requires a bridge between theoretical scholarship, social policy and lived experience. This includes consideration of how various structured and social locations such as diversity and advanced age may create more complex understandings of transitions and models of ageing in late life than those currently depicted in the literature.

Critical perspectives and the reconsideration of transitions in late life

Critical perspectives on the study of ageing provide a useful vantage point from which to reconsider transitions as they relate to late life. Following the path set out by critical perspectives in ageing[1], the aim is to address the interface between levels of academic discourse, public policy frameworks, organisational practices and lived experiences. Drawing attention to the connections between structural analysis, socio-cultural interpretations and subjective meanings, the theoretical approach taken throughout this book emphasises the interconnectedness of a range of variables:

- socio-cultural constructs on ageing that exist in policy frameworks and public services;
- the impact of major social divisions and cumulative disadvantage on the experience of ageing;
- the social construction of the process of ageing and transition;
- the perceptions of older people's experience revealed by the narratives of the subjects themselves; and
- discrepancies between structured and lived experience.

Critical perspectives to the study of ageing can be used to consider how interpretations and expectations about late life form models that can influence socio-cultural constructs and the lived experiences of older people (see Chapter Four). In relation to transitions and late life, critical gerontology suggests that ageing is a process that occurs throughout the lifecourse, and is in part socially structured and constructed through biomedical and socio-cultural practices related to the later part of the lifecourse. The prevalence of discourse on transitions in research and policy suggests that understandings of continuity and change comprise powerful models that guide expectations around health, productivity and decline that are organised differently in specific periods of the lifecourse. For example, transitions structure eligibility for service, as well as set expectations such as those of decline that are associated with the fourth age (see Laslett, 1989; Baltes and Smith, 1999, 2002). As explored in Chapter Four, the relationship between policy, society and experience plays a major role in guiding interpretations of age. Therefore, models of transition in late life, whether expressed in policy discourse, research or society, can be considered to influence the socio-cultural and personal expectations of ageing. Yet, the possible discrepancies between the experiences outlined in socio-cultural practices, dominant expectations, and older peoples everyday realities often remains unquestioned.

An analysis that is grounded in a critical perspective leads to exploring how the transitions outlined in macro-level policy or socio-cultural discourses may or may not correspond with older people's experience. These questions of 'fit' may be interrogated at two levels, the first related to changing contemporary conditions, and the second to subjective interpretations of age. Drawing attention to the structured experiences of ageing reveals that contemporary conditions may alter the factual details related to major transitions such as retirement. For example, the retirement age is subject to change – as contemporary debates in policy and practice indicate. At the same time, attention to the subjective experiences that accompany these structures is also telling. For example, although the age criterion is normally set at 65, older people may be subject to early retirement as a result of redundancy or business/factory closure; on the other hand, they may decide to continue working past retirement age (see Phillipson, 1998, 2004). In both cases, the actions taken would conflict with standardised interpretations of retirement as an age-based transition, as well as the expected time-based norms that accompany these changes. Contemporary conditions and the personal interpretations and motivations that surround practices such as retirement thus challenge fixed understandings of transitions. Yet, while the disjuncture between standard notions of transitions and contemporary conditions is most obvious in the example of retirement, where age eligibility at present is firmly noted (although the subject of much debate), differences between standards and experiences may indeed be more pronounced in relation to questions of advanced age and corresponding constructions of health, productivity and success. Exploring the forms of recognised transition through a critical lens can help to expose the discrepancies between standard expectations and lived experience in relation to late life. Having outlined the merits of critical perspectives to the study of ageing, the next section focuses on studies of the lifecourse that have come to represent a significant portion of scholarship on transitions, continuity and change.

The 'lifecourse perspective'

Approaches to the study of the lifecourse

As with critical gerontology, the lifecourse has been understood through a range of disciplines, but in particular sociology and psychology (see Clausen, 1986). The concept of the lifecourse is used to ground experience in the whole span of life, and has thus been cited as one of the most important analytical approaches in social gerontology today (Pescosolido, 2006; Settersten, 2006). In general, the lifecourse perspective is considered to incorporate a variety of approaches including age stratification, which relates the stratification of age cohorts to social structures over time (Riley, 1971; Riley et al, 1972); the personal and social forces shaping the lifecourse and development (Mills, 1959; Hareven, 1978a, 1978b; Elder, 1982, 1985; Hareven and Adams, 1982); developmental life stages as outlined within life-span psychology (Baltes, 1987a,b); and the cultural or intergenerational models of change (Kertzer and Keith, 1984). Encompassing such a vast scholarship, however, the lifecourse perspective can mean different things to different people. Over the years, the study of the lifecourse has been approached from socialisation, behavioural and adult development, and humanist and interpretive perspectives;

it has been used in studies drawing on a range of methods, including large-scale data sets and qualitative interviews.

Several attempts to clarify studies of the lifecourse exist. Dannefer and Setterson (2010) provide a useful distinction between a personological approach to the study of the lifecourse, primarily used in North America, and an institutional approach to the study of the lifecourse, largely used in Europe. While the geographical basis for such divisions is easily transgressed, the levels of distinction effectively identify two strands of thinking that are often confounded in references to the lifecourse. The personological approach, typified by Elder, is distinguished by its focus on explaining late-life outcomes for individuals and populations based on early lifecourse experiences (Dannefer and Setterson, 2010). Coined the 'lifecourse perspective' by Elder, this method has gained popularity in the social sciences as a means to theorise the lifecourse, especially in the context of the United States (Clausen, 1986; George, 1993). The institutional approach, on the other hand, focuses on the lifecourse as 'a social and political construct, often consisting of more or less explicitly defined age-graded stages that are reinforced in institutions created by social policy or legitimated by social and behavioural sciences' (Dannefer and Settersen, 2010, p 7). This approach, which takes accounts of structures and constructs, can be found in the works of Neugarten (1979a, 1979b), Kohli (1986a, 1986b), Kohli and Meyer, 1986), Mayer (1986), Hagestad (1990) and Settersen and Hagestad (1996). This book engages more closely with the understandings put forward in the institutional approach, and how interpretations of the lifecourse shape and guide ageing and late life. However, both the individual lifecourse studied by Elder, and the social and political constructs studied primarily in Europe, require detailed exploration for the contribution they make to understandings of transitions, ageing and late life. The distinction between personological and institutional approaches suggested by Dannefer and Setterson (2010) will be used in the next section in order to locate the study of the lifecourse.

Historical development of the lifecourse perspective

The personological approach

The emergence of the lifecourse perspective as exemplified in Elder's work represented a break from the traditions of socialisation and behavioural development that were dominant at the time. The ideas associated with the lifecourse perspective arose in the 1960s in the United States, prompted by C. Wright Mills' (1959) linkage of 'the study of biography, of history, and the problems of their intersections within social structures' (p 149) (see Hareven, 1978a, 1978b; Elder, 1982, 1985; Hareven and Adams, 1982). At the time, society was faced with widespread transformations and massive social change; scholars felt ill equipped to account for the social change occurring in the world, in particular how these transformations altered the experiences of people's lives. Leading theories of human socialisation and behavioural change, considered by critics as ahistorical and mutually exclusive, were seen as insufficient (Hareven, 1978a, 1978b; Elder, 1982; Hareven and Adams, 1982). The development of the lifecourse approach provided the means for scholars to move beyond socialisation and development, albeit in the separate disciplines of sociology and psychology, to account for the intersections between macro-level structures and micro-level lived experiences (George, 1993; Elder, 1994).

Crystallized in Elder's (1974) analysis of longitudinal data presented in *Children of the Great Depression*, the lifecourse perspective outlined how outcomes observed in late life could result from earlier experiences. As a perspective, it sought to link macro and micro levels of analysis in order to account for how social and historical variables could intersect with personal biographies across time (Elder, 1985, 1994; George, 1993). According to Elder (1994), the lifecourse is a 'multilevel phenomenon, ranging from structured pathways through social institutions and organizations to the social trajectories of individuals and their developmental pathways' (p 5). The language used by Elder can be somewhat confusing, however, referencing both individuals and structures; in practice, the approach tends to focus more closely on individuals and larger trends or shifts between cohorts and family units over time. It has been used in a variety of contexts, to demonstrate the impact of social change on social units such as the family (Hareven, 1978a, 1978b; Hareven and Adams, 1982); to demonstrate the effect of time and place on subjective states such as sense of self, level of distress and attitudes (Elder, 1974; Elder et al, 1991); to describe the lifecourse patterns of specific birth cohorts in particular regions (for example, Cook, 1983; Weil, 1987; Elder, 1994); and to understand persisting effects of social-psychological states (George, 1993, 1996). As the development of the lifecourse perspective grew in popularity, concepts of time, context and process became increasingly important dimensions of theory and analysis (George, 1993; Elder, 1994). What began as a marginal critique of dominant methods became a key means to understand how social change could affect people's lives, and has significantly shaped approaches to the study of transition across the lifecourse. Drawing on this approach, scholars have concentrated on how early experience can shape late-life outcomes, in particular to their predictive potential. In doing so (and perhaps indicated by Elder's title *Children of the Great Depression*), emphasis tends to be placed on earlier parts of the lifecourse considered as a whole, rather than the specificities of late life.

The institutional approach

The emergence of an institutional approach to the study of the lifecourse, primarily located in Europe, represents a different approach to the study of the lifecourse – and one that focuses more acutely on late life. Dannefer and Settersen (2010) root this approach in Cain's (1964) 'Life course and social structure', which established the lifecourse as a basis for social organisation, and Riley's age stratification (Riley, 1971; Riley et al, 1972). Both of these approaches will be discussed in more detail in Chapter Three as key contributions to the study of transitions. According to Dannefer and Settersen (2010), these studies paved the road for consideration of the lifecourse as a social institution or feature of social structure (Kohli, 1986b; Kohli and Meyer, 1986; Mayer, 1986, 2004; Meyer, 1986; Settersen and Hagestad, 1996). In this strand of thinking, institutions and structures shape ideas about what is appropriate across the lifecourse, and organise experiences into expectations of age- and stage-based norms (see Dannefer and Settersen, 2010). Here, age norms, social structures created through policies and practices, and cultural definitions are the elements of study. Norms, for example, become a way of constructing the experiences of individuals (Meyer, 1986), with institutions shaping the lifecourse (Mayer, 2004; Kohli, 2007) and thus late life. Embedded in this approach are assessments of patterns, norms and scheduling of events, including how constructs such as age become naturalised through normative expectations. Here, the early example of Neugarten's (1976) notions of events that occur 'on and off time' best characterise the relationship between timing and transitions across the lifecourse (see also Neugarten and Datan, 1973). More recent approaches draw attention to power dynamics and social cultural relations. This branch of lifecourse studies thus draws attention to the relationships between structures and interpretations of ageing that will be addressed throughout this book. However, while models that suggest humanist or interpretive versions of the lifecourse exist (see Holstein and Gubrium, 2000; Hockey and James, 2003), they are lesser referenced in mainstream interpretations of transitions in relation to late life. As discussed in Chapter Four, however, these perspectives can also be used to link the understandings of social and cultural structures with subjective experiences of transitions in late life.

Principles of the lifecourse perspective

In North America and increasingly abroad, studies of transition and the lifecourse are profoundly marked by Elder's (1985, 1994) lifecourse perspective. A brief review of Elder's key principles of the lifecourse perspective therefore outlines the conceptual and methodological principles from which transitions and the lifecourse have been approached.[2] The line of thinking pursued throughout this book argues that approaches to the study of the lifecourse should account for structural, socio-cultural and interpretive aspects as they relate to transitions in late life. Although calling for alterations to what has become known as 'the lifecourse perspective', Elder's themes cannot be dismissed. The lifecourse perspective is commonly cited as being comprised of four key principles: historical time and place; the timing of lives; linked or independent lives; and human agency (Elder, 1985, 1994). As discussed later in this book, the principles of the lifecourse perspective can be identified in older people's narratives. Chapter Seven demonstrates how the accounts of older people directly challenge dominant understandings of the lifecourse in ways that echo the four principles. Elder's themes are relevant signposts to the interpretation of variations in subjective experience and individual accounts; the insights from older people, however, take on greater meaning when their messages are also considered from interpretive and institutional perspectives that integrate attention to constructs, structures and meanings.

The first principle, the 'interplay of human lives and historical times' contends that the lifecourse of individuals is embedded in, and shaped by, the historical times and experiences over their lifetime. Individuals or groups, whether cohorts or otherwise, can experience 'different historical worlds' from those of previous generations (Elder, 1994).[3] This means that the lives of individuals may take different paths from their peers, and these individuals may, as a result, have different experiences of similar life events. The first principle outlines how individual lives are structured and affected by global and historical events, as well as family history, including experiences and events in their communities (Price et al, 2000; Szinovacz and Davey, 2007). The second principle, the 'timing of lives', states that the developmental impact of a succession of life transitions or events is contingent on when these happenings occur in a person's life. The timing of lives thus introduces the element of social timing, including, for example, factors such as the incidence, duration, role sequence, expectations and beliefs to the analysis. Elder's (1974) findings that one's location within a particular cohort affects the way that individuals fared during the Great Depression is key evidence of this differential impact of timing.

The third principle, 'linked lives', asserts that individuals' lives are interrelated and highlights the 'notion of interdependence and the idea that human lives are embedded in social relationships with kin and across the lifespan' (Elder, 1994 p 6; see also Elder and Pellerin, 1998). This conception of linked or independent lives moves understandings from a consideration of the social or the individual to experiences expressed through networks of shared relationships (Elder, 1998, p 4). The central idea is that actors position themselves vis-à-vis each other; therefore, the actions of one actor influence the experiences of another. Societal and individual experiences are thus linked by relationships, time and social location, including, for example, a convoy model where individuals continually affect and are affected by relationships with others as they move through time, age and history (Kahn and Antonucci, 1980; Antonucci et al, 1996). The fourth principle is 'human agency in choice making', whereby individuals are considered to have the freedom to act, to make choices and to adopt strategies that help them surmount structural constraints (Elder, 1994, 1998). Drawing on Clausen's (1993) understanding of constraints, this principle states that individuals construct their own lifecourse through choices and actions within the opportunities and constraints of history and social circumstance (Elder, 1994; Hitlin and Elder, 2007). While there is debate over the extent to which vulnerable groups can exercise agency within structural constraints (Hitlin and Elder, 2007), the notion of human agency suggested by Elder (1994) holds that all individuals have a certain degree of autonomy to reflect on their motivations and actions in order to better respond to events and protect their long-term interests. Together, the four principles set out what has become the dominant framework, at least in North America, from which to consider transitions as they relate to late life.

Transitions and trajectories

Regardless of the approach taken, studies of the lifecourse have resulted in the identification of transitions and trajectories as central frameworks from which to understand continuity and change. In both strands of thinking, the concepts of transitions and trajectories are central, if not inseparable, from the lifecourse perspective and lifecourse research (Elder, 1985; Hagestad, 1990; George, 1993). Although the understandings of these concepts does vary according to approach, transition is generally understood to refer to both periods of change, and the study of change over time, on a social or individual level (Hareven, 1978a, 1978b; Hareven and Adams, 1982). Transitions are considered to represent anchor points to observe social changes such as family type, timing of transitions and duration of roles, and to understand the impact these changes have on personal lives and subjective states. Writing from a sociological social-psychological perspective George (1993) defines transition as 'changes in status (most often role transitions) that are discrete and relatively bounded in duration, although their consequences may be observed over long-term' (George, 1996, p 250). In this interpretation, transitions are depicted as temporary states that individuals encounter as they progress through the lifecourse, or events that come to mark the beginning of new status-based roles and/or life stages. Examples of life transitions include the birth of children, entrance into adulthood or work life and retirement (George, 1993). While George's view tends to be more individual in nature, an institutional focus on how such experiences are normalised into marked stages or periods of life may also be taken. The various works associated with the lifecourse perspective establish transition as a central component of approaching change across the period of one's life.

Closely linked to transition is the notion of trajectories that are considered to account for multiple transitions and pathways across the lifecourse. Where transition tends to refer to short-term change, trajectories represent larger themes in the lifecourse as a whole. Trajectories are defined as 'long-term patterns of stability and change, that can be reliably differentiated from alternate patterns ... trajectories often include multiple transitions' (George, 1996, p 250). In this sense, transitions can be seen as embedded within trajectories that provide the transitions with distinctive form and meaning (Elder, 1994, p 5). Incorporating trajectories into the analysis, transitions are understood, not as isolated events, but as events that take place within the context of a lifecourse that includes the possibility of taking alternate pathways and therefore differentially shaping experience. This includes focus on the antecedent and consequences of the pathways (George, 1996, p 251). Making opportunity, choice and variable pathways a central feature of the lifecourse moves understandings of change over time away from predictable patterns towards more complex and fluid conceptualisation of change over time.

Analysis then becomes sensitive to how early events may affect later experiences, as well as constraints and choices. Yet again, while George's (1996) interpretation speaks primarily to individual experience, drawing on institutional understandings and constructivist perspectives can also be considered in relation to normative structures and expectations of ageing and late life. In this sense, the individual interpretations that George speaks of are firmly located within the normative expectations associated with transitions across the lifecourse and in late life. When considered from an interpretative or constructivist position (see Holstein and Gubrium, 2000), analysis of the intersections between individual experiences and social structures seem to hold enormous potential.

Rethinking transitions and the lifecourse in late life

Studies of the lifecourse offer several conceptual possibilities for the reconsideration of transitions as they relate to ageing and late life. This is especially the case where the ideas put forward by Elder (1994) can be understood in a historical, cultural and institutional context whereby individuals are positioned and relate to the societies in which they live. First, studies of the lifecourse draw attention to the constructions of age and the range of variables that may influence experience across the lifecourse and in late life (Dannefer and Settersen, 2010). Second, introducing the concept of time into the analysis of continuity and change enables timing, sequence and duration of events and experiences to come to the fore, allowing for a focus on the dynamic patterns that unfold across the course of a human life (George, 1996), in particular when time is considered from within a constructivist or interpretive framework. Development of an approach to the lifecourse that is interpretive in nature, as discussed in Chapter Four, introduces a more fluid understanding of how status, roles and identities can shift over time, and offers a complexity that directly challenges normative age- and stage-based models. Third, the lifecourse perspective offers increased attention to heterogeneity, and the possibility of heterogeneous patterns across time and place (Elder, 1994; Dannefer and Settersen, 2010). A focus on transitions and trajectories thus offers the possibility to introduce 'normative and non-normative changes that individuals experience over time' (George, 1993, p 353) as well as challenge such understandings as social and cultural constructs (Settersen and Hagestad, 1996). This focus could then be extended to a consideration of diversity that is based on differing social locations and the multiplicity of experience. Fourth, while articulated primarily in the interpretive and constructivist versions, the study of the lifecourse draws attention to the subjective interpretations of events and experiences, with subjective experience considered the means to link the macro and micro levels of analysis. Together, the intersecting aspects of age-based constructions, time, diversity and subjective experience form a solid platform from which to reconsider late-life transitions. Yet, while these merits have resulted in recognisable shifts to the study of continuity and change, the limitations in the study of the lifecourse, and in particular the lifecourse perspective, must also be considered.

The lifecourse perspective and its application in a research context reveal several weaknesses where the purpose of understanding the 'fit' between constructions of ageing and late life and subjective experience are concerned. For the purposes of this analysis, reconsidering transition in relation to late life, the lifecourse perspective has three key limitations. The first is the extent to which the macro and micro can be linked at a practical level. This is especially the case where the intersection between the two is often lost in a focus on the individual level. In emphasising individual-level interpretations, the lifecourse perspective fails to draw attention to structural constraints and the accumulation of disadvantage that can occur in relation to transitions to ageing and late life (see Dannefer and Settersen, 2010). Further, 'personological interpretations' do not address the ways in which expectations and social relations may be shaped by normative age- and stage-based perspectives. Second, the mechanisms of change and choice in social contexts and individual lives remain relatively unaddressed in the lifecourse perspective; choice tends to be overstated (Hitlin and Elder, 2007), and the links between constraints and opportunities are not often well explained (see George, 1993, 1996). The relationship between transitions, choice and structural constraints requires further attention, especially with regard to how marginalised or disadvantaged groups can exercise this agency and choice. Third, although the potential for heterogeneity exists on a conceptual level, the extent to which this diversity can be integrated into study samples and analysis remains a central challenge (George, 1993; Dannefer and Settersen, 2010). Diversity is rarely achieved in applied research. This is in part a result of the barrier imposed by ideas of representation and generalisation that operate in traditional understandings of research in the social sciences – that is, the expectation that samples be comprised to produce comparable groups and norm-based patterns, regardless of the fact that most individuals' lives do not fit these patterns (Dannefer, 1988). While the concept of heterogeneity challenges the assumptions that life transitions are patterned in predictable ways, lifecourse research often continues to function in relation to accepted and expected patterns primarily based on age, or composites that imply age, such as role or status. As such, the very structures of research work against the argument of the lifecourse perspective. In doing so, assumptions that operate within research can create a context where the integration of diverse social backgrounds is fraught with difficulty.

Conclusion: the lifecourse as constructed and meaningful

In sum, a critical perspective on the study of ageing combined with an understanding of the structured and social processes of the lifecourse provides a base from which to reconsider transitions in relation to late life. Such an approach provides a platform from which to question taken-for-granted knowledge, assumptions and practice in this domain. What emerges from the analysis of critical approaches to ageing and the lifecourse is a shared desire to understand the interplay of structures, history, context and experience. Key to this is paying attention to the challenges of linking the macro and micro, implementing envisaged ideals into the context of research and practice, and addressing diversity. Where critical gerontology provides the means to approach structural, socio-cultural and interpretive aspects of experience, studies of the lifecourse provide the channels to better understand variability, pathways, continuity and change at individual and social levels. Where the weaknesses relating to integrating micro-level and the macro-level experiences are concerned, critical gerontology and the lifecourse perspective seem to be located on two sides of the spectrum: critical approaches have tended to focus on an overly structural analysis that overlooks agency, and the lifecourse perspective as articulated in the 'personological approach', a focus on individual-level experiences at the expense of structures. The lifecourse perspective as it stands has therefore been unsuccessful in accounting for causation or structural aspects of experience, although this is not the case for the institutional approach, which has focused more specifically on the relationships between institutions, structures and experiences (see Dannefer and Settersen, 2010).

The institutional approach to the study of the lifecourse perspective is more closely aligned with critical approaches to the study of ageing, and the desire to understand the relationship between structure and experience. Drawing on lessons from critical gerontology, the lifecourse perspective must more seriously consider the constraints that exist for older people, the importance of subjective experience, and the ways that many of the transitions experienced in late life are not necessarily chosen, voluntary or reversible. Yet, drawing a lesson from the lifecourse perspective, subjective experiences of historical events and experiences can differ greatly. Echoing the humanistic and cultural perspectives in gerontology, the personological lifecourse perspective can be used to highlight how transitions may be interpreted differently by various individuals; that individuals may cope differently with life events depending on their histories and subjective states; and that they may interpret their experiences within the context of group, family or community notions. The institutional perspective can also highlight how older people's experiences may correspond or conflict with the normative expectations of ageing. When considered through a constructivist or interpretive lens, studies of the lifecourse can provide fresh insight into the lifecourse and transitions in late life as constructed (Holstein and Gubrium, 2000). This frame may be used to understand the socio-cultural constructs of age, relationships with policies and practices, and negotiated identities across time and in relation to existing models. Considering transitions and the lifecourse from an interpretive or constructivist perspective can further complement the approach in order to bridge understandings of the intersections of structures, practices and experiences, discussed in Chapter Four.

Critical perspectives that draw on the strengths of the various approaches to the study of ageing and the lifecourse have much to offer the analysis of continuity and change across the lifecourse. As outlined by Dannefer and Setterson (2010), thinking about the accumulated practices and experiences of older people represents a significant departure from normative age- and stage-based understandings of ageing and late life. What a critical analysis of transitions and the lifecourse offers is the possibility to move beyond the predictive potential that is implied in the lifecourse perspective, and towards recognising transitions and the lifecourse as social and cultural constructs. This includes taking account of the varying meanings that constructs can hold on social, cultural and personal levels, and in particular, identifying the differences that may exist between suggested macro-level 'shapes of ageing' and the subjective interpretations of older people that may, in part, be shaped by such models. Examples of the benefits of this potential amalgamation include the merging of the strengths of an analysis concerned with the structural, cultural and social issues of ageing with attention to the trajectories and pathways of lived experience; increased attention to the influence that age relations and structured locations can have on cumulative disadvantage across the lifecourse; and a better understanding of the relationships between institutional and organisational practices, as well as the subjective interpretations of experience and change. It is in this sense that understandings of transition as rooted in the lifecourse reveal their true potential of acknowledging continuity and change across time and lives, and amid relationships, in a socio-cultural context. Merging an analysis of policy frameworks with socio-cultural and personal interpretations of age can reveal that transitions may not be as fixed as research, theory and practice consider them to be. The issue of how to link the study of social policy with experience is explored further in Chapter Four. Prior to this, Chapter Three provides an overview of the specific approaches taken in relation to transitions, in order to better situate a reconsideration of transition as it relates to late life.

Notes

[1] See, for example, Cole, 1992; Cole et al, 1993; Featherstone and Wernick, 1995; Moody, 1995; Katz, 1996, 2005; Gullette, 1997, 2004; Minkler and Estes, 1997; Phillipson, 1998; Blaikie, 1999; Woodward 1999, 2003; Gilleard and Higgs, 2000; Andersson, 2002; Estes et al, 2003; Gubrium and Holstein, 2003; Baars et al, 2006.

[2] Those relating to the institutional approach have closer links with the field of social gerontology, and will therefore be reviewed in greater detail in Chapter Three.

[3] This principle integrates the possibilities of 'cohort effect' – that is, the idea that social change differentiates patterns of different cohorts – with 'period effects' – the idea that history can produce changes that are uniform across birth cohorts.

THREE

Multidisciplinary approaches to transition

This chapter launches a critical exploration of the state of knowledge on transitions in late life. Transition is a standard concept used in social sciences and policy to anchor notions of continuity and change throughout the lifecourse. As such, it is relevant to the study of ageing in contemporary society. This chapter outlines prominent academic approaches in the social sciences; reviews the contributions from the multidisciplinary fields of anthropology, sociology and psychology; and outlines how these ideas have been interpreted in social gerontology. Key themes developed in each of the disciplines are presented according to the following subsections: transition as a passage of rite or ritual; transition as movement between roles or status; and transitions as adaptation or development. Although the organisation of the material roughly corresponds with the disciplines, the intent is to clarify how ideas in each of the fields have influenced contemporary approaches to late life in social gerontology. As such, this chapter provides a multidisciplinary base from which to compare and contrast personal, social, and cultural shapes of ageing and late life.

Questions to be explored in this chapter include:

- What is meant by transition in the social sciences? How have transitions been understood across varying disciplines?
- How has social gerontology approached the study of transition? What key themes, debates and dilemmas can be identified?
- How do dominant understandings of transition contribute to, or shape, expectations of stability and change in late life?
- What relevant notions are worthy of re-examination?

The academic study of transition

Multidisciplinary approaches to the study of transition are linked by common threads as well as separated by distinctive interpretations. Consistent among the approaches is the underlying basis of studying change and movement across time, assessment of the degree of conformity or difference, and concern for timing or predictability. Differences relate to the primary focus, level of analysis and disciplinary boundaries of study. Anthropology tends to focus on cultural meanings and practices related to change; sociology on roles and status; and psychology on developmental tasks and coping. They also differ in whether changes are considered on an individual or social level, as well as whether transitions are viewed as fixed moments or constructed accounts. While the widespread use of the concept transition in academia, research and policy suggests a uniform interpretation, reflection on the multidisciplinary approaches reveals key differences. A focus on transitions as they apply to the case of ageing and old age takes us deep into the debates related to age structure, the constructions of age, and the ways in which age has been approached in the social sciences and more specifically gerontology. Careful consideration of key strands developed within each field can draw together the academic study of transitions into an interdisciplinary approach, such as the one taken throughout this book. Fixed age- and stage-based interpretations can therefore be reconsidered according to relational processes, contested claims and subjective interpretations in relation to late life.

Anthropological perspectives: rites, rituals and being in-between

In anthropology, culture and process are central to understanding the transitions that take place in Western and non-Western societies. Originally developed in the early work of van Gennep (1960 [1909]) and elaborated in the work of Hertz (1960 [1907]), Turner (1969) and others, the discipline of anthropology can be considered to have set the foundations for interpretations of the study of transition. At the centre of scholarship on transition is van Gennep's (1960 [1909]) groundbreaking work *The rites of passage*, which established the basis for explaining movement between status groups, roles or structures, and has come to influence studies of transition within and outside the discipline. Key contributions and debates in anthropology focus on the structures or functions of transitions; the rituals or ceremonies that mark transitions; the processes and symbolic meanings for individuals, groups and societies; and cultural variations that may exist. The following section outlines the main ideas from this field.

Transitions as 'rites of passage': a three-part structure

Studies of transition in the social sciences are traced to van Gennep's (1960 [1909]) classic text on the structural and process-related interpretations of transitions.[1] Van Gennep (1960 [1909]) argued that ritual events such as the 'coming of age' in various cultures could be characterised by a pattern of passage between places and spaces. He claimed that the 'life of an individual in any society is a series of passages from one age to another and from one occupation to another' (van Gennep, 1960 [1909], p 3). In the following quote, van Gennep (1960 [1909]) uses the parallels he witnessed across groups and cultures to establish a generalised model of transition. In doing so, he makes reference to a stage-based structure, a process of movement that occurs through ceremony or ritual, and outlines the types of transitions that occur:

Transitions from group to group and from one social situation to the next are looked on as implicit in the very fact of existence, so that a man's [sic] life comes to be made up of a succession of stages with similar ends and beginnings: birth, social puberty, marriagehood, fatherhood [sic], advancement to a higher class, occupational specialisation, and death. For every one of these events there are ceremonies whose essential purpose is to enable the individual to pass from one defined position to another which is equally well defined. (van Gennep, 1960 [1909], p 3)

Based on his ethnographic observations of ritual across cultural contexts, van Gennep (1960 [1909]) developed a typology comprised of a three-part structure. In this typology, each ritual is characterised by two end points and a process that exists between. The premise for van Gennep's theory is that any distinction creates a binary classification that implies a tertiary structure. Examples of these binary classifications include alive/dead and young/old. The process that exists between the two end points is considered the transition. Transitions marked by ceremonial practices are considered 'rites de passage'.[2] Van Gennep's three-part structure thus established the groundwork for the form and order between types of rituals across several contexts, profoundly influencing understandings of transition in sociology and social gerontology.

The importance of ritual: processes, meanings and change

The study of ritual processes used to mark change represents another key aspect of the anthropological study of transition. Studies of ritual, and in particular end-of-life rituals, represent a wide body of scholarship in anthropology (see Bell, 1992). Studied in depth by van Gennep (1960 [1909]), Hertz (1960 [1907]) and Turner (1967, 1969) among others, rituals related to death have been used to understand socially set roles that occur in a given culture (van Gennep, 1960 [1909]); symbolic meanings shared by individuals, groups and societies (Turner, 1969); and the cultural values expressed through these and other acts (Hertz, 1960 [1907]).[3] The literature on ritual includes three prominent themes relevant for the study of transition in relation to late life: first, that ritual can be used to mark passage between roles or status; second, that ritual processes are imbued with socio-cultural meanings related to this change; and third, that ritual can be performed according to the meanings made of them or an intended purpose (that is, transitions are performative).

Hertz's (1960 [1907]) attention to the social impacts of the funeral rite highlights the processes used to mark and symbolise change. This awareness of the social meanings surrounding funeral rites drew attention to the symbolic significance of rituals, social and collective representations of death, and has highlighted how social and emotional reactions to death vary across cultures. Hertz's questions, 'What happens to the corpse?' and 'Why is the corpse feared?', linked ritual processes with socio-cultural values and emotion, articulating how reactions can vary across cultural contexts and between individuals. Building on Hertz's work, scholars have continued to study the 'exit ritual' as a means of understanding the cultural values and assumptions of a given society, resulting in the sub-discipline of death studies (see Mitford, 1963; Becker, 1973; Huntington and Metcalf, 1979). For example, scholars have focused on the fear, guilt and anxiety that can be associated with death on individual and social levels. The following quote, offered in Huntington and Metcalf's (1979) classic book on death, reflects the deep emotions suggested by 'the corpse':

> The power is one of evocation and association. At the sight of a corpse, emotions surge through the individual chaotically: fear, rage, curiosity, sympathy, even joy, for he or she is dead and you are not. (Huntington and Metcalf, 1979, p 211)

Linking emotions and cultural practices is relevant to the study of transition in late life, and in particular, constructs such as the fourth age that are intricately related to decline and mortality. The focus on ritual, and the connection between practices, culture and emotion, can help us reconsider late life, in particular, where the ageing body may remind us of the corpse, and cause emotional anxiety related to impairment and growing old.

In a similar strand of thinking, Turner (1969) highlights how ritual is a meaningful event and process, and not merely a normative function of transition. For Turner (1967, 1987), ritual is transformative, ceremonial and confirmatory, and renders visible the values of a society (Bell, 1992; Parkin, 1992; Hockey and James, 2003). The process-based and performative aspects of Turner's work have been recognised as relevant to contemporary understandings of continuity and change. Hockey and James (2003) argue that rather than simply protect the coherence and stability of society, Turner's work highlights how ritual can be considered, in part, to produce the social and cultural – that is, ritual is linked with performance; it becomes a flexible guideline rather than movement between fixed points, with each ritual used to reformulate boundaries of 'belonging' (Baumann, 1992; Parkin, 1992). This interpretation of ritual as a series of meaningful events performed in a socio-cultural context illustrates how transitions are linked to individual, social and cultural processes, and the interpretations that occur within each. While the works of van Gennep and Hertz were originally translated and interpreted according to the structural functional framework of the time (see Bell, 1992), their works have been reconsidered from contemporary perspectives of rituals as conveyors of cultural values and socio-cultural variations. Edited collections such as Spencer's (1990) *Anthropology and the riddle of the sphinx: Paradoxes of change in the lifecourse* and de Coppet's (1992) *Understanding rituals* have turned to more critical readings of the relational and interpretive processes of early anthropological works. This occurs in part through more detailed attention to Turner's work on the concept of liminality that draws greater attention to the process of 'being between' (see also Hockey and James, 2003).

Liminality: transition and the time in-between

Although it has received less attention than rite and ritual, the concept of liminality has much to offer a contemporary analysis of transition in relation to late life. Introduced in *The rites of passage* (1960 [1909]), liminality referred to the existence of a transitional or liminal period. Van Gennep (1960 [1909], p 1) outlined this period as follows: '... a man [sic] cannot pass from one to the other without going through an intermediate stage', and that 'whoever passes from one [zone] to the other finds himself [sic] physically and macro-religiously in a special situation for a certain length of time: he wavers between two worlds' (van Gennep, 1960 [1909], p 18). A key aspect of van Gennep's thinking is that a move from one status to another is accompanied by a period of time spent in a transitional or liminal space. During this time, the individual exists temporarily outside society, until reintegration, labelled as 'incorporation' in the three-part structure, occurs.

V.W. Turner (1967, 1969) developed van Gennep's 'transitional' or 'liminal period' into the now well-known concept of 'liminality', used to refer to an in-between state. In van Gennep's (1960 [1909]) analysis, the liminal period is a phase where the individual exists outside society but is planning to re-enter it. Differing slightly, Turner's (1969) notion of 'liminality' captures the state of being 'between' as a process rather than outside normal social roles. Turner defines liminal individuals as 'neither here nor there; they are betwixt and between the positions assigned and arrayed by law, custom, convention, and ceremony' (1969, p 95). For both van Gennep and Turner, the liminal period is defined in relation to action. Individuals have little social status until they are integrated into the next stage. The idea of being between therefore draws attention to the process of transition, rather than transition as a movement between two fixed positions. Yet, both the interpretations of van Gennep and Turner depict the time spent between as temporary, with the individual exiting the liminal period at some point, in order to enter a new phase. This difference between being 'inside' or 'outside' social roles is an important distinction as far as the questions of growing old are concerned. As noted by several scholars, when understood as a process of being 'betwixt and between', liminality holds great potential in relation to understanding transitions in late life (Spencer, 1990; Hockey and James, 2003). For example, liminality can be used to understand how older people may exist between ages and stages – with the fixed points considered as frames that influence what is known or expected of transitions in late life – themes that will be explored later in this book.

Contribution: continuity and change as passage and process

Anthropological understandings have influenced the state of knowledge on transitions and made several significant contributions. First, scholarship in anthropology has established the foundational knowledge regarding forms, structures, and processes used to study transitions within and across cultures. Beginning with van Gennep's (1960 [1909]) *The rites of passage*, anthropology outlined a three-part structure used to define and set the types of transitions expected throughout the lifecourse. Through studies of ritual, it has also clarified how individuals move through periods of change, and the social and cultural values that accompany such processes. It has introduced notions of passage between roles, statuses and membership, and has linked understandings of ritual with cultural values and meaning making processes. As such, it provides the base to consider the rituals used to mark age (including the absence of such rituals); the socio-cultural expectations of continuity and change in late life; and the processes of being in-between that may be encountered. Considering the rituals or processes by which older people negotiate transitional turning points has much to offer understandings of late life.

Second, anthropological scholarship points to the meaning of transitions as culturally relevant. Although van Gennep's (1960 [1909]) early scholarship was typically read in relation to generalised patterns of transition that were similar across contexts, the focus on cultural values and meanings articulated in contemporary readings of Hertz's and Turner's works points to the cultural relativity of transitions. The focus on the symbolic and interpretive processes of transitions highlights variations that may exist within and between cultures, and across contexts. These interpretations thus draw attention to individual variations in meanings, and the cultural imperialism that exists in many Western approaches to the study of transition. They reveal the extent to which dominant assumptions are rooted in Western understandings of transition and late life, and call attention to the lack of diversity in taken-for-granted notions of change. Questions on the meanings of transitions in late life within and outside Western contexts, and according to diverse social locations, thus become paramount.

Third, a striking feature of anthropology is its explicit focus on the body and death through attention to the 'exit ritual' or funerary rite. Focus on the body, or the corpse, and the rituals used to mark or celebrate death, form the basis for many of the accepted understandings of transition. This focus, however, is in direct contrast to disciplines such as psychology, sociology and even social gerontology that have for the most part overlooked late life and death, including the socio-cultural values and anxieties related to the end of the lifecourse. Knowledge about death and the cultural values and practices related to death rituals can inform understandings of late-life transitions, in particular, where socio-cultural discourses of decline are concerned.

Review of foundational works and contemporary interpretations of transitions in anthropology outlines the classic interpretations that have influenced the study of transitions, as well as suggesting pathways from which to reconsider change in late life. While structural understandings of transitions are relatively straightforward where binary categories such as that of single/married, or rituals such as 'coming of age' are concerned, they are more problematic in the case of experiences that occur over longer periods of time, with fewer fixed end points, such as the lifelong process of ageing. While much of the scholarship has been devoted to identifying stages or types of transitions, more attention could be devoted to the meanings and processes that underlie these experiences. Rethinking the structure, process and meanings of marked transitions into age provides an entry point into the contested models of 'growing old'. A focus on processes and, in particular, those that may exist 'within and between' fixed transitions and patterned expectations, is particularly relevant to reconsidering transitions in late life. Lessons from anthropology provide the opportunity to reconsider the binary structure of transitions; explore the potential of fluid processes; and understand meaningful cultural makers, including those related to death, as well as the differences that may exist between cultures and contexts. Relevant directions include pursuing the concept of liminality as a temporary space between, the presence or absence of ritual in relation to ageing and late life, and how ideas about death and decline can shape interpretations of the lifecourse.

Sociological perspectives: normative age- and stage-based roles

Sociology has responded to contemporary questions relating to social change, shifting social structures and social roles across time. Sociological scholarship forms a large body of scholarship on transition and the lifecourse, with contributions focused primarily on normative movement between roles, generalised structures and age- or stage-based groups in society. Approaches to transition and the lifecourse in sociology range from the study of large-scale social trends to that of cohort variations, families and social roles over time, identification and movement into particular types of transitions, and the meaning of such experiences (although the latter tends to be found in more specialised fields such as health and illness studies). In the 1980s, the study of transitions was believed to have enormous potential for studying social change, which resulted in collaborative projects led primarily by Hareven (1978b) and Hareven and Adams (1982) that are now considered the foundational texts on the subject. Taken together, the majority of scholarship on transition tends to take for granted normative understandings of the lifecourse rooted in a structural-functionalist paradigm. The study of transition in sociology is also reflective of the larger disciplinary tensions between expectations of social cohesion and integration, and those focused on conflict and social change. At the same time, there is a growing perspective based on social constructivism that challenges the naturalisation of transitions as age- and stage-based, especially in social gerontology (Holstein and Gubrium, 2000; Hendricks, 2003).

This section outlines major sociological contributions to the study of transitions and the lifecourse. Although difficult to summarise as a result of the extent of scholarship, key contributions to the study of transitions relate to how movement is understood to occur through age- and stage- based roles across the lifecourse. While approaches to transition have shifted over time, the viewpoints of socialisation and structural functionalism have retained considerable influence in the field, especially where understandings of age and transition are concerned. Focused on stability and change, sociological perspectives exhibit a clear tension between expectations of transitions as smooth changes that occur across a stable backdrop and ideas whereby structured transitions are considered to be characterised by conflict. As with psychology, the field of sociology tends to operate according to a model of normative stages such as adulthood, or roles into which one becomes socialised, such as parenthood. There are clear assumptions about a 'normal' trajectory framed around adulthood and maturity that are closely linked to labour force participation, and in age, exit from the labour force (see Irwin, 1995). Movement across normative age- and stage- based markers are thus central to understandings of transition in the field of sociology. Conflict, lifecourse perspectives and interpretive perspectives have been summoned as counter-arguments, but age- and stage-based assumptions continue to underscore even these approaches. Sociological understandings of transitions have had the greatest influence on social gerontology and are the most well known. As such, they will only be briefly reviewed.

Early models of transition: socialisation and structural functionalism

Early approaches to the study of transition and the lifecourse in sociology were developed from within a structural-functionalist paradigm (Parsons, 1951, 1960, 1977, 1978). The structure of roles, status and age-based groups came to form the backbone for interpreting change, with the idea of transition in relation to ageing and late life articulated as movement between normative age- or stage-based roles. In the structural-functionalist perspective, the concept of socialisation was used to describe the ways that an individual became a socially functioning member of society, normally through institutions and systems. This process of socialisation was considered to prepare the individual for the roles he or she would play, and instilled the accepted social and cultural values of a given society. In relation to transition and late life, socialisation was seen to establish the normative roles one was expected to fulfil as a normal adult, with movement understood to occur between relatively fixed ages or stages in society. The underlying assumption from this perspective was that the transitions between roles or stages were discrete and had a relatively fixed and defined point of entry or exit. Not surprisingly, the majority of work on transition focused on attempts to delineate the structure, types and nature of each role, as well as the timing at which individuals pass from one role to another. This perspective stamped dominant understandings of transitions and the lifecourse, with transitions conceptualised as movement between standard normative roles, status or age-based groups in society that were assumed to maintain the social coherence or stability of society. Scholars, however, have criticised the stronghold that this perspective has on the study of transitions, and in part, inherent flaws of fixed and normative patterns (see Cole, 1992; Dannefer, 1996) that do not take account of various social locations and/or culture. The idea of 'choice guided by norms towards ends which were determined by values' has also been challenged (Turner, 1989, p 589).

History: development of the 'lifecourse perspective'

Although it is difficult to pinpoint a specific event that marked the appearance of 'transition' as a central sociological concept, the turn towards this perspective seems to have been established, at least in the North American context, by Hareven's (1978b) edited collection entitled *Transitions: The family and the lifecourse in historical perspective*. This collection publicised the work of several North American and European scholars – many of whom worked from a perspective that was later coined the 'lifecourse perspective' (see Elder, 1975). In the UK, it was Cohen's (1987) edited text entitled *Social change and the lifecourse* that designated transition as an area of sociological inquiry. Although taking place in two different geographical sites, these publications can be contextualised in the wider environment of the 1980s, where models of socialisation and behavioural development were considered insufficient to address broad social change. What emerged was that the concept of transition was considered to hold potential for studying social change, resulting in collaborative projects grouped together by Hareven (1978b); Hareven and Adams, 1982) that are now considered the foundational texts on the subject. For example, Hareven and Adams' (1982) edited text *Aging and lifecourse transitions: An interdisciplinary perspective* united authors in an attempt to examine transitions and changes in work and family as a process rather than an isolated event or experience.

Such academic developments led to an important distinction of the lifecourse as a process, and drew attention to the changing role of the family. From this lineage, sociological scholars in the United States focused primarily on large data sets in order to identify patterns of change in family (Antonucci et al, 2007; McIlvane et al, 2007), as well as cohort and generational units (Ryder, 1965). Scholars wanted to better understand how social change or changes in history affected individual level health and wellbeing (see Bengston et al, 1985, 1997; Gilleard, 2004). After this, the study of transition branched off into related traditions such as the sociology of the family, lifecourse studies, and specific fields such as sociology of illness or disability studies. One of the most prominent articulations of the study of lifecourse and transitions was how early experiences could affect outcomes in late life. As discussed in Chapter Two, this approach is best encapsulated in the lifecourse perspective articulated in the United States (Elder, 1974; Hareven, 1978a,b). One of the key challenges to this line of thinking, however, was that the structured aspects of ageing outlined by critical scholars, and the intersections between structures and experiences, were not always taken into account in relation to defining transitions, especially in late life. This was especially the case in relation to ability, ethnicity/'race', gender, socioeconomic status and sexual orientation (see Calasanti, 1996; Dannefer, 1988; McMullin, 2000) and the interpretive aspects of experience (Holstein and Gubrium, 2000).

Conflict perspectives: structured conflict between roles, status and groups

Although representing the majority of studies on transition, the inherent consensus of the structural-functionalist model was challenged by scholars focused on conflict. Conflict theorists maintained that relationships between different roles and status groups in society were characterised by conflict rather than consensus, in particular, by unequal economic conditions relating to the labour market. Conflict perspectives drew attention to structures, power relationships between individuals and society, and the need for change. Their argument was formed in opposition to the normative framework and the assumption that coherence occurred between roles and statuses according to the structural functionalism paradigm. As such, conflict perspectives identified structured differences between groups such as those organised according to age differences. Although this body of work – especially in earlier forms – did not take up the language of 'transitions', it did focus on issues such as dependency and age stratification that represented important transitional markers (see Estes, 1979, 2001; Townsend, 1981). Questions relating to the structured dependency created by the institution of retirement, for example, have evolved from conflict perspectives.

Conflict perspectives have created pathways to consider how social structures and institutions shape the lifecourse. These pathways link with the critical approaches to the study of ageing and the 'institutional perspectives' (see Dannefer and Settersen, 2010) discussed in Chapter Two. In this view, transitions may be understood as creating conflict or disadvantage, especially where income or exclusion is considered. Rather than change being seen as normative and standard, transitions can be seen to structure tensions or differential status between groups. Conflict in society is thus in part located in the structures of transition and changed roles or statuses such as retirement or ageing itself. The best articulation of conflict perspectives on transitions in late life can be found in the mid-range theory of age stratification that will be discussed in the gerontology section. Conflict perspectives have remained prominent where criticisms of diversity and the structural inequalities of social locations are concerned. At the same time, while conflict perspectives have challenged the normative models of integration, they often remain rooted in chronological age differences structured by social relations, and therefore inherently replicate age- and stage-based understandings in late life. It is in many ways impossible to get outside age- based divisions, as the idea of conflict is considered to be rooted in the very distinctions between groups in society. Challenges to age- and stage-based norms in sociology have also been made, therefore, by drawing on process-based arguments similar to those in anthropology (see Crawford, 1973; Spencer, 1990; Irwin, 1995) or interpretive frameworks (Holstein and Gubrium, 2000; Hockey and James, 2003).

Contributions from sociological perspectives on transition

In sum, sociological perspectives have made three key contributions to the study of transition as related to late life. First, sociology has solidified the dominant viewpoint that change across the lifecourse takes place as movement across normative age- and stage-based roles. It has outlined the types of transitions that are expected, the social and cultural expectations that exist, and the problems that can occur when one's life path differs or deviates from expected stages. For the purposes of this analysis, it has set the typified frameworks by which continuity and change in late life are measured and understood. Second, the sociological focus on conflict over cohesion has outlined the types of structured inequities that exist, can be sustained across the lifecourse, and even become more prominent in late life. They have established how experiences such as dependency are structured, and how experiences are constructed through relationships with institutions such as retirement. Although facing challenges in relation to incorporating diversity in a meaningful way, conflict perspectives in sociology clearly delineate that transitions can be marked by inequalities across the lifecourse, as well as exacerbated or improved through constraints, opportunities or social benefits.

Third, sociological perspectives on transition draw attention to the extent to which success and failure are defined through the binary of independence and dependence that characterise age- and stage- based segments of the lifecourse. This includes the emphasis placed on work, and the extent to which success, integration and independence are linked to the labour market. Drawing attention to independence and dependence highlights how this binary influences expectations and assumptions about transitions across the lifecourse, setting the status of 'normal' at the poles of adulthood and late life (see Walker, 1981; Phillipson, 1982, 1998, 2004; Irwin, 1995). The paradox is that in the case of youth, the transition into adulthood is marked as independence, whereas in late life, the transition is one of dependence. Yet, despite these constructs, both adults and older people are expected to achieve independence – the movement into independence in early life, and the maintenance of independence despite challenges of dependence in late life. Challenging the normative construct of adulthood as entry to the labour market, Irwin (1995) argues that independence should be unhinged from wage labour. Doing so would have important implications for late life, whereby the automatic association between dependence and late life would be destabilised. This could then inform dominant assumptions of late life as a time of dependence, decline or decreased social engagement (see Burgess, 1960; Guillemard, 1980). The lesson learned from critical approaches in sociology is that rethinking the possibilities between the states of independence and dependence throughout life provides a more complex understanding of the influences that shape late life, and therefore, the suggested and contested models of late life. What remains less developed in this field, however, is the meaning of moving into these ages, stages and roles; the impact of diverse social locations across the lifecourse; and a focus on the aspects that allow individuals and groups to achieve continuity despite change.

Psychological perspectives: development and adaptation

In developmental psychology, perspectives of transitions are centred on adult development across the life span (Levinson and Darrow, 1978; Levinson, 1986; Baltes, 1987b, 2003; Erikson and Erikson, 1998; Baltes et al, 1999). Developmental psychology and lifespan psychology offer insights into the internal and personal processes that accompany continuity and change. The field of psychology contains models to explain individual growth, development and change across the lifecourse, or rather life span,[4] which is the preferred term in this field. While the models used to explain change and maturity differ, the psychological study of transitions across the lifecourse tends to be delineated into various developmental stages. The most relevant for this analysis are those that extend consideration of development into late life. One such perspective is the lifecycle model of Erikson (1982), another is the life–span perspective advocated by Baltes and colleagues (Baltes et al, 1980, 1999; Baltes, 1987a).

Transitions as marked stages of development

In psychology, the study of transition originated in the stages of development outlined in classic developmental models. These models divide the lifecourse into stages that are anchored in chronological age. Rooted in biological understandings, models in developmental psychology outline 'normal' stages of development through which an individual progresses, such as childhood, adolescence and adulthood. The focus in each stage is to achieve growth through the successful movement from one defined stage to another. Underlying the developmental approach is thus a view of development as a biological and psychological process of growth until maturity.

Developmental models have influenced knowledge and practice relating to transitions. However, the majority of the models consider adulthood as the point of maturity, and in doing so overlook late life. The most widely known models used to explain human development include Freud's (1910) psychosexual stages of development, Piaget's cognitive model (1952 [1936], 1972 [1966], 1990 [1929]), and Erikson's lifecycle model (1982), focused on psychosocial developmental stages set in interaction with the world. While these lifecycle perspectives are considered to have set the foundations for the study of transition in psychology, they are less helpful where age is concerned. Piaget's model focused primarily on children, and Freud considered the therapeutic model impossible beyond the age of 40, thus marking adulthood as the end of development (Davenhill, 2004). The exception to the perception that maturity is reached in adulthood is Erikson's (1963, 1982) stages of the lifecourse, developed from a psychosocial perspective.[5] Although

Erikson's (1982) model draws on staged distinctions, it differs from psychological models by addressing development into late life. Understandings of transitions that are entrenched in models where maturity ends in adulthood are problematic for the study of ageing, particularly where youth is linked with positive potential and maturity beyond adulthood is associated with loss and decline.

In addition to the focus on youth, many developmental models have shortcomings in relation to the study of late-life transitions. First, models of development tend to focus on the universal rather than the individual, and thus have a tendency to overreach their claims of generalisation (Rutter and Rutter, 1992). Second, as predictive and normative models, they frequently fix expectations according to stage-based norms, making them out of synch with the dynamics that characterise change (Rutter and Rutter, 1992). This is particularly the case where the timing and final point of maturation are concerned. As will be seen in Part Two of the book, illustrations in the form of lived experiences and narrative accounts demonstrate the differences that are possible within and between individuals, including variations that deviate from expected paths. Third, developmental models have been criticised for gender and cultural bias (Wilkinson, 1988; Fine and Gordon, 1989; England, 2008), in which age bias could also be added to the list. The following section will elaborate on Erikson's contribution as one of the only developmental perspectives available to address ageing and late life.

Erikson (1982) outlined eight progressive stages, each characterised by a major tension.[6] Late life, or old age as it is referred to in Erikson's theory, is characterised by the tension between integrity and despair, and the developmental goal of 'wisdom'. This stage is considered to build on themes developed in adulthood, characterised by the tension between generativity and stagnation, with 'care' as the developmental goal. Erikson's model emphasises that developmental tasks do not end at maturity, but shift in focus to interdependence and interactions with younger generations through a concept he terms 'generativity'. In doing so, Erikson's work challenges the relationship between ageing and decline. In his later work, Erikson (1997) argues for the importance of rethinking old age under contemporary conditions:

> Thus, a historical change like the lengthening of the average life span calls for viable re-ritualisations, which must provide a meaningful interplay between beginning and end as well as some finite sense of summary and, possibly, a more active anticipation of dying. For all this, *wisdom* will still be a valid word – and so, we think, will *despair*. (Erikson, 1997, p 63, emphasis in original)

While framing late life as a time period characterised by wisdom or despair has been subject to critique (see Woodward, 2003; Gullette, 2004), Erikson's thinking outlines a developmental stage for late life that occurs in a wider social, political and cultural context, and includes both negative and positive experiences in late life.

Lifespan psychology

A second model for understanding development and change in late life is the lifespan approach of Baltes and colleagues (Sugarman, 1986; Baltes, 1987a; Baltes et al, 1980, 1999). The lifespan model focuses on development in late life, including what is considered post-maturity. It combines biological interpretations of development that were considered to end at maturity, with an understanding of development as a psychological process that continues through the life span. Built to address the aforementioned oversights of ageing in existing models, authors from the lifespan perspective argue that the process of ageing should be included in understandings of the life span:

> The periods of adulthood and old age represent extreme testing grounds for a life-span developmental posture, at least with regard to the long-term impact of infancy, childhood, and adolescence on subsequent development during the lifecourse. (Baltes et al, 1980, p 97)

Echoing the lifecourse perspective, their argument draws attention to the impact early stages can have on late life. They also focus specifically, however, on identifying the developmental tasks that occur in late life (Baltes et al, 1999). As such, Baltes and colleagues offer a model that reaches beyond the predictive models that tend to typify the lifecourse perspective discussed in Chapter Two. In this line of thinking, physical deterioration (Bühler and Burgental, 1968), life review (Butler, 1963) and impending death (Baltes et al, 1980), for example, all represent important developmental processes in late life.

In the lifespan approach, developmental tasks are framed in terms of adaptation and coping. Lifespan psychology considers individual development as a lifelong adaptive process of acquisition, maintenance and transformation (Baltes et al, 1999, p 472). It maintains that development can occur at any point in the life span as influenced by the past and future of the individual, and is therefore not necessarily linear (Baltes et al, 1980; Honzik, 1984). Emphasis in lifespan psychology is on change in behaviour that occurs within an individual over time, can occur across individuals in different ways, and be accounted for in late life.[7] As such, the lifespan perspective has important implications for the study of transition as experienced across the lifecourse. It challenges standard models of transitions considered to end at adulthood, and outlines the types of developmental tasks that can successfully be accomplished in late life.

The best-known model to explain psychological adjustment in late life is Baltes' (1997) model of selective optimisation with compensation. In this model, Baltes and colleagues suggest that biological deterioration is offset by individual mechanisms that allow older people to compensate for decline and optimise their function to the greatest extent possible (Baltes and Baltes, 1990; Baltes, 2003). According to Mayer (2002), this model rests on assumptions of potential growth, maintenance/function, resilience, and the regulation of losses that are considered central to development. This model is unique in its explanation of how processes of adaptation can be used in late life in order to compensate for loss and decline. Despite its challenge to psychological perspectives, however, it remains linked to biological and psychological models of development that are predicated on the basis of decline in late life. Baltes' model is thus limited where suggested models for late life are concerned. For example, Baltes and Smith (1999) themselves note that this model may have less explanatory power in relation to those in the 'oldest old' category, whose resources for coping may be depleted by the extent of the illness of impairment (see also Smith and Baltes, 1993; Smith, 2000; Baltes and Smith, 2002). As will be explored in the second part of this book, the two models that reach into late life – Erikson's focus on wisdom and Baltes' selective optimisation compensation – are relevant where late-life transitions such as the fourth age are concerned. Where Erikson's model speaks of care and wisdom as developmental tasks, the lifespan perspective focuses on adaptation and coping with age-related changes and impairment as key developmental tasks of this period. The questions of whether and the extent to which these resonate with older people's experiences, however, remain.

Contribution: continuity and change as development and adjustment

As outlined above, the psychological study of transitions and the lifecourse contribute to understandings of development and adjustment experienced at the individual level. The central themes of continuity and change are understood in psychology as movement across developmental stages, the successful accomplishment of developmental tasks, and adaptation or adjustment across the lifecourse, and in late life. Three themes are important where psychological understandings of transitions in late life are concerned. First is the idea that change is a normal part of the lifecourse. Individuals are expected to move across stages by building on previous stages. Herein lies the normative concept of 'success' that is embedded in understandings of transition in relation to ageing and late life. Movement into a new stage of development is considered healthy, whereas remaining in a particular stage is considered stagnation or a failure to mature. One of the problems, however, is that most available models offer little past adulthood, thereby linking normal process of ageing with decline and devalue. The tension between success-based models and those focused on decline will be explored as themes throughout this book.

Second is the understanding that change can be experienced as a difficult process that requires adaptation and adjustment. The psychological literature contains a substantial body of scholarship focused on adjustment and adaptation to change across the life span, in particular, the possible disruptive impact of life events or transitions, and the psychological adjustment required to cope with these changes. Considering that models either assume the dominant association between ageing and decline, or articulate developmental tasks of late life in relation to coping, the focus on adjustment and adaptation is particularly relevant for understanding transition in late life. An underlying theme in the psychological literature on transition is that late life is characterised by difficult developmental tasks of coping (Baltes, 1997) or outlining a different set of tasks focused on a more existential or spiritual base (Erikson, 1982), both of which suggest that late life is distinct from the rest of the lifecourse. Questions relating to continuity and change will be explored throughout this book.

Third is the implicit idea that threads of continuous experience can be located in one's personality or identity. While the discussion in psychology points primarily to experiences of change, there is also a body of scholarship on identity that draws attention to the theme of continuity across the lifecourse (see Kaufman, 1986; Atchley, 1989, 1999). In these interpretations, identity can become the means to move smoothly across transitions, and therefore the means by which 'success' can be achieved in late life. Understandings of continuity and change tend to differ from the majority of the psychological scholarship, with continuity rather than change the guiding force. Here, change is rooted in the identity of the individual, and possibly combined with ideas of coping or adjusting to normative stages of development. Success is therefore framed in terms of continuity of the identity or self. What is central to such understandings is the question of whether the individual is able to integrate change into their identity without experiencing rupture, crisis or breakdown. It is not surprising, therefore, that identity remains central to the strategies used to discuss difference and variation from standard interpretations of transition (see Hockey and James, 2003). In particular, identity claims are cited as the key location from which to challenge or confront normative models (see Kaufman, 1986; Hurd Clarke, 2002; Jones, 2006). Strands of psychology focused on personality and identity highlight how threads continue across time, throughout various stages and developmental tasks of the lifecourse. In this sense, the development and maintenance of an identity can provide older people with the means of self-definition and adjustment across time. Personality and identity can thus be seen as a means to overcome fixed definitions of expectations associated with developmental stages, as well as the idea of decline in late life. The questions that remain unaddressed at this point relate to how identity may be used in relation to difference, including varying social locations and impairment in late life, as well as the tensions between self-definition and the realities of impairment in late life.

Understandings of continuity and change as linked to development, adaptation and identity, and the tensions that exist between such explanations, are particularly relevant for the study of transitions as they relate to late life. The prominent themes in psychology reveal three significant gaps relating to the study of late life. First, there is a need to develop an interdisciplinary model that links insights from psychology with those of anthropology, sociology and gerontology (see Mayer, 2002). While arguments for linking the insights of sociology and psychology are long-standing (Clausen, 1986; George, 1993, 1996; Mayer, 2000), less attention has been paid to multidisciplinary models as they apply to ageing and late life. However, in isolation, the psychological perspectives focused on age norms, developmental goals and individual adjustments are generally unable to account for institutional forces, structural conditions and social roles that may also play a role in older people's lives. Second, there is a need to better understand diversity and the variations produced in adapting to continuity and change across the lifecourse. Third, scholars must understand the ways in which conditions of late life such as impairment and decline may intersect with psychological interpretations of ageing, specifically whether the developmental tasks of late life are indeed different from the rest of the lifecourse – the lines along which such tasks may be understood, and the extent to which identity and self can contribute to continuity in late life, especially where diversity and impairment are concerned. Such challenges as articulated by older people are explored as central tensions throughout the book.

Social gerontology: approaches to transition in late life

Trends from anthropology, sociology and psychology can be identified in the gerontological approaches to the study of transition in late life. Ideas such as those articulated by van Gennep (1960 [1909]) have been applied in the field of ageing and further developed in order to explain stability and change in relation to late life (see Cain, 1964, 1967; Neugarten, 1969, 1976, 1979a,b; Riley et al, 1972; Foner, 1975; Neugarten and Hagestad, 1976; Atchley, 1989, 1999, 2000; Laslett, 1989). Drawn from the various disciplines explored throughout the chapter, the predominant frameworks for understanding transitions in late life are age- and stage-based, accompanied by an emphasis on coping with change. The study of transition in social gerontology draws on distinctions from developmental models, thereby framing transitions as normative events that occur between these stages. For example, studies of widowhood and retirement have received dedicated attention in the field (Arber and Evandrou, 1993). While the literature on social gerontology in part sustains the key themes of anthropology, sociology and psychology, a closer look reveals how the field of gerontology also contains themes helpful to challenging the fixed interpretations of ageing and transition in late life. The following section will highlight perspectives that have been solidified in studies of transitions, focusing on prominent mid-level theoretical perspectives in each area.

Age- and stage-based expectations

The most prominent understanding of transition in social gerontology is that transitions occur in relation to age- and stage-based models and expectations. These ideas can be traced back to van Gennep's structure and process of transition, and the ways in which his ideas were interpreted in the dominant functionalist frameworks of sociology in the 1960s. In gerontology, the initial attention to transition and the lifecourse is credited to Cain (1964, 1967), who introduced van Gennep's model of transition, structures and rites of passage into studies of age. In doing so, Cain's work is considered to have set the foundations for contributions such as age stratification, articulated by Matilda White Riley, and Bernice Neugarten's timing of transitions. The anthropological notion of rites of passage became influential in studies of ageing in the 1960s and 1970s, especially as applied to retirement (Crawford, 1973). Although extremely influential in introducing the study of transition in social gerontology, Cain has been criticised for rendering an overly structural reading of van Gennep's work that overlooked the contributions of process and passage (Spencer, 1990; Hockey and James, 2003). The view of transitions adopted by gerontology, and that became dominant, was thus marked by structural-functional concerns for normative models, fixed end points and coherence. More recently, however, anthropological interpretations have been revived in relation to lifecourse identities and process-based readings of ritual, fluidity and socio-cultural meanings of transitions, that challenge long-standing interpretations in the field (see Spencer, 1990; Myerhoff, 2000; Hockey and James, 2003; Bytheway, 2009).

Stratification based on age

Drawing on the conflict perspective articulated in sociology, Riley's age stratification (Riley and Foner, 1968; Riley 1971; Riley et al, 1972; Riley et al, 1994) has also profoundly influenced the study of transitions and the lifecourse. Working from the starting point that age is structured in society created a base from which to consider transition in relation to social structures, and in particular, structures characterised by conflict rather than stability. Central to the age-stratification approach is the idea that age alters the social relations between older and younger people in society, changes social relationships and produces inequities between these strata. Age-stratification considers age as 'a pivot around which social relationships are formed' (Foner, 1975, p 145) and emphasises how age affects and is affected by the structure and dynamics of society (Riley et al, 1972), that is, it draws attention to the unequal power relations within society and, in particular, how practices entrenched in age create social divisions that result in an unequal distribution of social resources (Riley and Foner, 1968; Riley et al, 1972, 1994). This perspective has influenced thinking in relation to ageism (see Bytheway, 1994) and other conflict-based interpretations. It has also been used to build a more complex stratification that considers ageing in relation to economic class, political inequalities and cultural lifestyles (Turner, 1989). In Turner's (1989) model, age-stigmatisation is explained in relation to dependency, social exchange and reciprocity, whereby 'the politics of ageing' can be conceptualised as a series of conflicts between interacting economic, political and cultural dimensions. This reciprocity-maturation model outlines how interaction between the economy, political, social and cultural contexts creates disadvantage and decreased prestige. As adults age and become more bound within the social and cultural system, their social status and personal self-esteem rise; they decline, however, as adults move from this system, into retirement for example. In this sense, interpretations such as Turner's link development, structures and socio-cultural relations. This perspective implies that the transition into age-related categories is more dramatic than other periods and involves different lifestyles (Turner, 1989), or is likely to be accompanied by greater social implications, such as those characterised by Guillemard's (1980) concept of the 'social death'.

Age stratification reflects various strands of thinking in relation to continuity and change across the lifecourse that, when taken into account alongside other strands of thinking, challenge taken-for-granted understandings of transition in late life. Age stratification is in some ways aligned with the psychological view that age is potentially difficult, yet the interpretation here is not an individual developmental challenge, but located at the systemic level, with late life structured by social relations that create inequality, disadvantage or devalue. As such, it calls into question the individual focus on responsibility, as well as the expectation of a smooth and coherent progression through the stages of the lifecourse. At the same time, its attention to the decreased levels of prestige and power associated with age challenge the normalcy of psychological models of development, including those that replicate associations of decline in late life. Negative social experiences and a decline in status represent social relations that must be altered from an age-stratification perspective. A question that surfaces, however, is the means by which these changes may be achieved. Stratified understandings of age, therefore, have made central contributions to what is known about transitions in social gerontology, especially from a critical perspective. It is not surprising that the detailed attention to structures of disadvantage sprouted critical gerontology and a strand of lifecourse research focused on institutions and structures (see Dannefer and Settersen, 2010 on the institutional model of lifecourse research). The poignancy of age stratification's contributions becomes apparent in relation to transitions such as the fourth age that occur at the intersections of age, impairment and socio-cultural values of decline.

Timing and continuity

Two prominent strands of thinking in relation to transition and late life were developed around the concepts of timing and continuity. Although Cain (1964, 1967) was the first to incorporate van Gennep's model into social gerontology, interpretations of transitions as applied to the study of ageing and late life were popularised through Neugarten's work, and in particular, the idea that transitions can be experienced 'on' and 'off time'. According to Neugarten (1976), one moves across age-based stages in a way that is considered 'on time' as it corresponds with standard expectations or 'off time' in that it differs from them. For example, an early retirement at age 50 would be considered 'off time' as would a late retirement at age 75. In addition to the idea of on and off time, a distinction is made between expected or normal events, and unexpected or unanticipated events. The work of Neugarten (1976) asserts that events may not be experienced as difficult if they occur as expected (also Neugarten and Hagestad, 1976). In this line of thinking, it is the unexpected events that occur 'out of time' that can cause a potential crisis where adjustment is concerned (Tennant and Pogson, 1995). Nodding to the psychological processes of adjustment, such interpretations highlight the importance of an interdisciplinary perspective that considers meaning, structure and interpretation. Neugarten's contributions linking timing and expectations have become widely accepted in social gerontology. While her work has been criticised for its rigid interpretation of van Gennep's (1960 [1909]) work and more generally for its reliance on coherence and stability, characteristic of a structural-functionalist approach (Spencer 1990), her contributions in relation to timing are now taken for granted in understandings of late life. Neugarten's contributions of timing were central to early understandings of transition in social gerontology, as well as to a reconsideration of transitions under contemporary conditions, where the process of ageing is seen to occur over a long process. Her contributions linked structures with experience, and introduced the idea that culturally defined norms can alter the meaning of the experience and that timing can affect successful development or coping. As such, they contribute to a more institutional consideration of the lifecourse and transitions in late life.

In a related but slightly different way, Atchley (1989, 1999, 2000) is credited with bringing psychological ideas about coping and identity into sociology and social gerontology. Writing initially in relation to retirement, Atchley (2000) linked psychological perspectives on coping and adaptation with sociological perspectives on change. In his work, he created an understanding whereby the individual could achieve continuity despite change. Continuity theory, as it was called, made a significant contribution to the understanding of transition in social gerontology. Rather than focusing on development or tasks that rely on a distinction between early and late life, Atchley's continuity theory provided the possibility for a cohesive thread achieved through identity. Atchley (1999) maintained that continuity of identity could be achieved across transitions such as retirement. Introducing this blend of psychological and sociological perspectives, Atchley (1999) created the space for consistency based on a continuous thread that was located in an individual's lifelong identity (also see Meyer, 1986). Atchley's (1989) continuity theory thus drew attention to the concepts of success and failure, and in particular, whether the individual is able to negotiate the change into their sense of self or identity without experiencing rupture, crisis or breakdown. This has been most influential in the field of identity and lifestyle where continuity offers a possibility to negotiate or resist the fixed normative patterns and expectations of age. The possibility of continuity across the lifecourse, and especially in late life, has become deeply embedded in understandings of transition, with the concept of continuity often used as an implicit frame for experience in late life, and in older people's accounts.

The third and fourth ages: transitions in ageing

In addition to the elements discussed earlier, the division between the third and fourth age is crucial to understanding transition in late life. Scholarship in ageing contains an inherent separation of 'younger/ healthier' and 'older/ill' older people that reflects not only the dominance of age- and stage-based perspectives on transitions, but also socio-cultural ideas about illness, impairment and decline. In part, the distinctions made between the third and fourth age can be read as an attempt to more accurately depict the heterogeneity of older populations and the changes that may occur in late life. Rooted in biological understandings of expected physical and psychological changes, the constructs of the third and fourth age were used to differentiate between a 'younger' subgroup of the older population and those that are slightly 'older', that is, the periods of early and late ageing. The most common age-based divisions are thus between what is known as the third age (normally people aged 65-74) and the fourth age (normally people aged 75 and over, although some authors consider this category to begin at 80).

Over time, movement from one group to the other came to represent an expected age-based construct denoting change. As outlined above, Neugarten's work described how movement into the third age (that is, ageing), and between the third and fourth ages, represented separate transitions in late life. The expectations that accompanied the third and fourth age were popularised in Laslett's (1989) work *A fresh map of life*, which discussed the lifecourse as represented by four stages, the first being that of childhood, the second of adulthood, the third of ageing, and the fourth of decline.[8] Echoing normative stages of development, and age- or role-based social norms outlined in developmental psychological and sociological perspectives, each of Laslett's distinctions are accompanied by a set of expectations:

> First comes an era of dependence, socialization, immaturity and education; second an era of independence, maturity and responsibility, of earning and of saving; third, an era of personal fulfilment; and fourth an era of final dependence, decrepitude and death. (Laslett, 1989, p 4) [9]

Over time, the distinctions, best exemplified in Laslett's (1989) articulation of the third and fourth age, have become solidified as important thresholds at least on socio-cultural and practical levels. The separation of the third and fourth age has become commonplace in the conceptualisation of late life and has been taken up in great detail (Baltes, 1987a, 1987b, 2003; Baltes and Baltes, 1990; Baltes and Smith, 1999, 2002; Gilleard and Higgs, 2000; Midwinter, 2005).

The divisions proposed by Laslett, however, are not only age- and stage-based boundaries for transitions, but are also deeply reflective of social and cultural values assigned to these periods. Laslett's (1989) main contribution was in challenging the naturalisation of age by articulating the third age as a time of opportunity and freedom characterised by choice, related not to chronological age, but to potential and possibility. In this way, it most closely corresponds with notions of lifestyle that are based on choice and the negotiation of experience (see Turner, 1989; Gilleard and Higgs, 2000). Yet, while claiming that the third age has no fixed end point, Laslett's (1989) distinction between the third and the fourth age implies that the fourth age is a period of decline and decrepitude that brings this potential and opportunity of the third age to a halt. Gilleard and Higgs (2000) have argued that indeed, 'the positive notions of opportunity associated with the third age are entirely dependent on the existence of the fourth age being defined as dependence, decrepitude and death' (p 199). Divisions between these stages of late life underline socio-cultural notions, and stamp understandings of late life change with decline – topics that will be addressed in detail in Chapter Nine. On a conceptual level, this period of the fourth age represents one of the major contemporary challenges where continuity and change are concerned – a tension that establishes the fourth age as a transition worthy of reconsideration.

Conclusion: alternative base for the study of continuity and change

This chapter has highlighted the varying influences that can be found at the root of models in social gerontology. It has drawn attention to the tensions between ageing as a lifelong process and age as a separate period of life; to debates between assumptions based on coherence and conflict; and to the role of structures, processes and meaning making. It has outlined psychological explanations of development and adjustment, and how these are seen to be linked with the internal, personal and emotional processes of transitions throughout the lifecourse. Threaded across the approaches, however, is a concern for understanding continuity and change across the lifecourse, and a recognition that the current fixed models based on age and stage do not necessarily correspond with contemporary questions and experiences. Contemporary issues call into question the centrality of age, the dominance of age-based models and the blurring of life stages, and emphasise the importance of subjective interpretations in shaping the form, timing and meanings of changes. Together these challenges suggest that alternative forms of understanding transition be considered. Yet, gerontology is not at a loss for how to proceed; several available strands offer insight and innovation where the reconsideration of transitions in late life is concerned.

The differing disciplinary approaches to the study of transition in late life provide direction to consider alternate lines of thinking, and in particular, paths from which to reconsider age- and stage-based models of transitions and the lifecourse. As highlighted in earlier chapters, dominant age-based interpretations of transitions have been critiqued on several fronts: the relevance of age-based stages (Featherstone and Hepworth, 1989; Featherstone and Wernick, 1995; Blaikie, 1999; Gilleard and Higgs, 2000); diversity and diverse social locations (Blakemore and Boneham, 1994); the complex relationships between body, psychological, social and cultural aspects of ageing over time (Cole, 1992; Dannefer, 1996; Estes et al, 2003); and the geographical context within which transitions occur (for example, urban/rural; Western/Non-Western states). Drawing primarily on standard age- and stage-based concepts, however, social gerontology has overlooked important insights for understanding transitions in late life. It now faces contemporary challenges related to the fluidity of growing old, challenges to social-cultural norms, and questions of diversity and difference – issues that will be explored in remaining chapters. Lessons learned from the multidisciplinary approaches to the study of transition allude to age as a contested terrain; the growing recognition of diversity among ageing populations; socio-cultural interpretations of age; and the global challenge of growing old within various contexts – all of which highlight the need to reconsider transitions in late life. Concepts that are relevant for contemporary questions of ageing, transitions and late life include process, passage, liminality, diversity, continuity and adaptation.

The exploration of varying disciplines reveals that multidisciplinary approaches to the study of transition have, in part, become interdisciplinary when applied in social gerontology. In drawing on perspectives developed in anthropology, sociology and psychology, social gerontology has benefited from differing perspectives, but at the same time has been marked by them. What seems important for a reconsideration of transitions in late life is attention to how structures and experiences inform and influence understandings of ageing and late life. Questions of age, for example, are crucial to social gerontology. Although arguments against age-based discrimination may cause one to question the relevance of a discipline based on age, analysis of the structured social relations that are created and maintained in relation to age emphasise the importance of an analysis that takes account of age relations and early experiences of disadvantage (Ferraro and Shippee, 2009). Articulating inequalities in late life as disadvantage that occurs over a lifecourse, as implied by the 'personological' approach to the lifecourse, would change the nature of how social gerontology approaches transitions. Yet, such a decision may overlook both the age-specific features and socio-cultural practices that alter older people's experience. Less dominant interpretations focused on the intersections of diverse structured and social locations, social and cultural interpretations of transitions, and subjective interpretations suggest that there may be an alternative basis to understanding transition in relation to late life. In these alternate models, age may be seen as one of many intersecting variables, with age considered a subjective and negotiated process. Transitions, for example, may be comprised of flexible or relational aspects that include a liminal period of being and feeling in-between. Emotions and subjective interpretations may feature more prominently than the scholarship would lead us to believe, with transitions more nuanced than fixed ages or stages suggest. Questions of 'fit' between the suggested models of transitions and late life become important, as do the models of continuity and change that older people use to negotiate their experiences. Chapter Four thus turns to the methods used to understand older people's experiences in relation to the dominant approaches.

Notes

[1] While the language used in the English translation and subsequent interpretations of van Gennep's (1960 [1909]) work refers to 'rites of passage', Kimball (1960), who wrote the introduction to van Gennep's work, notes that the term 'passage' could have been translated as 'transition' rather than 'rites of passage', and 'schema' as 'dynamics' rather than pattern. He notes how this difference may have affected the way that the work was taken up, and that using transition and dynamics may have better captured the sense of both process and structure found within van Gennep's original work.

[2] Van Gennep's (1960 [1909]) process of passage consists of three main phases: separation (termed *separation* in French); transition (termed *marge* in French); and incorporation (termed *aggregation* in French).

[3] What is interesting for the purposes of this analysis on transition in late life is that the key foundational studies for transition sprung from ethnographic observations of ritual at the end of life, with studies of death therefore providing the basis for much of what is known about lifecourse transition – roots that are rarely acknowledged in dominant understandings of transition. In fact, Huntington and Metcalf (1979) entitled one chapter in their book 'Death as transition'.

[4] The term life span tends to be used as two separate words when referring to a span or period of a life, and as one complete word when referring to a discipline of study, as in lifespan psychology or lifespan biology.

[5] It is noteworthy that Erikson's wife elaborated on a final ninth stage of 'old age' after Erikson's death in 1994 (Erikson, 1997).

[6] These include infancy (basic trust versus basic mistrust); early childhood (autonomy versus shame, doubt); play age (initiative versus guilt); school age (industry versus inferiority); adolescence (identity versus identity confusion); young adulthood (intimacy versus isolation); adulthood (generativity versus stagnation); and old age (integrity versus despair, disgust). The strengths or ego qualities emerging from each respectively are hope, will, purpose, competence, fidelity, love, care and wisdom.

[7] The lifespan model includes three influences to explain individual variation: normative age-graded influences that are biological and socio-cultural, and that correlate with age, such as physical maturation or education; normative history-graded influences that are environmental, cataclysmic events, such as historical events that characterise entire cohorts; and non-normative influences that are significant for a particular individual, but not part of the overall pattern of the lifecycle, such as a traffic accidents, disease or winning the lottery (Baltes, 1997).

[8] Laslett (1989) drew on studies conducted on mortality, longevity, the survival curve and the fourth age conducted by Fries (1980) and Fries and Crapo (1981) to define his construct of the fourth age. In doing so, the link between the fourth age and frailty is clearly established, as is the reliance on biomedical definitions focused on decline and death. As will be discussed in Chapter Nine, the fourth age has yet to be defined from a social perspective.

[9] Of note is that Laslett's (1989) concept of the third age became a stepping-stone for the development of the University of the Third Age in the UK.

FOUR

The intersections of policy, practice and experience

This chapter outlines how discourse in policy and practice can be linked with older people's experiences of transition in late life. It moves beyond academic understandings of transition, providing the conceptual background and methodological means to reinterpret transitions as they are presented in social policy discourse. Rather than treating the study of social policy and the analysis of lived experience as separate, this chapter is drawn to an understanding of what happens at the intersections of these sites. First, it outlines how policy discourse may be understood to represent and shape socio-cultural interpretations of ageing and late life. Second, it outlines how a narrative approach can be used to access the storylines told in public policy and older people's accounts, and the link between the two. Third, it outlines how these ideas were used in the Late Life Transitions project that forms the basis of the book. This linked approach provides the foundation to consider the models that shape late life, and the ways in which older people may use these ideas to negotiate socio-cultural and personal constructs of ageing. Together, a storied approach to late life can provide new ways of understanding expectations and interpretations of transitions in late life as taking place in the intersections between policies, discourses, organisational practices and lived experience. In doing so, the approach builds on and links critical traditions in gerontology from structural and humanist perspectives. It outlines both how older people's experience may be shaped through ideas such as those articulated by academic study and public policy practices, and how older people may draw on, negotiate or contest the expressed ideas about ageing and transitions in their own lives.

Although focus on policy has always been central to the study of ageing from a critical perspective (Estes, 1979; Phillipson, 1982; Walker, 1982), contemporary planning issues have brought debates on ageing to the fore. In recent years, concerns for transitions related to ageing and late life have resurfaced through debates on the age of eligibility for retirement benefits, and ideas on how to best achieve productive and successful ageing (see Moody, 2001). Underlying the attention to issues of ageing are concerns for financial stability amid shifting demographics, ensuring productivity over the lifecourse, and attempts to reduce fiscal expenditure on costs such as pensions (Gee and Gutman, 2000). These debates and ongoing reforms have an impact on 'what it means to be old' (Cole and Gadow, 1986), with definitions of ageing and late life evolving, and being redefined and contested. They also contribute to an ideological context whereby ageing and transitions are increasingly shaped within specific types of discourse.

This is particularly the case where the ideological commitments of governments and policymakers are concerned. The most notable examples of change are in the areas of retirement and health, where age boundaries and expectations are shifting dramatically.

Contemporary debates and policy responses to late life are imbued with tensions between theoretical thinking about the lifecourse, such as the normative models outlined in Chapter Three, and more contemporary ideas. Where earlier models addressed lifecourse changes through the desire for a stable and coherent integration into society along age- or stage-based lines, current thinking tends to challenge these integrative models by drawing attention to fluid experiences across the lifecourse. Policy models, dominant ideas and older people's experiences increasingly draw attention to the fact that expectations of transitions as smooth movement between two fixed age- or stage-based states are no longer realistic. Currently, understandings of transitions experienced throughout the lifecourse are shifting and have left commonsense understandings of ageing in a state of confusion or flux (Phillipson, 1998; Biggs, 1999, 2004b; Gilleard and Higgs, 2000, 2005; Powell and Longino, 2001). Yet amid these various interpretations and powerful socio-cultural discourses, accessing the meanings and models attributed to growing old can be a difficult process. Reconsidering transitions from a critical perspective is thus a crucial step in understanding and planning for ageing societies.

Models that structure and shape expectations of late-life transitions can be found at the intersection of social policies, socio-cultural discourses and older people's accounts. Each of these sites contains notions of what constitutes a positive or negative experience of ageing, including expectations of how individuals move between ages, stages and roles, and the challenges they may experience in this process. Yet approaching policies as sites that shape understandings requires the conceptual and practical means to explore these locations from the inside. Both critical gerontology and the lifecourse perspective outline the theoretical argument for blending macro and micro perspectives. However, as discussed in Chapter Two, each has experienced difficulties in bridging these levels, and both have tended to focus almost exclusively on studies either of society and institutions, or individual experiences. This tendency to concentrate on one level is also reflected in the differences between approaches taken in anthropology, sociology and psychology, as explored in Chapter Three. Yet, current scholarship points to the increased relevance of linking disciplinary approaches in ways that integrate these levels. Approaching the interface of policy, practice and experience brings one closer to understanding how messages from each may be read in socio-cultural contexts. Understanding the intersections between policy, institutional practices and lived experiences is thus central to the task of reconsidering transition in late life.

Policy: shaping expectations and experiences of transition

Policy is a fascinating site where the questions of late-life transitions are concerned. Policy efforts have played a major role in understanding, shaping and responding to ageing and late life – especially in contexts such as the UK where reconfiguring age has figured prominently in the policy agenda (see Biggs, 2004b; Biggs et al, 2006). Focusing on the messages that are articulated in public policy show how ideas about the lifecourse can become fixed into social practices that influence interpretations of ageing. Policy contains a mixture of ideas and practices. Although policy discourse is considered to reflect contemporary concerns and interpretations not yet integrated into practice, it also contains long-accepted strands of thought – many of which are political and ideological – that remain at the core of social and organisational practice. These include structured understandings of transition that are rooted in the idea of successful integration into society through work and timely withdrawal from the labour force. Such ideas can profoundly shape practice, expectations and the interpretation of experience of ageing and late life, albeit not in predictable ways. According to Leonard (1997), social policy is both a response to, and an attempt to engineer, 'the problem of ageing', and is a bridge between macro-social discourses and everyday experiences. The models of transition that are embedded in public policy can thus be seen as ideas that inform understandings of late life and guide the interpretation of experience. Nowhere is this contradiction more evident than in recent examples of pension reform or treatment of issues of frailty, whereby contested classifications and definitions of eligibility for social programmes are influencing ideas about contemporary experiences of ageing, and in particular whether or not they are deemed successful. With questions of planning for ageing societies at the forefront of policy debates, an exploration of the intersections between policy, practice and experience can highlight the tensions and contradictions that exist between dominant models and personal constructions of age.

Policy as a reflection of contemporary views on ageing and late life

Policy discourse, debates and definitions are considered to reflect contemporary views of social problems and social groups. When considered across the lifecourse, public policy can be seen to reflect themes of successful development, education, social issues, integration into society, productive work and retirement. As such, policy can be seen as an active representation of what is known as an 'institutionalised lifecourse' (Dittmann-Kohli and Meyer, 1986), reflective of larger social and cultural understandings of the divisions that occur across the period of a life. It can also be seen to incorporate socio-cultural beliefs such as the focus on the individual, independence and the primacy of youth. Some of the prominent ideals that can be identified in contemporary policy on ageing focus on active, productive and healthy ageing. Further policy can represent the ideological commitments of government and policy in shaping discourses on age. With the upsurge in recent attempts to shape discourses of ageing and late life (Moody, 2001; Katz, 2005), policy discourse and practice form an excellent site from which to explore how social and cultural views of ageing have shifted over time and, in turn, how policies can influence transitions in late life and vice versa.

Policy as a structure for practice

At the same time as reflecting contemporary views, policies also represent macro structures that guide organisational practices. Comprised of discursive practices whereby language defines and influences the directions taken, policy can be considered to set the boundaries for 'legitimate' claims for public and social resources in a particular social and cultural context. In doing so, policy establishes – or at minimum reflects – ideals and expectations to be pursued in a given society. In some cases, policy solidifies a consensus of the day into practice – for example, the idea of older people as having made lifelong contributions. In others, the notions integrated into policy are more in line with political ideology that pushes a particular view of ageing in order to alter programmes and public expenditure – for example, the notion that social programmes and services targeting retirement and older people's health are too costly (see Gee and Gutman, 2000). And while policy is increasingly shifting to a lifecourse perspective, direct programmes tend to be population-based, with older people representing one major group deemed to need services. The potential to shape or influence the definitions of ageing is thus considerable. Policies implemented at a given time, and in a particular socio-cultural context, form guidelines for practice that result in specific interpretations of the population group at hand. Retirement policy, for example, has resulted in tensions between portrayals of older people as rights–demanding seniors and as dependent older people (Townsend, 1981; Walker, 1982). This classic example demonstrates how policy frameworks are often considered to be connected to the release of social expenditure, as well as the creation of frameworks within which to 'grow old' (Biggs, 2001, 2004b; Hendricks, 2004). Drawing on Calasanti and Slevin's (2001) term 'age relations', policies such as those relating to retirement can be considered as sources of power that create and sustain power relations that ultimately affect understandings of late life.

Focusing on policy as practice reveals how particular groups such as older people become the objects of disciplinary knowledge (see Foucault, 1994). This focus also allows for an analysis of how powerful practices referred to by Smith (1984) as the 'relations of ruling' can be used to structure, define and regulate experience. While policy is not an institution per se, it does play a central role in creating the structures for the administration of public resources, and defining eligibility. As such, the practices of policy, and the accompanying organisational practices, highlight how policy is representative of an institution that shapes late life. The overall visions of ageing that are being promoted in public policy, such as those of active or successful ageing, are case in point and will be further discussed in Chapter Five. The linkage of language and practice are integral to understanding definitions of social issues such as late life, including the ways in which notions and practices established in public policy can block or facilitate claims for access to services (Fraser, 1989, 1997).[1] Focusing on the ways in which policy sets guidelines for particular groups such as older people can help understand the composition and definitions of groups, the formation of social identities over time, and the way in which dominant notions are secured and contested (see Fraser, 1997). Long discussed in critical gerontology, the policy definitions and accompanying practices that shape and structure experiences across the lifecourse need to be better understood (Fraser and Gordon, 1994; Walker, 2006a, 2006b). Examination of policy structures and social relations can point to the experiences that exist within and between these structural relations of age, and draw attention to the relations that are necessary for negotiation and resistance within these structures and services. This is particularly the case in the shifting context whereby age is being redefined simultaneously by policies and older people themselves.

Policy as a frame of reference

One of the ways researchers can link explorations of policy and lived experience is to consider public policy and policy discourse as a 'frame of reference' for what is taken to be real (Goffman, 1974; see also Schutz, 1962, 1970; Bateson, 1972). Such frames of reference can be seen to influence or shape interpretations of ageing. Asking questions such as 'Under what circumstances do we think things are real?', Goffman (1974) draws attention to the ideas and assumptions that construct events and experiences. He says the following of frames:

> I assume that definitions of a situation are built up in accordance with principles of organization which govern events – at least social ones – and our subjective involvement in them: frame is the word I use to refer to such of these basic elements as I am able to identify.... My phrase 'frame analysis' is a slogan to refer to the examination in these terms of the organisation of experience. (Goffman, 1974, pp 10-11)

Drawing on this understanding, policy can be seen to frame experience through the creation of typified constructs that establish models for growing old, structure responses to older people, and in turn shape social and cultural expectations of late life (see Schutz, 1962, 1970 on typification). Such a perspective has been taken by Holstein and Gubrium (2000), who have explored the discourse and practices of institutional contexts ranging from legal proceedings to schools to long-term care. In ageing policy, fixed notions of age- and stage-based transitions, as well as those of 'success' or 'dependence' in late life, can be considered as representational frames for making sense of growing old. Drawing on frame analysis and the constructivist interpretations of the lifecourse, policies can be considered to frame expectations of late life, providing typical constructs or representational frameworks from which events and interactions are perceived and experienced.

In providing typified frames for experience that are reflective of dominant and contemporary interpretations of age, policy can also be considered to influence subjective interpretations and lifestyle choices. Older people may use typifications such as those available in public discourse to construct or attach meaning to their experiences of ageing and the lifecourse (Holstein and Gubrium, 2000). They may, for example, draw on the discourses of health and success in retirement to make sense of their experience. They may on the one hand look forward to their retirement as a time of freedom, activity or enjoyment, or they may on the other hand dread the symbolic 'social death' (see Guillemard, 1972, 2002) that retirement can be seen to represent. This is not to say that older people directly take and apply a typical view, but that they may relate to these frames, accepting some aspects while negotiating or contesting others. Thus, making sense of transition in late life comprises a complex mixture of strategies. Yet while there is a growing sense that older people negotiate their experience in relation to powerful policy constructs or socio-cultural discourses (Biggs, 1997, 1999; Hurd Clarke, 2002; Grenier, 2003; Jones, 2006), we know very little about the processes by which some messages are embraced while others are rejected. Scholarship on late life lacks a complex understanding of how the decisions and viewpoints of older people relate to the internalisation of socio-cultural ideas of age, and a subsequent application of them in relation to other older people and themselves.

The reverse relationship also exists, where cultural beliefs and the interpretations of individuals or groups can influence the definition of problems and social responses. This can range from changes in the language used to refer to older people, to older people's ways of organising their services and those ideas judged to be popular. For example, the beliefs and practices of older people from diverse social locations can alter the types of discourse or frames of reference used to discuss experiences of ageing (see Grenier and Brotman, 2010). Structured and social locations may affect older people's ability to draw on such frames for their experience, that is, the experience of a particular social location may provide opportunities or barriers in relation to the dominant or expected frames. Take for example the location of a lifelong athlete who remains healthy and active in late life and can draw on the typification of physical activity with ease (see Tulle-Winton, 1999, 2000). Also take for example the case of an older person who has experienced racism and discrimination throughout the lifecourse, and as a result may reject any label deemed stigmatising (Grenier, 2006b, 2007b). Older people's subjective interpretations of ageing take place across varying locations in a socio-cultural context where they make use of their lifelong experiences in order to shape their understandings of late life. This may be even more so the case when they become directly involved with practices that require them to accept classifications and the accompanying associations such as frailty or the fourth age, discussed in Chapter Nine.

The link between policy discourse, practice and experience draws attention to issues of 'experiential fit' with regard to constructs of transitions in late life. As Gubrium and Holstein (2000) maintain, the experience of ageing includes an amalgam of macro-level societal discourse and micro-level personal narratives. Questions of 'experiential fit' – that is, whether larger concepts used to frame ageing resonate with older people's interpretations of ageing – are particularly important in the contemporary context. Take as an example the tensions that occur as a result of disparities between dependency models based on adult ageing and those based on productive ageing (Katz and Green, 2002). Yet, while scholarship in critical gerontology continues to flag these discrepancies as requiring attention, there are few available methods to link the models expressed in policy discourse with older people's subjective experience. After brief comment on current discourses related to transition in late life, this chapter turns to a narrative method aimed to explore the discrepancies between suggested models and late life experiences. In particular, it discusses how narrative methods may be used to understand how expectations about late life that are embedded in policy models can influence socio-cultural constructs and lived experiences of older people and vice versa.

Discourse in current policies

Approaching policy as a site that shapes knowledge and provides interpretive frames for late life reveals the increasing attention devoted to two divergent strands of discourse: the biomedical or functional aspects of ageing and the healthy, productive and social aspects of ageing. These two strands correspond with dominant interpretations of late life as either marked by continuous lifecourse trajectories characterised by health or discontinuous life events of illness, decline and rupture. In this context, older people receive conflicting frameworks regarding the 'best ways to age'. On the one hand, they receive messages about healthy and successful transitions into ageing and late life, and on the other they are told that decline and loss of autonomy are inevitable. It is within this binary that anti-ageing practices, for example, gain their strength as a powerful discourse. The opposition of these constructs, however, draws attention to the powerful assumptions made about the lifecourse, and, more importantly, the questions of 'experiential fit' between dominant models and personal experiences of ageing and late life. It is these questions that can be explored at the interface of public policies, organisational practices and the lived experiences of older people. From a critical perspective, attention can be drawn to the types of contemporary model that are suggested, the tensions that exist within and between these models, and the degree to which the experiences of older people correspond with the emerging policy and practice picture.

Yet, exploring policy in the current context reveals a growing trend whereby policy is actively attempting to 'engineer' the shapes of ageing by altering the frames of reference. International policy, for example, increasingly reflects ideas of ageing as a time of productivity and social engagement – ideas that are at the core of a major shift from decline-based models. Several similar attempts can be found in initiatives such as the United Nations' (UN) 2002 International Plan of Action on Ageing (UN, 1982), the UN Economic Commission for Europe's Regional Implementation Strategy for this plan, A Society for all Ages, and the UK's 2000 Winning the Generation Game (see Biggs et al, 2006). Rather than viewing ageing and late life as a time of decline and dependency, these strategies embraced active and productive visions of an ageing society along socially inclusive lines, and shifted the image of older people from dependent to active, healthy and successful (Biggs et al, 2006). Although countries such as Canada have been slower to develop vision statements that set the frame of reference in Canadian society (for example, the 1998 Principles of the National Framework on Aging), changing interpretations of ageing can be found through the thematic focus of projects such as Population Aging and Life-Course Flexibility taken up by the Policy Research Initiative (see PRI, 2004). What becomes evident in a close reading of policy is how competing discourses such as those focused on function and decline increasingly come to exist in polarised compartments. Such interpretations of ageing are particularly pronounced in practice settings, where levels of health despite impairment can reduce eligibility for service, and where decline itself is used to reinforce the importance of health and activity as success. To date, there has been little critical attention focused on the way these tensions between discourses of success and decline manifest themselves in policy discourse and guide the late-life experiences of older people.

Narrative storylines of policy discourse and older people's experiences

Understandings and assumptions about transitions in late life become available in the language and practices of policies and services. Turning to language and discourse can thus provide access to the powerful ideas that shape expectations and responses to ageing and late life. Approaching language as dialogical, representative, and performative (Bakhtin, 1978; Mischler, 1986; Eakin, 1999) can help to guide this analysis. First, language is a form of dialogical communication – the product of interaction between two forces, including policy texts and older persons in this case. Whether in print or person, language always involves a speaker and a listener, and the relationship between the two (Bakhtin, 1978). In this case, policies can be considered to represent and communicate a particular point of view as well as shape practices and expectations of transition in late life. Second, language is a social construct that provides access to our worlds, meanings and experiences of social reality (Berger and Luckman, 1967). In the case of policies, these can include representations of health, activity, dependence and decline, and include the ways in which such constructs are interpreted in practice and experience (Holstein and Gubrium, 2000). Third, language is a performance in the sense that it is intentional, purposeful and useful (Hall, 1998). Language is thus used by policymakers and older people alike to articulate particular directives or expectations at micro and macro levels. As such, language is at one and the same time the basis for the individual to make meaning of experience and actions (Goffman, 1959); a means to influence eligibility criteria and define need (Fraser, 1997); and a way of giving shape to social and cultural experiences (Hendricks, 2003, 2004). A focus on the language of policy therefore represents an important channel to identify the models suggested for transitions in late life, and the discrepancies that may exist between policy and lived experience. The following section elaborates how the sites of policy and experience can be considered for the stories they tell about ageing and late life.

Rooted in the study of language and experience, narrative methodology can play an important role in exploring the stories and shapes of late life. Although a storied approach is more commonly practised in relation to biographical accounts, reading policy as a story can shed light on the socio-cultural discourses that operate in society and inform older people's interpretations of late life. Macro-level policy discourse in this sense can be seen to inform expectations. Focused attention on the narrative storylines of policy and practice can demonstrate how a particular account develops over time, and can take precedence in socio-cultural discourse and practices. When local stories are set against larger interpretations of ageing and late life, the comparison between the official storylines of public policy and those experienced in everyday lives of older people provides glimpses into the coalescence or disjuncture between the suggested and the experienced. The language used provides an inroad into how public and personal models are used to make sense of late life, including how the two may intersect where social programming is concerned, or break down in relation to particular social locations or identities, for example. This understanding of language and discourse draws attention to the multiple and competing discourses that can influence models for growing older, and as a result, shape older people's lives and experiences. Policy and lived experience embody two dynamic sites of interpretation; narrative methods provide a guide to analyse what happens at these intersections.

The study of narratives derives from various disciplinary sources dedicated to exploring the interpretative aspects of experience from the perspective of the subject. Stemming from the multidisciplinary fields of linguistics (Labov and Waletzky, 1967), psychology (Sarbin, 1986), sociology (Maines, 2005) and cultural studies (Bal, 2004), storied accounts are understood as an intrinsic way of articulating and understanding human experience. Narrative approaches thus take account of the structure used to organise experience through storied accounts, and provide a window into the subjective interpretations of individuals. Narrative research aims to understand how respondents make sense of events and actions in their lives (Riessman, 1993; Clandinin and Connelly, 2000). In the words of McAdams (1993), narrative 'seek(s) to explain events in terms of human actors striving to do things over time' (p 30). It is not surprising, then, that most narratives begin with a participant-directed flow of the interview, intended to highlight meaningful experiences, themes and ideas. On a conceptual level, narrative provides access to fluid accounts of experience (Polkinghorne, 1988), and situates stories within a particular context and across time (Randall and Kenyon 2001; Kenyon et al, 2001). On a subjective level, narratives provide participants with authority over the content and presentation of their stories (Czarniawska, 2004; Labov and Waletzky, 1967) and grant the power to articulate their perceptions in ways meaningful to them (Reissman, 1993). These underlying premises of narrative approaches closely align the stories told by individuals with their subjective interpretations of experience. They also, however, point to the ways by which policies may also form accounts of experience packed with meaning.

Whether articulated in relation to the study of policy or older people's accounts, narrative research draws attention to the frames of reference, the centrality of meaning making, the context, and the rhetorical purpose of the stories told. In narrative, the account told is intricately linked with the context within which it is told, and its relationship in time. Bruner (1986) suggests that individuals think of the world through two perspectives: a paradigmatic mode where experiences are understood according to a tightly reasoned analysis, and through stories where events are explained in terms of meaning-making processes. His approach highlights how the subject makes meaning of their experience through the very telling of a story. While locating a subject within policy is a slightly more complicated matter, the storylines of policy can also be approached as a frame of reference that is used to represent experience or socio-cultural notions of the time. In this sense, the language of policy can be considered to convey interpretations of ageing in a particular society. Narratives told at both the levels of policy and experience provide insight into socio-cultural models of late life, including how these models become frames of reference that are integrated into the storied accounts of older people. Discourses, for example, may appear as characters or ideas against which older people measure themselves, their ageing, and the sense of success or failure that is deeply ingrained in understandings of transition in late life. On the other hand, the storylines of older people can reveal how the dominant age- and stage-based models may or may not correspond with their conceptions of ageing. Attending to the context and purpose of each storied account allows the researcher to move beyond narrative as a voiced expression of experience, and into a more profound understanding of what is being conveyed within the larger socio-cultural context of growing old.

One feature relevant for exploring the fit between policy and lived experience is the rhetorical purpose of an account. Polkinghorne (1995) outlines how texts include elements by which the rhetorical purpose of a story is achieved. He argues that narratives contain plots where individuals purposefully organise their thoughts and selves according to their experiences over time (Polkinghorne, 1988, 1995). Points to consider include the storyteller's intended message, the reason they have shared this account at this particular point in time, and the techniques they have used to achieve a particular outcome. Although narrative approaches can differ in the attention or weight given to rhetorical purpose, as a feature, rhetoric seems relevant to an analysis of policy and practice. For example, data can be analysed in order to explain why the stories told through public policies are presented in particular ways. Following this line of inquiry, the researcher can delve into the reasons why particular frames of ageing may take precedence over others, and draw attention to change over time. Accounting for rhetorical purpose as such also makes resistance against particular models or social constructs possible. For example, older people's storylines may be used to contest a particular reading of their life whereby they are marginalised or stigmatised. As such, attention to the rhetorical purpose of a story can unmask power relations that exist at a given point in time in a particular socio-cultural context. While narrative approaches have been used to challenge powerful classifications related to illness and disability in the medical discipline (see Frank, 1991, 1995; Williams, 1996; Kelly and Dickinson, 1997; Charmaz, 1999), the consideration of context and purpose in older people's accounts could also be used to understand and challenge the suggested models for growing old. Scholars in the field of social gerontology have drawn on narrative in their studies (Ferraro and Johnson, 1983; Chambers, 1984; Chambon, 1999; Ray, 2000; Kenyon et al, 2001; Bornat, 2002; Chapman, 2005; Grenier, 2007a); however, few studies have connected narrative inquiry with more macro-level structured locations of social policy discourse (see Neysmith, 1995; Bornat, 2002; Elliot, 2005; Neysmith et al, 2005; Reissman and Quinney, 2005 for exceptions). This combination, however, seems highly suited to understanding the socio-cultural models of transition that are deeply integrated in public and personal models for late life.

Rooted in the study of language and experience, narrative is an extremely relevant method from which to explore the intersections of public policy, socio-cultural discourse and lived experience. Narrative accounts share a fundamental relationship with continuity and change. Since narrative is a method concerned with trajectories and pathways and the ways in which experience may unfold over time (Riessman 1993; Kenyon and Randall, 2001), it provides a useful base from which to explore transitions across the lifecourse. It allows the researcher to move away from fixed interpretations and into considerations of fluid processes and variations in pathways. Narrative lends itself to reconsidering the constructs that shape transitions in late life, and rethinking social programmes based on how individuals might be expected to respond to significant transitional events. Using narrative to understand the models of ageing that take place in policy, socio-cultural discourses, organisational practice and narrated accounts is thus the next logical step in assessing the 'experiential fit' between social policy and lived experience.

Late-life transitions: exploring the fit between policy and lived experience

The following section outlines the details of the Late Life Transitions project,[2] which contrasts the storylines of public policies with lived experience. The methods used are described briefly as an illustration of using a narrative approach in practice, as well as to contextualise the examples discussed throughout the remaining chapters. The majority of the discussion will focus on the interview portion, as these accounts directly inform the second part of the book. Drawing on a critical perspective, the Late Life Transitions project explored the shapes of ageing that were promoted in international and local policy frameworks in Canada and the United Kingdom and compared these with the narrative accounts of 60 older people in Montreal, Canada. The objective of the research programme was to understand the public discourses expressed in social policy, and the personal narratives used to make sense of, and plan for, late-life transitions. Of particular interest was the 'fit' between macro-level social programming and micro-level personal experience. Stories told at the sites of policy and experience were intended as a means to better understand accepted and contested models for growing old, with narratives approached as anchors of experience situated between social policies and socio-cultural discourse. The research was divided into three main phases: document analysis, in-depth interviews and an analysis of the fit between the two locations. The tensions between universal and normative models, population diversity and continuity and change, were important conceptual markers in the study.

Policy discourse

The first phase of the research documented how transition and late life were understood in relevant policy documents and literature on ageing. In this phase, the focus was to identify how national and global policies interpreted and construed transitions as they related to ageing and late life – specifically the qualities attributed to ageing populations, the timing of transitions, and the balance between various explanations of hypothesised age- and stage-based transitions. In this phase, attention was given to change over time, geographic specificities, stated thematic threads and the unintended or unexpressed aspects of policy. Inspired by Foucault's work on discourse and power, analysis focused on the dominant and suppressed discourses in policies on ageing and late life (see Foucault, 1972, 1973, 1980a,b, 1994). This phase consisted of collecting relevant public policies and conducting a document analysis that identified ideas, themes and tensions. It was not the specific policies themselves that were of interest, but the overarching frameworks for transition into ageing and late life conveyed throughout. This phase resulted in the identification of constructs that shaped expectations of growing old. It highlighted the development of ideas such as success, productivity and decline, and their changing context with respect to biomedical and social aspects of adult ageing. The analysis of discourse as such explored underlying assumptions; began to unlock alternate possibilities; provided a framework for coding and categorising socio-cultural constructs of age; made links between the types of language used; and offered an understanding of both dominant and alternative themes in the policy documents. As explored in Chapter Five, in some cases, it was the absence of discussion of a dominant strand of themes such as function and decline that was of interest.

Narrative accounts of older people

The second phase, interviewing, focused on identifying how older people made sense of transition, and the degree to which they turned larger discourses into mental maps to guide their own trajectories of ageing. Interviews were conducted with 60 community-residing, English-speaking people aged 60+ from diverse social locations[3] over an eighteen-month period. The original sample proposed a purposeful (Ritchie and Lewis, 2003) and theoretical (Strauss and Corbin, 1998) sample comprised of 75 persons loosely nested in the conceptual age-based divisions of 55+, 65+ and 75+ that were considered to represent interpretive frames. The first group comprised a group deemed to be 'anticipating ageing' (55-65), who in preparation for ageing receive messages about prevention, activity and health. The second was reflective of the third age (65-75), considered 'old' and receiving messages about active aging and body maintenance. The third group was reflective of the construct of the fourth age, or 'old old' (75+), who received standard messages about disability and decline.

Drawn from a self-selecting sample, however, the resulting sample differed somewhat from that proposed. The resulting sample primarily comprised seniors from two distinct groups: the first was a group of healthy and active seniors participating in a late-life education programme comparable to the University of the Third age model, and the second was a group of older persons involved in a programme for people with visual impairments. Although not intended in the original design, and falling outside of what would traditionally be considered as comparable groups, these two groups proved fruitful in relation to the intersecting effects of age and impairment. As the study progressed, the contrast between the two groups characterised by visual impairments and a late-life learning programme provided an opportune example of exploring groups of older people polarised by health and illness. As will be elaborated in Chapter Five, this polarisation reflects strands that are evident in the policy and academic approaches to transition in late life. The differences between the two groups corresponded with constructs of the third and fourth age, and as such, provided unique standpoints. Narrative accounts from both locations were considered in relation to the messages targeted at their respective groups, creating an otherwise unavailable opportunity for comparison and contrast. For example, older people in the education programme would be considered to have experiences of health and freedom that corresponded with expectations of the third age, and older people with visual impairments would be more typically categorised as experiencing a decline considered within the realm of the fourth age. Further, participants came from social locations that varied according to gender, disability, visible minority ethnic status and socioeconomic status.

Interviews drew on a narrative technique that included a composite of open-ended unstructured questions and probes, and questions inspired by varying narrative studies of the lifecourse. As the sample was comprised of numbers much larger than normally used within narrative studies, a decision was made to supplement the open-ended process with selected questions, rather than a completely participant-directed interview. Each interview included a section informed by the narrative or life-story approach as told in their own words (Frank, 1995; Mishler, 1999); direct questions about experiences of transitions and turning points across the lifecourse – taking account of the past, present and future; and personal models or strategies used. In the first instance, older people were asked: Could you tell me a bit about yourself and your life? The interview guide was developed in order to glean an overall sense of their storylines, and draw comparisons within and between individual accounts, as well as with policy and socio-cultural discourse (see Table 4.1). After elaborating on their stories,

Table 4.1: Analytic questions for the Late Life Transitions project

Phase of research	Questions	Intent
Review of policy documents	• What is visible or overtly stated in documents? • What emergent strands or themes run through these documents across time? • What remains unexpressed?	• What is the dominant message and intent of each policy document? • What is known or assumed about ageing in each document? • What models are being suggested within and across documents? • Which ideas have become dominant over time? Which suppressed?
Narrative interviews	• Tell me about yourself. • Looking at your life, could you identify three to four key events? • Could you tell me about the major turning points in your life? • Throughout your life, what expectations did you have about growing older? • How is your experience of ageing like that of your friends? How is it different?	• What are the key identities? • What does this person select as important? • Are there similarities or differences in paths or turning points? • What types of transitions do older people identify? • What are the major points that are used to frame and interpret their life trajectories?
Assessing experiential 'fit'	• What is assumed or taken for granted in each policy document? • How does this relate to the general shapes of ageing suggested by policy discourse? • What are my reactions to these discourses? • What does this say about older people? • How might they react? • How do older people's accounts correspond or contrast with suggested models?	• What remains unexpressed? • What is hidden below the surface level? • What emotional associations are being made? • What is being assumed about older people? • How might this influence their storied accounts? • How might differences between suggested models and experiential accounts be understood?

participants were asked at an appropriate point in the interview to identify key transitions and turning points in their lives. This approach was used to open the frame of transition, and transcend the established age-based boundaries that are normally used to organise experience. Although sceptical about supplementing their participant-directed accounts with a series of open-ended questions, the ease with which older people identified, discussed and integrated key events and turning points into their storylines was pleasantly surprising. Questions comparing their experiences with their personal expectations and that of their friends were less helpful; social and cultural discourses emerged more naturally through the use of characters and actors than through prompting. Results from this phase provided insight into older people's transitions, including discussions on how locations such as impairment affected their experience of ageing and late life.

The third phase focused on exploring the experiential 'fit' between policy discourses and personal experiences – examining the relevance of current age- and stage-based transitions experienced across the lifecourse. The analysis included consideration of the extent to which 'fit' varied according to age-based groups, social location and experiences of continuity and discontinuity across the adult lifecourse. Questions focused on identifying how older people use the suggested strategies, and in what combination and circumstances, and the degree to which policy was effective in helping people rethink what it means to 'grow old' (see Table 4.1). Data from each interview were analysed as an individual narrative, as well as across interviews. Features for the analysis included attention to timeline, intention, moral of the story, turning points and transitions (Frank, 1995; Froggett and Chamberlayne, 2004). Informed by the exploratory potential of narrative (Frank, 1995; Chamberlayne et al, 2000; Roberts, 2002), and explanations provided by grounded theory (Glaser and Strauss, 1967) that are often necessary in a policy context, the analysis sought to achieve a balance between highlighting unique experiences, and comparing and contrasting issues along the lines, for example, of 'typical' and 'extreme' cases (Patton, 2002). Comparisons revealed variations in the types of transition, the prevalence of socio-cultural constructs of age, and how such understandings can guide and reflect social and personal responses to later life – all of which will be discussed later in the book. A central aspect that emerged from older people's accounts was a consideration of the feelings and emotions that exist in socio-cultural practices, discourse and older people's interpretations. Rendering their stories explicit made available the assumptive realities that operate in policies related to ageing and late life. Together, the approaches of document analysis, narrative interviews and exploring the 'fit' between policy and experience inform the reconsideration of transitions as they relate to ageing and late life.

Conclusion

This chapter has explored how a focus on language and narrative storylines offered at the sites of policy and experience helps to understand the relationships between policy frameworks, socio-cultural responses and older people's accounts, where transitions in late life are concerned. Drawing on constructivist and interpretive readings of the lifecourse (Gubrium and Holstein, 2000; Holstein and Gubrium, 2000; Hendricks, 2003, 2004), combined with an interest in policies as frameworks for experience (Phillipson, 1982; Walker, 1982; Estes et al, 2003; Neysmith et al, 2005), has provided the conceptual and methodological means to link an understanding of macro-level structures with micro-level interpretations. From this perspective, the storylines of public policy and older people can be read as current and purposeful interpretations of transitions in contemporary conditions. Yet, viewing them in terms of their similarities and differences highlights the discrepancies that can exist between the two. The approach outlined in this chapter provides the space to reconsider the larger suggested shapes of ageing, as well as the various ways in which older people may contest the accepted notions of ageing and late life. The chapter points to the complex process of integration, negotiation and resistance, whereby older people may, for example, draw on socio-cultural notions that are deemed as acceptable to shape and construct positive aspects of age – thereby including themselves in an ongoing discourse. At the same time, the approach linking policies and experience also provides the methodological means to break away from dominant and standard notions of age and stage, and toward a recognition of subjective pathways, the impacts of cumulative experiences and diversity.

When considered in relation to macro-level constructs such as those of public policy, older people's accounts highlight two specific sub-themes that will be developed throughout the book. The first is related to the diversity and variability that may exist between accounts, and the second is related to the feelings and emotional processes that may affect storylines at all levels of policy, practice and experience The accounts highlight how making meaning of continuity and change across the lifecourse must be considered as a personal, social, cultural and emotional process. Exploring the stories of policies and individuals in a socio-cultural context provides the space to reconsider the extent to which suggested models of transition are informed by personal fears, political interests and economic expediency (see McAdams, 2003, 2006). When considered alongside dominant models, older people's accounts draw attention to themes including the subjective or intuitive aspects related to ageing and questions of 'what it means to grow old' (Cole and Gadow, 1986) in Western society that may be hidden by experiences of ageism (Butler, 1990; Bytheway, 2005); competing assumptive realities between generations (Dittmann-Kohli, 1990; Jones et al, 2008); the cult of youth (Gullette, 1997, 2004; Woodward, 1999); and personal and socio-cultural fears of ageing (Grenier, 2009a). Attention to the underlying emotional processes and meanings, for example, may be used to consider how perceptions such as those related to mortality may affect views and responses to ageing in policy and practice. Thinking through what is taken for granted, and what often remains unsaid, can allow critical gerontologists to move beyond what is immediately available in order to consider various socio-cultural and personal processes involved in the construction of experience in late life.

Notes

[1] Fraser (1989) refers to the process of making claims through language as 'needs talk' and the context of validation, interpretation and satisfaction as the 'politics of needs interpretation'.

[2] Late Life Transitions: Understanding the 'Fit' Between Policy and Personal Experience was funded by the Social Sciences and Humanities Research Council of Canada (Grenier, 2005-08, project 410 2005 1928).

[3] This 'heterogeneous' sample (see Patton, 2002; Robson, 2002) is not meant to be representative or generalisable, but to reflect the growing number of older persons from ethnic and minority backgrounds in the city of Montreal, thereby addressing the neglect of diversity in previous research and theory on age (see Hendricks, 2003).

FIVE

Socio-cultural constructs of late life

This chapter outlines social and cultural constructs that influence everyday contemporary experiences of growing older. It considers the contemporary strands of thinking that are available in public policy and socio-cultural discourses as sources that reflect 'what is known' about late life and can inform interpretations and practices. Drawing on the critical perspective outlined in Chapter Two, and the related methodological approach outlined in Chapter Four, this chapter explores key discourses that form the backdrop for expectations of transition in late life – that is, it focuses on the qualities attributed to older people, and the behaviours expected from older populations. Rather than discuss the examples of retirement and widowhood that characterise the transitions literature, this analysis is primarily concerned with the discourses related to health and illness in late life. As such, it refers to the transitions that mark movement into 'old age', as well as the changes older people are expected to experience once they are considered 'old'. Focusing on these issues through the lens of transition raises questions of whether such broad-based expectations of health and success are possible, and for whom. In doing so, this analysis moves the state of knowledge on transitions beyond models that rely on social integration or conflict, toward understandings of the socio-cultural and personal processes that take place in a complex contemporary context.

The link between policy, socio-cultural discourse and experience, is a central aspect of this analysis. Notions of transition that are prevalent in socio-cultural discourses and public policies on ageing contain tensions between earlier theoretical thinking of ageing as age- or stage-based, such as dependency for example, and more recent ideas about continuous or discontinuous experiences across the lifecourse. At a superficial level, policies, and the resulting organisational and institutional practices, can be taken to reflect two prominent types of discourse: the biomedical aspects of ageing as decline, and the social aspects of ageing framed around productivity and success. Yet, on closer examination, these seemingly contradictory discourses intersect in the structures and practices related to health and illness in late life. The polarisation of health and decline, and the reinforcement that occurs between them, results in conflicting messages about ageing. On the one hand, older people are instructed on healthy and successful ageing, and on the other, the inevitable decline and loss of autonomy. What is missing from the existing framework is an understanding of the complex connections and contradictions that underlie the suggested models of ageing, and how these articulations influence socio-cultural expectations and personal interpretations of late life. While the immediate context is Western, illustrations from international, national and local policy frameworks can also be used to guide analysis in a non-Western setting.

In order to understand the complexity of transitions in late life, this chapter begins with the expectations that accompany the continued presence of age- and stage-based thinking. Following this, it draws attention to four powerful ideas that inform understandings of transitions: the increasing polarisation of health and illness in late life; the emphasis on anti-ageing and changing biomedical and technological advancements; the prevalence of success-based models of age focused on healthy and productive forms of ageing; and the role of lifestyle and identity as a means to better understand the subjective experience of age. In reviewing these, the chapter demonstrates that contemporary policy discourses contain notable pathways, many of which point towards the positive notions rooted in 'success'. These include, for example, being healthy in late life; continuing meaningful and active social roles; taking advantage of biomedical and technological developments; using anti-ageing products to defy ageing; and engaging in consumer choices to stave off the signs of ageing. The challenge is to understand how these discourses and suggested pathways shape expectations and inform interpretations of late life. The following questions are relevant for this chapter:

- What major socio-cultural discourses operate in society, culture and public policy? How do these discourses construe transitions in late life?
- What dominant and suppressed models are available to guide ageing and late life? Which elements have remained constant? How have these changed over time?
- How do the various discourses form a backdrop for late-life experiences? What tensions and contradictions exist? How do these contribute to and shape approaches in social gerontology, social policy and lived experience?

Boundaries and the expectations of age

Age- and stage-based assumptions that operate in discourse and practice create socio-cultural boundaries and sustain particular expectations in late life. Despite academic and practical challenges to the issue of chronological age, many of the socio-cultural interpretations of late life, including public policy, continue to be rooted in age- and stage-based thinking. Age and stage are implicit in many contemporary responses to transition and late life. Yet, the recent critical literature in social gerontology argues that discrete age- and stage-based differences are becoming outdated and less relevant (Blaikie, 1999; Featherstone and Hepworth, 1989, 1991; Gilleard and Higgs, 2000). Age- and stage-based models of transitions have been challenged on several fronts, including diverse social locations (Blakemore and Boneham, 1994); the complex relationships between body, psychological, social and cultural aspects of ageing over time (Cole, 1992; Dannefer, 1996; Estes et al, 2003); and the geographical context within which transitions occur. Take for example the differences in urban versus rural locations (Keating,

2008) and in non-Western contexts (Schröder–Butterfill, 2004, 2005). Yet, while chronological age may academically be considered less relevant in contemporary contexts, the social-cultural constructs and accompanying expectations that guide transitions remain firmly rooted in such 'dated' models.

Age-based assumptions found in policy and socio-cultural discourse are normative in nature, and shape ideas of how older people are expected to look, experience change, and, most importantly, treat their body. Age- and stage-based markers serve to separate older people from the rest of society, at least symbolically, if not also geographically and spatially (Rowles, 1978; Katz, 1996). Moving into the classification of 'old', for example, is based on chronological age in combination with role, function and socio-cultural markers of age. Expectations formed in relation to late life tend to correspond roughly with the distinction made between 'younger' older people in the third age (65+) and 'older' older people in the fourth age (75+ or 80+). Taking the specific transition of retirement as an example reveals how the very construct is related to expectations around contributions, productivity and independence versus dependence associated with advanced age. Similarly, the construct of the fourth age revolves around ideas of function, illness and decline that take place at the intersections of ageing and the body. As such, it is not simply age that marks the binary between groups, but the discourses of success and failure that are aligned with each of the groupings. Although originally organised to account for age-based differences in the broad-based category of people aged 65-100, the socio-cultural meanings of these groups have changed over time. While several authors have attempted to distinguish between these classifications (see Fries, 1980; Baltes and Smith, 2002), the analysis in this chapter is concerned with the socially constructed expectations that are associated with age-based distinctions rather than the groupings themselves.

Furthermore, the signs and symbolic evidence of ageing that are used to distinguish older people also inform interpretations of late life. Just as grey hair, wrinkles or adaptive equipment such as a walking stick signify the transition into being recognised as 'old', signs of functional decline or a loss of autonomy are also used to mark movement from the early period of the third age, and later age into the period known as the fourth age. Ideas that inform transitions, therefore, are not only based on crude or underlying measures of age, but complex systems of meaning that exist in socio-cultural discourses and practices. Making sense of ageing takes place in a context whereby transitions are accompanied by deeply ingrained ideas of success and failure, and the expected efforts to stave off the decline associated with 'growing old'. As such, the potential separation of older people from younger people, and further of the 'old old' from the 'young old', are rooted in understandings of age as illness and sustained through symbolic markers of decline – the responses to which are in part configured through biomedical and technological advances that will be explored later in this chapter.

Four types of account told about latter parts of the lifecourse are illustrative of the ways in which age- and stage-based approaches continue to structure and inform interpretations of late life. Each is rooted in a basic age-based construct that is accompanied by a particular response. The focus here is not on the chronological age distinctions, but the accompanying social expectations based on the combination of age, function, health and illness, for example (see Table 5.1). The construct associated with and up to mid-life contains the idea that one should prevent the signs of ageing and actively avoid the decline and disability that has come to be associated with late life. As it progresses into 'near old age', the emphasis shifts from prevention to an active maintenance of the body and health. The third age, originally set as the marker of ageing, is being redefined as a period where older people are encouraged to be active, healthy and productive. This shift is strange, as the preoccupation with the body issues remains, but this period is subject to overly emphasised messages of activity and health. On the contrary, the fourth age represents a time where older people are expected to experience decline and prepare for death. Together, these four accounts intersect to create and sustain socio-cultural discourses that shape expectations of transitions in relation to late life.

Table 5.1: Socio-cultural age-based expectations

Age-based construct	Discourse and expectations
Up to mid-life (45+)	• Prevent the signs and symptoms of ageing (active prevention) • Maintain the body at optimal level
Near 'old' age (55+)	• Prepare for ageing (finances, housing, expectations and so forth) • Maintain body strength and wellness
Third age (young old, 65+)	• Activity and freedoms of age • Monitor and maintain the body • Deny and avoid the 'signs of ageing'
Fourth age (old old, 75/80+)	• Expect decline and dependency • Integrate accumulated losses • Focus on adaptation and negotiation

The academic and practical response to this fourth group is particularly interesting. A review of the academic literature and policy documents reveals that the group characterised by decline and impairment is often excluded from dominant discourses on the lifecourse and ageing. This negation implies that ageing discourses can only accommodate healthy and active expectations. For example, the impact of these powerful discourses can be seen in how ideals of 'preventing the signs of ageing' have crept into earlier periods of the lifecourse, such as mid-life and the run-up to 'old age'. Considered to comprise predominantly healthy groups, the audiences of those in mid-life and those nearing old age are targeted by discourses of prevention and preparation that can be achieved through consumer lifestyles and/or technological advances. The fourth age increasingly becomes a distant period of the lifecourse that is feared and avoided.

The polarisation of health and decline in late life

Considering the age- and stage-based expectations alongside socio-cultural discourses highlights how the polarisation of health and decline in late life has the potential to shape individual and social interpretations of ageing. The distinction between healthy and declining groups, while rarely made explicit outside academic and research settings, operates through typified constructs and targeted social responses. For example, a stratification is evident in the differences between policies targeted at younger, healthy older people and those aimed at older people who are ill. This includes the tendency to assume a healthy and active population when referring to populations of older people, neglecting to include those who are older and possibly in less good health. Such separation of the third and fourth age groups of older people is also present in the conceptual and applied notions of age, including, for example, the use of age-based samples in research. As an effort to avoid chronological age, authors have suggested the use of constructs of the first age, second age and third age categories to study ageing (Young, 1988; Laslett, 1989; Young and Schuller, 1991; Midwinter, 1996, 2004, 2005). However, this suggestion fails to recognise how such concepts remain embedded in age- and stage- based expectations. As such, they do not challenge the binary polarisation of health and decline in late life, but sustain the differences between them. They also leave unexamined the ways in which most social science thinking has focused on the group best characterised as the third age.

In policy contexts, the polarisation takes place through definitions of target groups and the justification for programming decisions. Policy documents that are visionary in nature focus almost exclusively on the promotion of health and wellbeing in late life, while programmes for older people target a loss of autonomy. In doing so, practices mirror the distinction between younger/healthy older people, and older/ill people considered to be in decline. As a result, they sustain the socio-cultural expectations associated with the polarised third and the fourth ages – in particular, the notion that the younger group is capable of change, and the older determined to fail where health and success are concerned. According to Grenier (2009a), practices focused on late life as a period characterised by decline create a particular dynamic for those considered to be within the fourth age. First, they align this period with dependency, burden and vulnerability that are to be avoided. Second, they create differential public planning targets – with 'younger' older people the target of prevention, and 'frail' older people offered 'maintenance-only' programmes. Third, they represent unspoken associations of fear, failure and a general malaise toward older people with 'failing' bodies (see also Thomson, 1991; Clark, 1996; Hoggett, 2000; Clarke et al, 2006). Fourth, they marginalise or exclude a segment of older people through physical or social distance, and as a result may in the future affect intergenerational relationships or a commitment to public care (also see Froggatt, 2001).

These distinctions between groups can be seen to spill into the social, whereby groups for healthy active seniors tend to remain separate from groups for older people with a loss of autonomy. An example to be considered is the case of late-life education where older people, such as those in the Late Life Transitions project, participate in peer-learning programmes that are age- or stage- based. In such 'universities of the third age', universities or communities create education centres for older people that are primarily geared toward healthy and active older people. These programmes are very different from day-centre programmes designed for frail older persons that focus on function and rehabilitation. Although unintended, the resulting socio-cultural practices that take place in late-life education and other similar programmes is that active healthy ageing characterised by younger groups of older people is deemed exciting and filled with opportunity, and the decline associated with the fourth age feared and avoided. Consequently, socio-cultural practices that have a positive impact where health, activity and participation are concerned may unintentionally reinforce the separation of younger and older groups of older people, and, in turn, overlook the unique needs of the fourth age. The separation of, and failure to integrate, fourth-age issues into educational and social spaces, for example, reinforces decline and dependency associated with late life. These divisions become apparent in the experiences of older people who begin to experience decline while participating in groups intended for the third age, as will be explored in the second portion of this book.

The dichotomisation of health and illness in late life presents several challenges where the 'fit' between socio-cultural, policy discourses and personal experience is considered. First, it creates a context that sustains segregation based on age and socio-cultural markers of decline. A negative association is made between physical impairment and social value in late life whereby older people with impairments are separated from older people considered healthy and active as the norm. Second, as a result of stigmatisation, older people may distance themselves from the discourses and practices that are said to characterise their experiences. In the case of frailty, for example, older people may insist that their experiences do not correspond with the assumptions outlined in these classifications. They may deny their own impairments, or associate with healthier groups – decisions that may later affect their eligibility for services (Grenier, 2007b). Third, these models afford a lack of attention to the social structures and accumulated life experiences that may cause impairment and decline. For example, someone in the third age may experience significant levels of impairment as a result of lifelong poverty or repetitive manual work, while someone in the fourth age may not. Fourth, they fail to challenge the unrelenting connection between ageing and decline that is reinforced in such models. It is therefore important to consider what underlies the suggested models for continuity and change across the lifecourse. Examples of discourse and practice that create and sustain distinctions between the third and fourth age will be explored in the following comparative case illustration.

Case illustration: geographic and programmatic policy differences

A comparison between approaches taken in the contexts of Canada and the UK conducted as part of the Late Life Transitions project revealed similarities and differences where attempts to shape ageing and the suggested models for late life were concerned. In the UK, there was an active attempt to shape ageing that occurred without a Canadian equivalent. The best example of this can be found in the document *Opportunity age* (DWP, 2005), which represents an attempt to redefine the meaning of dependency ratios by altering the idea that older people are dependent (Biggs et al, 2007). In Canada, overarching visionary documents that grapple with the issues of ageing were notably absent, with the available models outlined primarily in provincial documents aimed at service delivery rather than society in general. While this is in part due to the federal/provincial structure whereby provinces administer programmes to population groups (see Maioni, 2004 on the differences between federal and provincial levels of responsibility), the absence of a Canada-wide vision statement represented a significant gap in thinking about ageing at the social level. In comparison with the UK, Canada was less actively involved in shaping expectations for age. At the provincial level, however, a different inclination was observed whereby documents from Quebec reflected a striking polarisation of healthy and dependent populations with the approach focused on either vision statements for healthy and independent seniors or services for impaired older people (Milette, 1999; Agence de développement de réseau locaux de services de santé et de services sociaux, 2004; Gouvernement du Québec, 2005, 2006, 2009; Agence de la santé et des services sociaux de Montréal, 2006). The documents from England and Quebec both demonstrate active attempts to participate in the socio-cultural shapes of ageing and suggest models within which to grow old. Expected themes related to demography/ longevity, health/productivity and function/decline were generally prevalent in the documents of both countries. However, a deeper exploration revealed how the presentation and suggested shapes of ageing varied by geographic and programmatic policy level.

In the UK, policy documents were used to outline a broad vision for ageing that suggested particular models for late life. In *Opportunity age* (DWP, 2005), former Prime Minister Tony Blair's introduction stated:

> An aging society is too often – and wrongly – seen solely in terms of increasing dependency. But the reality is that, as older people become an ever more significant proportion of the population, society will increasingly depend upon the contribution they can make. (DWP, 2005, p 8)

In a latter section, the document attacked former dominant models of dependency as ageist practice. Blair said:

> The impact of population change is often measured by looking at the ratio between the number of people over 65 and other adults. It is an example of exactly the kind of age-stereotyping we believe should be avoided ... we believe a more meaningful measure is the relationship between those who are active in the workforce and those who are not. (DWP, 2005 p 20)

The document continued to focus on ageing as a productive time, saying 'we want to build a society that focuses on what individuals can do, instead of making assumptions about capacity based on age' (DWP, 2005, p 23). Visions such as those suggested in *Opportunity age* represented a concerted initiative against social ageism and a model based on inclusion. Yet, they did so by means of financial and general independence, and replacing former notions of dependency based on age with the idea that work or work-like activity is the primary source of independence in later life (see Biggs et al, 2007). Of course, such messages belong in the context of active attempts to change the retirement age in the UK. However, what underlies the expressions of redefining dependency in relation to work and productivity is the implication that ageing and the likelihood of increasing infirmity are unrelated, and that older adults can continue to perform their work and work-like activities into late life.

Differing somewhat from those of England, a review of documents in Quebec revealed a striking tendency to polarise groups according to health or impairment. In vision-type documents, ageing was promoted as a time of involvement, health and leisure that corresponds with the third-age ideas of freedom and activity outlined earlier (Gouvernement du Québec, 2005, 2006, 2009). In service-level documents, however, policies described 'population needs' and the types of programmes and services available for impaired older people in Quebec (Agence de développement de réseau locaux de services de santé et de services sociaux, 2004; Agence de la santé et des services sociaux de Montréal, 2006). In order to understand the implications of these suggestions, the provincial context that anchors its perspective in health promotion must be taken into account. In this sense, the message is similar to that expressed in *Opportunity age* – health and continued productivity are the gold standard. Yet, in Quebec, health promotion remains rationalised by dependency models whereby ageing is depicted as costly for the state. This can be seen in the former Quebec Minister for Health and Social Services Phillipe Couillard's statement that 'the only way to truly control the impact of demographic change in the long run is to promote prevention and healthy habits' (Couillard, 2004).

In practice, what occurs is that success-based models of ageing are used to justify funnelling resources into earlier periods of the lifecourse in the name of prevention. Late life and ageing remain relatively unmentioned in larger health promotion policies or vision statements, except where the costs of demographic crisis are used to justify reduced spending (see Gee and Gutman, 2000). Yet, policies targeted specifically at late life focus on impairment or loss of autonomy. There is no room to consider what exists between health and illness. This pattern of polarisation has become even more common in recent years. Attention to notions of success through participation and involvement that closely correspond with international success-based models has increased (Gouvernement du Québec, 2005, 2006, 2009). At the same time, efforts have turned to developing eligibility models based on functional impairment over the lifecourse. While at the time of review the UK was more actively involved in defining late life, the predilection to focus on impairment and earlier parts of the lifecourse – almost overlooking age entirely – is becoming more visible in Quebec policy and practice. What remains to be seen is the extent to which the polarisation of health and illness across the lifecourse continues and how this affects ageing, older people and the social responses dedicated to issues of late life.

This brief illustration of the responses taken in two geographic settings of contemporary policy renders obvious the sizeable gap that exists between success- and dependency-based models, and more important, the fact that any attempted transition between the two will be difficult at best. With older people in the general public depicted as healthy, active and productive, and older people in services depicted according to dependence and functional impairments, the unexpressed sentiment is that success-based models are inappropriate for older people with impairments or at advanced ages. With movement between success and dependence unmentioned and seemingly improbable, critical scholars are left to wonder what happens to older people as they move between the available models of health and decline. Further, how can time spent within and between success and dependence be understood? Transitions into later periods of late life that are accompanied by impairment are left shapeless – devoid of guidelines or suggestions for these moments in late life. There are no accessible rituals, and the only available models are age- and stage-based combinations that polarise health, activity and independence at one end and dependence and decline at the other. What is missing in both countries is a vision that takes account of the various experiences in age, including how late life could include those who have moved beyond the third age.

Anti-ageing: biomedical and technological issues of ageing

Prominent biomedical and anti-ageing discourses also shape interpretations of late life. Biomedical understandings frame ageing in relation to risk, decline and longevity, and are central to understanding contemporary models of ageing. While criticisms of the biomedical dominance over ageing and late life are not new, medical and technological advances have altered contemporary understandings of these issues. In the 1980s, Estes and Binney (1989) wrote of the 'biomedicalisation of ageing'. In doing so, they set the stage to identify how older people were associated with illness and decline (Estes, 1991; Achenbaum, 1995; Katz, 1996), demonstrated how ageing was approached as an individual medical issue that favoured disease models and biological reductionism (Moody, 1993), and drew attention to the profit-based industry of ageing (Estes, 1979, 1993). While this critique remains valid, the landscape of the biomedicalisation of ageing has shifted. For example, dominant biomedical discourses have moved away from exploring ageing as a disease and towards the 'fundamental mechanisms' or root causes of ageing itself (Settersen et al, 2008). Contemporary interpretations focus increasingly on isolating causes and manifestations of ageing, as evidenced in the studies of neurological and hormonal aspects of ageing (Kokmen et al, 1977; Waite et al, 1996; Holliday, 2004) and studies of physical issues such as frailty (Rockwood et al, 1994; Fried et al, 2001; Bortz, 2002). Through such studies, former definitions of ageing as a disease are replaced by ageing as a period characterised by risk, classified according to severity, and considered in relation to debates on longevity. The approach taken is a type of 'science of ageing', whereby attention is devoted to the identification of the causes of ageing, and the means by which to prevent or cure these problems. It is not uncommon for policy documents to allude to scientific developments or technological aspects of ageing primarily as descriptions of a changed contemporary context or conditions within which to grow old.

Furthermore, the bodily signs of impairment and decline become characterised as risks in the contemporary understandings of late life. At the level of socio-cultural discourse, 'risk' plays a central role in how transitions are considered and accommodated. The work of Beck (1992) drew attention to risk and probability as central discourses of 'late modernity'. In late life, the relationship between the body and the risks of illness and injury, and the assumed associated costs, have become central to understanding the responses to ageing, and ultimately, the achievement of 'success'. Once defined and classified in relation to risk, the body is targeted for interventions ranging from consumer products to health and social care services. The ageing body is thus at the forefront of socio-cultural discourses of prevention and medico-technological advances that shape the body, and the expectations of late life. Underscored as biomedical risk, the processes of ageing require control, resistance and alteration. New technologies ranging from cosmetic surgeries to pharmaceuticals and stem-cell research are suggested to combat or solve the 'problems of ageing' (Katz, 2003; Liebing, 2010). In the context of human services, discourses on risk – many of which derive from biomedical interpretations – can be identified in professional classifications and binary divisions of social care practices (Grenier, 2007b). When connected with discourses on shifting demographics and the linkage of age, health and cost, risk discourses sustain the perception of older people as costly consumers of public services (see Gee and Gutman, 2000 on crisis demographics). Risk is, then, both the emotional rationale for pursuing scientific advancements aimed to ultimately discover a 'cure' for ageing, and the means to classify and make judgements about the distribution of services. As a result, discourses on risk shape contemporary definitions, responses and expectations of ageing and late life. This includes influencing the shaping of older subjects and their experiences (Phillipson and Powell, 2004). The result is a marked emphasis on biomedicalised interpretations of ageing, and an anti-ageing perspective designed to counter the signs of ageing. Such perspectives undoubtedly influence socio-cultural and personal interpretations and responses to late life.

Biomedical interpretations of age as illness and disease are mutually reinforced by socio-cultural discourses that emphasise the avoidance of decline and impairment. The proliferation of technological and anti-ageing consumer interventions is a prime example of the intersection of medicalisation and risk in relation to ageing. The anti-ageing movement is organised around assisting or enabling older people to alter their bodies in order to prevent ageing. Tracing the emergence of anti-ageing science, Fishman and colleagues (2008) highlight how anti-ageing efforts consist of one of two parallel forms: one comprising commercial and clinical enterprises offering products, regimens and treatments, and another comprising the research and development efforts of biogerontologists. They discuss the tensions that exist between biomedical researchers and the anti-ageing movement. They describe how, aided by scientific discoveries linking ageing, longevity and genes, the biomedical strand achieved legitimacy through distancing itself from the product-based stream (Fishman et al, 2008). This tension between science and consumer products operates as a backdrop to the interpretation of experience. Older people become aware of anti-ageing through commercial practices and ever-increasing access to technology. Older people receive information and are targeted for products that will help them to defy ageing. In this context, the ideals of anti-ageing become a feature of personal and cultural interpretations of late life (see Katz, 2000, 2005; Calasanti and King, 2007; Edmondson and von Kondratowitz, 2009). At the same time, biogerontologists continue to research the root causes of ageing and develop anti-ageing technologies in fields such as stem cell research, nanotechnology and gene therapy (Mykytyn, 2006), with research on genetics currently considered the leading explanation of age-based change (Fishman et al, 2008). Discourses and actions positioned against the signs and realities of ageing form an important backdrop to understanding and interpreting late life.

Also prevalent in the biomedical and technological strands of ageing is the often unstated association between ageing and death. Death is not directly addressed in social policy, socio-cultural discourses or biomedical and technological interpretations, and this omission can be considered to represent an unthought or unstated known that operates implicitly (see Bollas, 1989, 1992 on the 'unthought known'). Discourses on risk, for example, serve as a substantive link between the concepts of decline and mortality, with older people considered to be at risk of both. It is the strength of the association between the two, the desire to extend longevity, and the imperative to control costs related to ageing societies that, at least in part, drive biomedical responses to the problem of ageing. In other words, it could be argued that the fear of impairment, decline and death, fuels the search for a cure. In the academic literature, Gadow (1996) has recognised how the socio-cultural context of death can 'dictate the meaning of aging and ... control the experience of aging' (p 38). Yet, when combined with biomedicine's curative model, and more recent anti-ageing discourses and practices, the role death plays in shaping the political and personal responses to ageing cannot be overlooked.

Death represents a significant obstacle for medicine. It is not surprising, therefore, that scientists focus on identifying root causes of ageing and attempt to prolong life. With ageing positioned in accordance with risk and longevity, the solutions become focused on medical solutions and technological advances, many of which belong within the realm of the profitable ageing enterprise of which Estes (1979, 1993) spoke. Biomedical efforts focus on extending life for as long as possible and, in particular, on what Gruman (2003) refers to as 'prolongevity' – the desire to extend average human life expectancy to its maximum without extending suffering and infirmity. Such achievements in respect to longevity are often emphasised by citing the number of centenarians and shifts in life expectancy among men and women in the developed world. Making it to 100 years of age is deemed a major success that is set as a goal for which to strive (Bytheway, 1994; Baltes, 1997). The juxtaposition of such longevity with the risks of impairment and decline provides a solid socio-cultural backdrop for the interpretation of late life that shapes what is deemed success or failure.

Successful models of ageing

Successful ageing is a dominant model that informs interpretations of transitions in late life. Since the beginning of the 1990s, ageing has increasingly been interpreted within positive frameworks as a time of activity, success, productivity, health and leisure (Walker and Naegele 1999; Katz, 2000; Walker 2005b). At the heart of this thread is the idea that health and wellbeing in late life can be achieved through success and productivity. The current mainstream model of 'successful ageing' was born out of writing by Rowe and Kahn (1998). In its development, the concept represented a challenge to the idea of dependency in late life (Phillipson, 1998; Unger and Seeman, 1999). However, it has become a paradigm that embraces prevention throughout lifecourse as the key to an old age post-retirement that is active, healthy and psychologically fulfilling. Success-based models of ageing emphasise the positive potential in ageing, and have, as a result, become an attractive and powerful framework within which to interpret ageing and late life. The challenge at this stage is in considering the extent to which the pendulum of dominant discourse has swung from one extreme focused on dependency to the other in its overemphasis on success and productivity.

Despite its positive attributes, scholars have condemned the uncritical acceptance of successful ageing as a paradigm that outlines how one 'should' age. Authors writing from a critical perspective have expressed their scepticism about idealised notions of productivity, success and healthy ageing (Blaikie, 1999; Katz, 2000; Moody, 2001; Morrow-Howell et al, 2001). Labelling this approach 'the new gerontology', Holstein and Minkler (2003) expose how preventative efforts aimed to encourage 'successful ageing' focus on changing individual behaviour rather than social conditions or structured disadvantage. Furthermore, the paradigm of successful ageing has been considered ageist in its linkage of ageing with a youth-based and consumer culture (Featherstone and Hepworth, 1989). As a result, popular culture has come to associate ageing with a new sort of adult lifecourse, marked by an unwillingness to grow old, identification with youthful cohorts and the avoidance of bodily ageing (Gilleard and Higgs, 2002; Katz, 2005). While achieving lifestyles based on successful ageing may seem possible for particular groups of older people, the model of successful ageing has been considered unrealistic in the face of bodily ageing, particularly in the fourth age (Baltes and Smith, 2002). On an emotional level, the tendency to emphasise success has also been considered to represent an intolerance of vulnerability, an unconscious tendency to avoid impairment, and the projection of dependency on to 'the weak or needy' (Sevenhuijsen, 1998; Froggatt, 2001; Lloyd, 2004, 2006; Grenier, 2009a). There is also the problem that success is used to fund and target prevention in early life rather than late life. Although dominant in the current models of late life transitions, an uncritical acceptance of success-based models overlooks how experiences of ageing may differ in relation to disadvantage or impairment, for example. The discourses of success and failure take on a particularly powerful significance where they occur on or in relation to the ageing body.

The body plays a significant role in the consideration of success or failure that is implied in successful ageing. Located in a youth-based culture, the socio-cultural backdrop for transitions into late life is one that emphasises strong and able-bodied persons. This active view of the body is central to socio-cultural discourses on age and intricately connected to social perceptions and responses in late life. Considered as a political surface for health and policy talk, the body becomes the means by which socio-cultural judgements are made (Fox, 1993; Öberg, 1996). Success, and the inverse of failure, are thus performed, judged and inscribed on the body. This parallels the literature outlining how the 'disabled' body is considered in relation to success or failure (Oliver 1990; Morris, 1991; Swain et al, 2004). In the case of late life, the body is judged for signs of ageing, decline and impending failure. In the words of Fox (1993), 'the body ... has become along with its health or illness a text to be read, written and re-written by body experts be they doctors, beauticians, sports instructors or lovers' (p 20). In late life, this reading includes classifying the body in accordance with risk-based criteria, as well as individual and social expectations. The acceptable socio-cultural response from a successful ageing paradigm is to hide the signs of ageing. Consider, for example, the way older people may dress in ways to conceal or control their ageing (Twigg, 2007). The body thus becomes an important marker of success or failure in late life, and one whose role must be understood in relation to transitions in late life.

Another prominent theme underlying the success-based models of late life is the idea that bodies can be shaped and controlled. The premise for such interpretation is that the ageing body is somehow 'intolerable' and must be transformed (see Gadow, 1991). Several authors have discussed how older bodies require disguise, alteration or control (Blaikie, 1999; Tulle-Winton, 1999, 2000; Katz, 2005). Featherstone and Hepworth's (1991) notion of the 'ageing mask', whereby the youthful self is disguised, reveals how ageing requires concealment. In this line of thinking, the signs of ageing and decline represent powerful socio-cultural messages that come to be interpreted by selves and others. In a similar interpretation, Woodward (1991) speaks of 'checking ourselves' in the mirror for imperfection, while authors such as Tulle-Winton (2000) and Phoenix and Sparkes (2006) have focused on older athletes and bodybuilders engaged in ultimate forms of body manipulation. Whether the act of modification is subtle or more pronounced, each places emphasis on monitoring, surveillance and manipulation of the body, both by self and others (see Foucault 1979, 1980a, 1982). Further, it reinforces an ever-increasing model of strength, vigour and activity. Success becomes increasingly located in the achievements of the body, with illness, dependency and decline representing the failures of the body and self. Writing in the field of disability studies, Wendell (1996) argues that this refusal to accept bodily life in all of its forms perpetuates a 'myth of control' that causes an inherent desire to avoid illness, disability and death. Drawing on what may be thought but unstated is the notion that older people's bodies, like those with disabilities, will never quite measure up. Older people who achieve extraordinary feats, while hailed in the media as aspirational role models, will always be considered people who have successfully controlled their ageing bodies – they will be distinguished from those with younger/healthy bodies and older/ill bodies. As such, their successes subtly emphasise the failure of those unable to master their bodies, and the fleeting nature of those that do.

Further to this notion of the 'unrelenting' body is the emphasis on continued productivity that is also embedded in success-based models of transition in late life. From this perspective, the idea of activity is extended beyond the functions of the body to the acts of accomplishment, achievement and keeping busy (see Moody, 2001; Katz, 2005). Seen in the earlier illustration of the UK's attempt to reframe ageing, the discourses of productivity are most often targeted at work activities and professional achievements. In the context of ageing, these take the shape of continuing paid work past age 65 or an active volunteer life that replaces employment. In policy, these notions are enacted through debates such as raising the retirement age and encouraging lifelong work activities. This prominent emphasis on being productive throughout the lifecourse creates a 'cult of productivity', whereby all actions taken must be purposeful. The result is that the desired outcome of success, often aligned with early periods of youth and professional maturity in adult life, has been extended into later periods of the lifecourse (see Biggs et al, 2007). Making contributions deemed productive, and thus successful, is a marked socio-cultural trend against which the experiences of older people are measured. Yet, such a concentrated view of success through productive action seems to suggest internal emotional conflict related to rest, idleness and dependence.

The expectations of success and productivity that underlie socio-cultural and political understandings of transition represent a significant challenge for late life. On its own, success is a discourse that is difficult to challenge – it is practically impossible to outline an alternative to the positive agenda of success that is not rooted in failure. As with active ageing, expectations of independence and autonomy are steadfast in success-based models, overlooking possibilities such as interdependence as well as profound experiences of vulnerability (Lloyd, 2004). While the emphasis on success is problematic, it becomes more troubling where processes of impairment or dying are concerned. The augmented models of 'choice' and self-agency being promoted in policy discourse and practice is only likely to increase the disappointment directed at older people in the fourth age who may be unable to achieve these models. This is particularly the case when these models are combined with individualistic expectations of choice and self-agency that are increasingly expected from older people regardless of age or impairment (see Lloyd, 2004). A critical perspective can be used, however, to reveal the pervasiveness of such models and the extent to which they conceal the harsh reality that not all persons can achieve the health, productivity and independence in old age that they may desire. The promotion of success-based models must be criticised for the way in which they disguise an 'intolerance of dependency', reinforce expectations of individual autonomy, and fail to account for differences and inequalities between older people (see Hoggett, 1998; Lloyd, 2004). The dominance of success-based models thus requires reappraisal of the potentially hidden assumptions and perverse incentives that accompany this new model of ageing. As demonstrated in the case examples in Chapter Six, these positive notions of success and productivity play a powerful part in guiding what is 'known about' and expected from late life.

Case illustration: shifting shapes of ageing, Vienna (1982) to Madrid (2002)

A comparison of the policy discourses between the two international plans on ageing reveal that a dramatic change has taken place with regard to the social and cultural models suggested for growing old. The notions of ageing envisaged by the international policy documents from the First World Assembly on Ageing in Vienna in 1982 and the Second World Assembly on Ageing in Madrid in 2002 capture the contemporary concerns of each period and clearly demonstrate the shifting vision of ageing that has taken place over a 20-year period. Comparing the discursive statements articulated in Vienna (UN, 1982) and Madrid (UN, 2002) shows how the idea of success, not mentioned in the first plan, had, by the second plan, become the new dominant model.

The Vienna assembly focused on demographics, respect and age- or stage-based distinctions, while the Madrid assembly spoke of lifecourse continuity through activity and inclusion. To be more specific, the Vienna International Plan of Action on Ageing (UN, 1982) emphasised the demographic change likely to radically impinge on population structures by 2025, outlined the need for significant policy change and spoke largely of ageing within models of dependency and decline. At the same time, it illustrated a relatively gentle view of ageing, with an emphasis on reflection, wisdom and summation. Twenty years later, the Madrid

International Plan of Action on Ageing (UN, 2002) represented a move from the general acceptance of decline/dependency models towards a view of ageing as a time of reflection, individual 'achievement' (p 2) and 'potential' (p 3). Tracing the thematic changes between the conceptualisation of ageing put forward in the plans of Vienna and Madrid reveals how health and activity have become dominant over discourses of decline and dependency, as well as over notions of reflection. It also contextualises current tensions between age- and stage- based interpretations and more fluid models that have been surfacing in social gerontology for the past decade. The largest recognisable shift in thinking about transitions, however, is the shift in emphasis from a focus on the specificities of late life that were characterised according to demographics and dependency, to success-based models considered to take place across the lifecourse. Central to this understanding are subjective identities and lifestyle choices that are attributed with success.

Lifestyles and identities: subjectively shaping the lifecourse

A growing strand in the discourse on late life is the extent to which older people can shape their lifecourse and experience. Within this, two variations are evident. The first focuses on identity and subjective experience, while the second, albeit overlapping somewhat, focuses on lifestyle choices. Identity tends to refer to the individual ways in which one can negotiate the lifecourse, whereas lifestyle is considered to take account of the socio-cultural context, and the opportunities and constraints that may affect the choices made. Both, however, are recognised and encouraged to varying extents in the policy context. For example, portraits and illustrations from older people are used to understand the impact of public policies, and older people's groups are often called on to voice their concerns as active citizens and consumers. Despite the differences between these contributions, attention to identities and lifestyles provides new ways to negotiate continuity and change across the lifecourse. In doing so, the focus shifts from a one-way understanding of discourse as a force that shapes experience to the multiple ways that experience may also shape discourse and practice.

Identity claims are likely to be the most popular means by which older people are considered to voice their understandings of ageing and the lifecourse (see Hockey and James, 2003). Rooted in biographies, identities draw attention to authentic notions of voice and experience. Accounts from this perspective draw heavily on open-ended stories and observations collected through narrative methodologies or in-depth ethnographies of experience (Rowles, 1978; Bornat, 1999; Ray, 2000, 2007; Gubrium, 2001, 2005; Randall and Kenyon, 2001, 2004; Grenier, 2005). Meaning making and negotiation are key to this strand, with older people's accounts exposing how lived experiences may correspond or clash with set understandings. In the academic scholarship, authors have focused on identity in relation to self-perception (Biggs, 1997; Powell and Longino, 2001) and the differences between chronological age and 'true selves' (see Kaufman,

1986; Biggs, 1997; Kerner Furman, 1997; Woodward, 1999). Such approaches have also been used to contrast powerful institutional practices and highlight the resistance of marginal groups (Gubrium, 1975; Grenier, 2007a,b; Grenier and Hanley, 2007). When taken into account, identity can challenge fixed constructs such as professional classifications, age-based expectations and social norms. One such area concerns taken-for-granted knowledge and practices in relation to class (Savage et al, 2004; Savage, 2005). The argument on identity, however, is not entirely separate from that of lifestyle; identity choices may also be seen to represent an extension of lifestyle choice and signify status (see Warde, 2002; Jones et al, 2008). Consider, for example, the 'snowbird' identity of older Canadians travelling to Florida each year and the ways in which this represents both an identity and a lifestyle (Katz, 2005).

Discourses that draw attention to lifestyle choices in late life challenge fixed and determinist approaches to late life. In the lifestyle thread, attention focuses on socio-cultural dynamics in age (Featherstone and Hepworth, 1989) whereby the lives of older people can be shaped through cultural choices (Gilleard and Higgs, 2000). Consumer choice and culture figure prominently, with authors outlining the options and opportunities available in late life. For example, Jones and colleagues (2008) highlight how older people have moved from passive to active forms of consumption – with patterns of consumerism in late life beginning to resemble those in earlier parts of the lifecourse. Lifestyle interpretations also focus on experiences that link identities and social bonds in ways that speak to the consciousness and identities of generations (Gilleard and Higgs, 2002). It is not surprising, therefore, that attention to lifestyle is most associated with the third age, as it corresponds with the freedom and desires most commonly associated with this group. Reference to this type of third-age lifestyle is also present in policy discourses. While some are stated, as in the case of volunteering in late life or the social participation emphasised in the case of Quebec (Gouvernement du Québec, 2005, 2006, 2009), others are implicitly made available through the images that accompany online policies, such as those depicting 'retired' seniors on vacation or the golf course. This focus on lifestyle choice that is now available in socio-cultural discourses and public policy reflects a contemporary understanding of the lifecourse as blurred rather than age- and stage-based. It also reveals how choice is considered to play a role in individual assessments of transitions and late-life experiences, as well as the social-cultural models suggested for growing old.

This attention to identity and lifestyle represents contemporary concerns for making sense of ageing and late life. Together, they signify an important shift towards accepting the changing nature of ageing and the lifecourse, and the extent to which individuals can alter their experiences. Both identity and lifestyle claims provide a base from which the negotiation, rejection or subversion of dominant understandings of late life become possible. On an ideal level, this change in thinking creates the potential for involvement in processes related to public policy. In the UK, for example, policy contexts emphasise the importance of what Jones and colleagues (2008) have referred to as a 'voice and choice' discourse, whereby older service users are expected to have their voices heard and be provided with choices about their care in late life. As such, policy discourses that appeal to identities and lifestyles can be read as an attempt to integrate fluid interpretations of age and transition, and diverge from past conceptions of older people as passive recipients of social benefits. However, such attempts must also be considered with scrutiny. The extent to which older people are actually able to exercise 'voice and choice' in the context of the consumer market requires attention, both in relation to the problem of being defined through the purchases one makes and when disadvantage is considered, with unequal access and choice across the lifespan a matter of debate (Walker, 2006a, 2006b). Rooted in individual interpretations and mainly consumer choices, the pathways to success that are promoted in identity and lifestyle claims may be limited for those located at the intersection of unequal power relations, structural disadvantage and 'impaired' bodies. As a result, identity and lifestyle choices have been criticised for giving the impression that older people are able to exercise choice within an ageist culture and society. However, representing an important means to shape experience across the lifecourse and in late life, the discourses and practices related to identities and lifestyle require greater attention – in particular in relation to meaningful forms of choice and participation that extend beyond the individual level.

Conclusion

This chapter has outlined influences and assumptions about ageing that can inform political and personal interpretations of late life. It has reviewed key socio-cultural discourses and practices of age- and stage-based boundaries, the polarisation of health and decline in late life, anti-ageing, successful models of ageing, and lifestyles and identities. Yet, while reviewed separately throughout this chapter, these discourses and practices exist in a complex and intersecting pattern that shapes personal and socio-cultural interpretations of late life. Together, they form a backdrop against which expectations and experiences of ageing and late life may be interpreted. They are measures that older people may hold in mind as they experience continuity and change across their lives. They are also expectations that may find their way into policies and practices relating to age. The picture that emerges from the current discourses on ageing is that a shift from dependency models to success-based models has taken place. Considering the polarisation of health and illness and the forces of anti-ageing, the questions of how these new models shape the experience of late life, and the avenues that exist for reshaping, must now be reconsidered. The next chapter will consider the case illustrations of nine older people where the discourses discussed in this chapter are seen to operate in relation to transitions and late life.

Part Two
Contested models of ageing and late life

SIX

Narratives of transition on ageing and late life

This chapter marks the beginning of Part Two, exploring transitions as contested terrain in late life. Building on the foundations established in Chapters Two to Five, the second part of the book uses the illustrative experiences of older people to reconsider knowledge about transitions and the lifecourse. The interviews presented in this chapter highlight how contemporary trends and dominant views articulated in the academic literature, the socio-cultural context and policies related to age might be rethought. Drawing attention to older people's narratives exemplifies a critical practice of gerontology grounded in the lifecourse. Taking narrative interviews into account represents a move from fixed interpretations of age to more fluid accounts that may simultaneously correspond with and challenge, current conceptions of late life. Chapter Six presents nine case illustrations organised in relation to success-based models, ageing and decline, and varying social locations. Chapter Seven draws these interviews together, exploring questions that challenge dominant understandings of transition articulated in the first section of the book. Chapters Eight and Nine pick up on the specific issues of diversity and the polarisation of health and illness that may affect interpretations of transition in relation to late life. Chapter Ten draws together insights and raises questions that extend beyond the focus of this book.

The current chapter considers nine case studies that draw attention to older people's interpretations and expectations of growing old. It highlights variations that exist between accounts, and explores normative expectations alongside the atypical means that older people may use to make sense of transition in late life. For example, older people's life stories may reflect the expected transition types such as retirement or widowhood or age- or stage-based assumptions, or make use of dominant discourses such as activity or productivity to frame their experience. At the same time, however, their experiences and interpretations may differ from or challenge the taken-for granted knowledge and expectations, especially where age, relationships and diversity are considered. This chapter does not present older people's experiences as more 'authentic' voices, but rather considers their accounts as alternative understandings based on lived experience. Likewise, the accounts are not intended to articulate arguments related to identity that are explored elsewhere. While identity is one aspect of this experience, it is not the sole basis for the argument. Themes embedded in the illustrations include subjective interpretations of turning points and difficult moments; continuity and change; the role of health and illness in late life; interrelated lives or relational models; and the influence of diverse social locations across the lifecourse.

Questions to be considered in each of the case illustrations include the following:

- How does this person understand his/her lifecourse?
- What transitions has he/she experienced?
- In what way does his/her account correspond to, or conflict with, the accepted models of transitions in late life?
- What trends and/or innovations exist?

The cases presented in this chapter illustrate three main locations. In each location there are two cases that more closely typify the dominant expectations and one that contests them. That said, each case contains some element of challenge to dominant understandings of late-life transitions. In the first location, the cases of Charles, Anna and Edwin most closely typify the success-based models that are dominant in the academic literature, socio-cultural constructs and policy discourse. Together, these three cases build evidence for the privileged status associated with the successful ageing paradigm, the role of health, and the relational nature of transitions. The case used for contrast here is that of Edwin, whose adherence to a successful ageing framework is challenged when he becomes a primary caregiver for his wife. The second location is characterised by advanced age, illness or impairment, and the ways in which individuals respond or cope with these changes. Here, the stories of Dorothy, Sam and Peter highlight variations in the trajectories and responses to illness and impairment. This grouping demonstrates how illness or impairment in late life can represent a major rupture, how economic poverty can affect experience, and how coping mechanisms differ. Dorothy's case represents most clearly the adoption of an illness narrative that typifies the construct of the fourth age. Peter's story outlines a lifelong trajectory of disadvantage and demonstrates how illness and impairment can affect transitions and late life. While Peter's acquisition of impairment at an early age provides a certain amount of contrast, it is Sam's story of a smooth transition into advanced age, rooted in a positive perspective, that is most divergent. His story challenges the association of advanced age and impairment, and in doing so draws attention to the onset of illness and impairment as significant.

The third location discussed in this chapter is one that comprises varying social locations that challenge age- and stage-based understandings of transition. Here, the stories of Elizabeth, Elaine and Colin are used to illustrate how structured or identity-based locations can affect experiences across the lifecourse. Elizabeth's story is one of immigration and racism, and Colin's one of invisibility and marginalisation as a result of sexual orientation. In both cases, the strength of character built from these experiences and the identities derived from each were used to negotiate experiences of late life. Elaine's case of lifelong economic poverty and exposure to violence is used for contrast to highlight how continuous aspects of the lifecourse may be more negative than positive. While the cases differ according to the subject matter, together they challenge the dominant accepted understandings of age- and stage-based transitions. These three illustrations highlight how the intersection of locations structured along racialised identities, sexual orientation and poverty can shape and inform lived experience. In each of the examples, names, locations and organisations have been changed in order to protect the identities of the respondents. In some cases, individuals selected their own pseudonym; in others, researchers assigned names that corresponded somewhat with the history or background of their actual name.

Illustrations of the dominant success-based model

Case one: Charles

Background

Charles is a 72-year-old man born in Montreal to Jewish immigrant parents who fled Europe to escape the Holocaust. Charles' family pushed him to attain a good education and to excel in all aspects of life. Although raised in the French part of the city, he attended English school. Charles started university at McGill, but being the only child of a poor family, his parents asked him to leave education to work full time in the family grocery store. After working for several years there, he started what became a highly successful insurance agency. He then married, and, at the request of his father-in-law, took over that family business in the garment industry. His marriage ended after a few years, and Charles, who describes himself as 'one of the early divorcees in 1960', raised his son on his own – something that he admits was "quite rare in [his] community at the time". Throughout his life he built and developed various manufacturing businesses, and later moved into the import/export business with China, Japan and Taiwan. It was in this professional capacity that he developed what he refers to as the "next phase of [his] education – the world of travel". Charles speaks of his professional experiences as successful, and his home suggests that he is financially well off. He married a second time, describing himself as "beautifully married", and has a son from this marriage. In his retirement, he became involved in a late-life learning programme, and now gives talks to a variety of groups, including foreign students and older people in educational settings, nursing homes and cruise ships. He is active and involved in many aspects of society and firmly believes in the power of positive thinking.

Transitions

Charles' narrative focuses on three main transitions in his life: the discovery of music at an early age; his work life, and the way this afforded him the opportunity of travel; and his retirement, which allowed him to further his interests in music, learning and travel. A large part of Charles' narrative is focused on his passion for music, which was inspired at an early age. Charles identifies a moment that changed his life when he was six years old, living in the Little Burgundy area of Montreal. Rooted in this historical context, he links his current pursuit of music,

Table 6.1: Overview of transitions in nine narratives

Name	Corresponding constructions	Challenges to the typified construct	Identified transitions	Key contributions of this story
Charles	• Third age Success • Productivity • Activity • Leisure/travel	• Low income in early life • Left school • Divorce and single parenthood • Bout of cancer	• Role of music in his life • Opportunities of work and travel • Retirement	• Active ageing and contributing to society • Positive outlook • Connections and relationships developed throughout life
Anna	• Third age Success • Activity • Health • Involvement	• Perceptions of success and contributions • Control over the lifecourse • Injury in late life	• Immigration • Marriage and children • Accident and retirement • Lifelong learning programme	• Adjustment/adaptation to change • Importance of positive thinking • Introspection/reflection • Hard work and determination
Edwin	• Third age • Education • Social mobility • Success • Physical activity	• Upbringing in a deprived neighbourhood • His wife's illness in late life • Caregiving • Disappointment with retirement	• Support and influence of his father • Overcoming his youthful rebellion • Marriage and children • Retirement	• Decreased strength in late life • Interconnection of transitions • Discrepancy between expectations and life circumstance
Dorothy	• Fourth age • Impairment • Activity, productivity and involvement • Pain and loss	• Multiple losses • Lack of social support • Meagre financial resources • Desire to persevere/survive	• Sense of failure as a mother • Husband's illness and death • Adapting to impairment	• Loss overshadows coping and 'self' • Compounding effects of loneliness and depression • Impact of financial restrictions in late life
Sam	• Fourth age • Health and activity • Productivity • Creativity • Impairment in late life	• Adjusting to changes brought by impairment • Wife in long-term care • Visual and other impairments • Positive thinking	• Joining Air Force – friendships • Death of first wife and second marriage • Lifelong passion for art	• Accommodation to late life impairment by reducing activities • Active ageing through realistic adjustment • Creativity in late life • Disposition and positive thinking

Name	Corresponding constructions	Challenges to the typified construct	Identified transitions	Key contributions of this story
Peter	• Impairment in late life • Hard work • Community involvement • Illnesses • Poverty	• Multiple losses • Early experiences of impairment • Intersecting events • Desire for independence	• Family breakdown(s) • Death of parents • Workplace accident • Hospitalisation and rehabilitation	• Impact of illness • Intersection of age, illness and poverty • Disconnect between expectations and realities of ageing
Elizabeth	• Alternate transitions • Woman of colour • Success • Involvement • Leisure • Busyness	• Immigration as frame • Perception of age (not old) • Discrimination in work and society • Illness and rehabilitation	• Immigration • Education and workforce participation • Integration into Canadian society • Racism	• Impact of key events • Successful ageing through involvement • Drawing on personal strengths and qualities • Alternate frame for interpreting life (immigration over age)
Elaine	• Alternate transitions • Working poor • Involvement • Productivity • Independence	• Exposure to risk and injury across the lifecourse • Family support and close relationships • Resilience	• Death of son • Traumatic workplace event • Retirement as freedom and liberation	• Lifelong effect of poverty and poor working conditions • Strength and resilience as a lifelong strategy • Adaptation to change in late life
Colin	• Alternate transitions • Gay man • Productivity • Success • Involvement • Early retirement	• Sexual orientation • Late relationship • Conservative upbringing • Friendships • Stigma and discrimination	• 'Coming out' in mid-life (44) • Death of father and subsequent depression • Retirement and community involvement	• Centrality of identity and subjective interpretation • Impact of timing, linked lives and key events • Intersection of social locations (sexual orientation and age) • Shifting socio-cultural contexts

and in particular jazz, with the purchase of a Benny Goodman record. He said:

> 'I was approximately six years old at this time when one of our neighbours ... said, "It's time you learned about music of the area we're living in." We're living in old Montreal ... we had 'Black folks' living around us, and you gotta learn the music!... And it begins the story of my musical life.'

Charles' passion for music was threaded throughout the account, in particular in his descriptions of his early life and of the renewal of this passion through teaching in late life. He described the period of his work life as 'not affording him the time to concentrate on this interest'.

Charles' narrative includes a detailed focus on his work and subsequent retirement. He outlines the details his work life with enthusiasm and describes his various ventures as opportunities afforded throughout life. For Charles, these opportunities became his central motivation to share the knowledge he had acquired with others. When speaking of his retirement, he outlines how it allowed him the occasion to renew earlier life interests despite being a significant adjustment:

> 'You suddenly become aware that you are no longer earning money from your work....You make small adjustments, and that takes like a bit of time. And then you find a new goal....And so, in my case, I took it over as a challenge and so earning was replaced by doing. And the satisfaction of remuneration was replaced with the satisfaction of a good job done. Of creativity. Of development of mind enhancement....] I suddenly became like this crazed happy guy doing what I really wanted to do probably for many years. But suddenly here it was.'

For Charles, 'doing' involves physical activity and travel, as well as teaching and learning: "I work out four days a week in the gym. I run all over the world.... I do it because I want to see, I want to learn, and I want to exchange thinking and ideas with people." He defines himself as a champion of causes like the University of the Third Age, and emphasises how such groups transform into social opportunities that play an important role in the activity and involvement of older people in society.

Contributions

Charles' account outlines the gold standard of 'success' that is exemplified in policy and socio-cultural discourses. Charles' account typifies the notions of active ageing and success, and corresponds with ideas of continued productivity through activity and involvement. Further, it is a story that demonstrates how a positive outlook can be enacted across the lifecourse through a strategy of keeping busy. However, this strategy is often expressed in a way that creates distance between oneself and age. He says: "I've got so much to do. I haven't got time to get old.... So many new thi ngs are coming at me, new ideas, new opportunities, new challenges." At the same time, however, he does briefly reference an unanticipated event of "a bout with prostate cancer". He says:

> 'I'm fortunate enough to have health, reasonable health.... I had cancer
> 13 years ago ... but, um, I have been given a lease on life and I hope
> to carry this very message.... The power of positive thinking.'

Yet, Charles does not refer to this event as a transition, simply an event in his storyline that reinforces his desire to live life according to positive thinking. Charles links his life motto to a quote from the famous Hebrew scholar, Hillel, saying: "'If not now, when?' And that's my motto. If not now, when? So everything that I have to do and accomplish, I do now, I can't wait for tomorrow." A second major contribution can be found in the connections and relationships throughout his lifecourse. His story emphasises the importance of opportunities and supportive relationships, including the discovery of music, access to education, meaningful work and travel. His focus on relationships is best exemplified in a lesson he learned from his father:

> 'He said use life like it was a bank account. Always leave a little
> something in for someone else. Leave a little in for tomorrow. Leave
> a little in for another person. Extend yourself. And, I guess that's what
> I'm trying to do now ... I'm just trying to be a good human being if
> I can ... and I think if you do a little bit of good, you'll get a little bit
> of good back. And that makes life a little bit more bearable.'

Case two: Anna

Background

Anna is a 71-year-old, Czech Republic-born woman living with her husband in Montreal. Originally from a privileged background, she immigrated to Canada in her early teens and now describes herself as 'typically Canadian'. Her narrative is set against a historical context of political change, the resulting emigration to Canada, and the unfolding of her life in Montreal. Anna describes her background prior to the war as one of advantage: "I am quite privileged to have lived that life." In 1949, aged 13, she left for boarding school in England while her parents moved to Canada to get settled. Two years later, she emigrated to Canada (1951) to join her family. Her narrative highlights how her experience of immigration under difficult circumstances established a lifelong pattern of adjusting to change:

'I certainly enjoyed my life here except at the beginning.... And, you know, when you are almost 16, it is quite a chore to get adjusted, but I somehow got through it. And, um, of course, when you lose your roots, your extended family, and all your familiar surroundings, it is not very pleasant.... Well, I just adopted [sic] and adjusted.'

In Montreal, she attended McGill University (BA degree), where she met her husband. She has lived in Montreal ever since, raising her three children, and engaging in what she refers to as 'satisfying work life' in public relations and work with volunteers. Anna describes herself as an as an older woman who is 'confident', 'in pretty good health' and 'still quite presentable for a woman her age'. Her narrative is threaded with a positive perspective and an emphasis on adapting to change and enjoying her late life:" I'm 71, with a lot of expectations, a lot of things to be done yet. And can't turn back the clock so you might as well enjoy the later years."

Transitions

Anna's transitions centre on immigration, getting married and raising her children, and an injury that prompted her to retire and subsequently join a late-life learning programme. In each of these cases, she discusses the importance of adapting to events and circumstances as a means to integrate change. When asked about the transitions in her life, she says: "I think that the immigration was perhaps the greatest catalyst in my life. But, then, I think somehow or other I have come to terms with this, I can't do much about it." This strategy of adapting and adjusting occurs several times throughout her narrative, in relation to each of her identified transitions:

'I think, you have to realise that there are certain things you cannot change, so you just have to adapt.... I always feel that everything is good for something. One door closes, another one opens. It is cliché, of course ... and one has to be positive, I guess, and adapt.'

In late life, this strategy is applied to a fall that she experienced in 2004, when she broke her hip and femur:

'I had a lot of health problems three years back.... Slipped on ice and fell ... I spent about six months out of my life just getting better.... So, that was certainly quite traumatic, I would say ... but I got through it, life goes on.'

As with her experience of immigration, the fall represents a turning point in her life. Following her accident, she began to rethink her work and decided to retire:

'During that time, I just thought, "Well, you know, 30 years later – how much more can I contribute?" ... I found that quite upsetting for a while, but then I thought ... a time comes when you have to admit to yourself – time to move on.'

On retirement, she joined a peer-based educational programme for seniors where she is now enrolled as a learner and a teacher. Anna attributes her growth in old age to joining this club, claiming to be better prepared for her own ageing as a result. She teaches courses on ageing and retirement that encourage experiential perspectives and the exchange of ideas about growing old.

Contributions

Anna's narrative draws attention to the myriad of events that require adaptation across the lifecourse, the realities of ageing that vary according to the individual, and the need to critically appraise success-based models. Her narrative emphasises the connection between past, present and future in making sense of one's life experience. She says:

'A past is very useful because you can always use it as the out-stick – measure your experience against it and see how things have changed.... One has to evaluate and select.'

While Anna's narrative is an example of success based on activity, social involvement and reflection, it is also critical of the dominant interpretations of success. Her account does not promote success and activity at all costs, but takes account of how the enjoyment of late life is predicated on good health: "It is, uh, fun being a senior, in a way, as long you are in reasonably good health." She realises that her experience of ageing thus far is privileged, yet is subject to change:

'So, so far, I am at a point where I have, I guess, all the right ingredients. You know, good family, good friends, a lot of interests ... can't complain too much.'

Her model of success is less about feats of 'sailing the world' and more about introspection, confidence and acceptance. Based on her experience, she encourages older people to accept the changes they cannot control, saying:

'There are stages in life. They [older people] have to be open. And you can't be frustrated when things don't go your way. Because life is never, you know, cut and dry ... you can only plan so much.... You cannot control much but you can control your attitude obviously.'

Recognising limitations and differences, she strongly believes in the power of positive thinking, determination and hard work:

> 'If you do have a successful retirement, it doesn't happen overnight, you have to work at it.... Like everything in life you have to work at. Things don't happen. They don't fall into your lap. You have to work at marriage, you have to work at family, at your job. So you have to have certain self-discipline and just have to get through it. And retirement is one of them too.'

While life may present unexpected events, she highlights how an openness to adaptation and change can, in the end, work out well:

> 'As I said, you can only, uh, expect so much and then you have to cope with whatever else comes up and ... deal with it. And, uh, sometimes it turns out to be very beneficial, it can turn out very well.'

Case three: Edwin

Background

Edwin is a 72-year-old retired man living with his wife in an owned home in the suburbs of Montreal. Edwin was born, raised and schooled in a working-class neighbourhood in the north end of Montreal. Speaking of his neighbourhood, he says:

> 'Back in the thirties, it was a very, very rough area, there was a lot of poverty ... very few people went to high school. And still fewer people who ever dreamt of going to university.'

His father, who was a liberal union leader at the time, raised Edwin to become a critical thinker; this upbringing allowed Edwin increased social mobility from a working class into a professional background. He says: "Some people say that he had brainwashed me. Well, of course, he did ... and I took to it. And I've always seen the world from that perspective." Influenced greatly by his father, he pursued academic studies in history, culminating in a PhD, and embarked on an academic career. Edwin attributes his career choice and life trajectory to the support of his father and the opportunities that came his way:

> 'I'm not trying to inflate my position in any way whatsoever, but I do know for a fact that these were incredible strokes of luck. 'Cause on a rare occasion, I do meet people from my former neighbourhood and it's rather sad.... I think to myself, hell, you could have been just the same way.'

Transitions

Edwin identifies four transitions in his life: the influence of his father, overcoming his anger and rebellion in young adulthood, getting married and having children, and his retirement. Speaking of the influence of his father, he says:

> 'One of the key events in my life was that my father was my father....
> That by the time I was 13, 14 years of age, I knew that there was
> another world outside of the world we lived in, uh ... the world of
> art, and literature and poetry, and these were not foreign words to.'

He discusses the legacy from his father as one of the magic of learning, discovery and knowledge:

> 'Then my father died ... there was nothing in the will. There was no
> property, there was no money ... somebody pointed out, the only
> thing you ever got from your father were a box full of rusty tools....
> But something that this individual couldn't understand. Ah, he left me
> with magic. He left me with an understanding of things that other
> kids in the street didn't have ... he saw things and understood things
> ... that's what he left for me. Not the ... rusty tools, but something that
> fundamentally affected my existence, my life.'

Edwin's narrative is one of success through professional achievements, physical activity and the maintenance of good relationships. He took up jogging and rock climbing, which he continues to do to this day, recently climbing Mount Whitney at 75 years of age. He also describes himself as an avid reader and a family guy. The continuous aspects of success and physical activity were not automatic and Edwin is still uncertain about a stage in his life where he describes himself as a 'problem child' with 'a lot of anger'. He describes how this misbehaving led to him leaving high school and going straight into a job – an error that prompted him to go back to school after one year: "I realised that I had made a terrible mistake ... and working in a factory was just doing the most repetitious thing." On returning to his studies, Edwin met his wife and after a brief courtship they got married. In order to survive financially, his wife took on a job while he completed his PhD. He discusses their poverty during this early period of marriage and her 'sacrificial act' of working in order to support him. Once he completed his studies, he took up various academic posts in the United States while his wife raised their three children, whom Edwin describes as 'a very big part of his existence'. His wife later returned to school to pursue her PhD. His story of professional and familial success is intricately connected to the efforts of his father and his wife. He continued to work as an academic until about 10 years ago, when he 'surprised himself by retiring'.

Yet, his transition to retirement differed from his expectations. Shortly after he retired, Edwin's wife suffered a heart attack, which significantly affected her physical mobility and health, propelling Edwin to assume caregiver responsibilities. He describes this moment:

> 'And then a very unfortunate thing happened early in our retirement.... she had a – what we refer to in our family as an "event".... She took it very, very badly. Ah, came to the conclusion that her life was over.... This was hard.'

His wife's illness was also a shock for Edwin, who had expected his retirement to be a period of leisure and self-reflection. In discussing his expectations of late life, he highlights how some of his expectations never materialised:

> 'It hasn't been as wonderful as I had hoped. Ah, my biggest resentment is the fact that ah, I now, I saw retirement for a short period as endless time for myself which is really selfish.... And my wife, as I said, got sick.... So that's a very frustrating thing.'

In an effort to adjust to this new reality, he began to read books on late life, and recently joined a late-life learning programme. In relation to late life, he says: "Of course, what you learn, if you learn anything, is that you have very little control in life."

Contributions

Edwin's narrative provides three main contributions. First, it outlines the decrease in strength that can occur in late life, and as such challenges dominant interpretations. His description of his recent climbing feat was a mixture of pride and sadness:

> 'It was wonderful. Also sad, though, because I had the feeling ... [pause] I may not be able to do those things much longer. Yeah, age takes its toll. I've begun to sense it, physically.... Less strength, tire more easily.... I'd love to do [another climb] but, ah, I just don't have the energy for it.'

Second, his narrative clearly highlights the interconnections between his life and that of his father and wife, demonstrating how transitions are not experienced as individual events, but intertwined with the experiences of others. Third, his account highlights the discrepancy that can exist between one's expectations and the realities or circumstances of one's life. The clearest examples occur in relation to his retirement and the subsequent event of his wife's illness. Despite this, he says: "If I were asked the question, 'If you could re-live your life ... what would you do differently?' And I would say nothing differently. I would pursue the same thing."

Illustrations of impairment in late life: the fourth age

Case four: Dorothy

Background

Dorothy is an 82-year-old widowed, Jewish-American woman. Dorothy worked outside the home in the marketing industry, raised two children and cared for her ill husband for a period of 30 years. Dorothy was raised by her mother in New York, her father having died when she was a young girl. She describes her family as consisting of herself, her mother and her sister as 'the three musketeers'. Living in New York City during the war, she had an active social life and met and fell in love with her husband. She says: "I was young and enjoying my life at that time." Family is important to Dorothy and she uses her childhood as a comparison with her own relationship with her three children. Dorothy was always an active volunteer, and returned to university in her 1970s. She says: "I was with the young kids studying, and I loved it!... I really don't enjoy being with older people. Everybody has aches and pains, and that's not what I want to hear when I go out." Over her life, Dorothy has acquired a number of injuries she attributes to extended caregiving, and developed visual and physical impairments in her 80s that she reports have significantly affected her quality of life. Her ability to see and walk is affected by macular degeneration and rheumatoid arthritis. She walks with an unsteady gait, using a zimmer frame [walker] and sometimes, a wheelchair. Formerly an active person, Dorothy considers her transition to old age difficult and speaks of 'adapting' as a major challenge. Despite her various losses, however, she considers herself a survivor:

> 'I was a very active … raised my family; took care of a sick husband; went to work to support the family.... My husband ... died … my kids have grown up … I'm suddenly alone … with no job, nothing to do. I was left without insurance.... My eyes have gone, my bones are pretty much shot. And I've become something I'm not happy with.... But I'm a survivor. That's what keeps me going.'

Transitions

Dorothy's narrative is dominated by loss, a sense of failure and dissatisfaction with her current situation. Three issues are of note: what she considers her failure as a mother; her husband's illness and death, which followed shortly after her retirement; and her struggle to adapt to physical impairments in late life. Dorothy feels that she was unsuccessful in developing a sense of family togetherness, as her mother had done: "I tried to do that with my kids, but I think I failed a little because my husband got sick and I had to work." Yet, in responding to the question of the transitions experienced in her life, Dorothy describes her pride in her children's achievements. These include her daughter's marriage, her son and daughter's graduation from university, and living long enough to meet her great-grandchild. Yet, even in these illustrations, she quickly returns to discussions of loss. For example, she says:

> 'When my daughter got engaged, I made her a big party in my house. There was a time I had my own home. But my husband had a stroke and he couldn't work, so I lost my home.'

The death of her husband shortly after her retirement represents the dividing line between her former and current life: "I suddenly, I left my job because he needed me.... He was sick for 30 years.... So I quit my job, I retired. And then my husband, six weeks later, he died." His death left her feeling alone and purposeless, with all of her meaningful roles removed: "Suddenly there was no one to make a cup of tea for. No one to do anything for. No one needed me. It's a terrible thing not to be needed."

Also prominent in Dorothy's narrative is the emotional impact of the physical impairments she experiences in late life. Dorothy speaks of the difficulty she has in adapting to changes of late life: "Life is not easy. Life was never easy but when you're younger, you're able to cope. As you get older, coping becomes more difficult." Her narrative draws attention to what she can no longer do – losses she connects with her dissatisfaction with her increasing dependence:

> 'I can't get about. I can't do the things that I did before.... I'm stuck in the house day and night.... When I was 80 ... I was still driving and running out to go here and there. But when I lost the car, that was a terrible blow ... I had to rely on someone to bring me something.'

Her narrative outlines how she requires assistance in every aspect of her life, including the daily acts of bathing and dressing. Dorothy clearly outlines that in the face of impairment and chronic pain, coping becomes more difficult:

> 'You say to yourself, what good is all this? And you're not going to get better, and it doesn't [end up] to be that rainbow at the end. So what if you live another year ... they want you to live longer, but there isn't that quality to your life. I think it's useless. I didn't want to touch on the death subject, but I guess it just comes out automatically because that's the way you think.'

According to Dorothy, her impairments affect her sense of self: "I hate being the way I am." When asked how she deals with this, she replies: "I just keep going." She says: "All these things start to bring you down. So you think someone like me can rise above it – very difficult."

Contributions

Dorothy's account highlights the difficulties in coping that can be experienced in relation to severe impairment in late life, including how a narrative of loss can come to overshadow one's sense of self. Dorothy's feelings of loneliness and depression are exacerbated by her meagre financial resources. She is currently uninsured because of her husband's illness, and spends most of her pension on medication and rent. A sufferer of chronic pain, Dorothy has to pay for a morphine patch among other medications, which total $300. The lack of freedom that results from her financial situation is particularly difficult. Dorothy describes herself as a social person, but is unable to go to plays or museums as a result of her reduced mobility and strained financial situation. She has the television on all day to keep her company. She tries to keep active by baking:

> 'I just cannot sit idle.... It takes me three days to bake a cake because I'm so handicapped ... one day I'll measure my flour and my sugar and I put 'em in a plastic bag and put away.... I don't do it all at once.... But I like to do things myself rather than buy them ready-made. And it keeps me busy.'

Case five: Sam

Background

Sam is an 87-year-old married, French-Canadian man of Irish descent. He is a retired World War II veteran who lives alone in an apartment in Montreal; his second wife resides in long-term care. Sam identifies himself first and foremost as an artist, although he spent the majority of his working life employed in a large steel company: "I've been an artist and I still am. I took courses in art, sort of hoping I could make a career but it didn't work out. So I got a job." His passion for art developed when he was in his 30s, when he met a number of artist friends in the Air Force. Painting has been Sam's hobby and part-time job throughout his life, and he has organised and displayed his work in 18 exhibitions, many of which have taken place since he retired. During the war, he was overseas for four years, working behind the scenes to prepare bomber planes. After the war he returned to his work in the steel company. He stayed with this company for the majority of his career, taking early retirement at 62 when the company moved to the United States. He married shortly after the war (1947) and had three children, although his wife died of cancer early in life. He married for a second time and his wife helped raise his children. Sam's second wife now lives in a long-term care facility and requires 24-hour care; he visits her four times a week. Sam has a visual impairment and some health conditions, but these do not play a large part in his life story. Instead, he focuses on his activities and the positive aspects of his life, the major one being his painting. In addition, Sam discusses his accomplishments in electrics, woodworking, metalwork and sailing. Sam has a positive disposition and considers himself a flexible person: "You know, everybody has a complaint of something. And this is human nature, but I try to be reasonably adaptable to almost anything because I have a lot of patience."

Transitions

Sam's narrative highlights three transitions: joining the Air Force and meeting a group of lifelong artist friends; the death of his first wife, and subsequent second marriage; and adapting to impairments in late life. Sam speaks positively of his time in the Air Force: "Fortunately, I was able to come back home. It was a great experience, I wouldn't have missed it for the world." During this time, he befriended a group of artists, with whom, for the most part, he maintained lifelong contact. He says: "There ... were seven boys in all... I'm the only one that's left alive right now.... Three of them were killed in action.... And the other three ... eventually passed away." Sam's second major transition, which he identifies as the saddest part of his life, was the death of his first wife at age 41. Talking about the most difficult moments in his life, he says:

> 'Maybe I can answer that in this way: I don't want my life to change. I'm quite happy with it now, in spite of the fact that I lost my first wife.... We all have big disappointment in life for some reason or another. That was mine.'

After the death of his first wife, he met the woman who became his second wife. Although disappointed that his second wife currently lives in institutional care, he discusses his love for her, and how they maintain daily contact. The third transition discussed in his narrative is the adjustment to illness and impairment. While Sam does not identify this as a transition in the same way that he does his experiences in the Air Force and his marriage, his account includes several examples of adjusting to these changes in order to maintain his sense of self and pleasure. He says that he has had good health across his lifecourse, and takes his health challenges of recent years in stride:

> 'My health, I would say, has been exceptionally good ... I had nothing too serious until this February. I fell and broke and fractured my hip ... I didn't suffer too much from it.... Now I'm going into the hospital to get a knee replacement. But that's about the extent of my sickness.'

He also mentions briefly being injured in the war: "I get a benefit from the Department of Veteran Affairs ... because we got shot up pretty badly ... they still don't know if that's the reason my eyes are the way they are today." Sam uses a white cane to compensate for his macular degeneration and tries to keep as physically fit as possible, something that has always been important to him: "I'm quite exercise-prone. I do a lot of exercise ... years of aquafit ... I ran into this knee problem, I had to give up the long walking ... I played a lot of tennis. I was a skier." Sam considers himself to be young with an active mind:

> 'I mean, I know I'm 87 but ... my age is one thing, and what I feel is something else.... I've been coming here [to a centre for people with visual impairments] 10 years because of the company. It's not because they're doing any good for my eyes. My eyes get worse. But the company is wonderful.'

Contributions

Sam's narrative is an example of advanced age and impairments that do not come to define him or his experience. His story includes several examples of the many ways he has accommodated change into his life. For example, he has changed the way he paints:

> 'So I've let the portraiture go.... In the interim, I'm still painting.... The portrait started to get me agitated.... I said, "Well maybe you should give it up because of the detail and the eye" ... and so, anyways, I gave it up.... While I still paint to today, I have, uh, I have halogen lighting.... They say, "How do you do it, you're blind?." "No I'm not blind! I have trouble seeing." But if you want to, you can do it! ... It takes a hell of a lot longer than when I used to do it.'

He has also changed the way he exercises. Staying in shape has always been an important part of his life, and he is still active despite having to stick to less vigorous activities. Speaking of adjustments, he says: "I was always interested in everything, and the one's I liked, well, I really dove into them....Yeah, so I've had to adapt myself to ... things like that." He views these adjustments realistically, however. He believes that one's mentality has a great impact on one's perception of age and experience of late life: "You have to adapt your body and yourself realistically to what you know you can do." Sam describes himself as easy-going in many parts of the interview: "I'm just a rather friendly type of person. And, uh, get along with almost anybody. I can adapt myself to any, any character." His narrative highlights how he is satisfied with what he has done in his life: "So if I don't do any more in this life, I've done a lot of it. I've done a lot."

Case six: Peter

Background

Peter is, to use his own word, a 'young' 76-year-old, divorced man from a working-class background, who grew up, and is currently living in Montreal. Peter describes himself as 'tough' and worked his way up through various positions in the railway industry: "I was never a 'roughie'. I worked very hard. At the age of 15, I started shovelling coal in the railroad." Starting with a number of temporary jobs, Peter eventually acquired a more permanent run as a locomotive engineer. He was married and divorced three times, widowed twice. He has five children, three from his first marriage, and two from his second, but is estranged from them. Sobriety is a theme that runs through Peter's account. Ill for about 15 years with heart trouble and prostate cancer, Peter suffered a stroke in 2007 that left him with more serious physical impairments. Until recently, he was married to his third wife, a woman sponsored from Russia who cared for him after his stroke, until she left him for his son. He currently shares his rented two–bedroom apartment with a lodger, who provides care in exchange for rent-free accommodation. Peter is disadvantaged financially and lives, as he says, 'hand to mouth'. Of his $1,200 income per month from the Old Age Security pension and the Guaranteed Income Supplement (GIS), $800 is allocated to rent, $100 to electricity and heating bills and $200 to medications; he relies on donations from charities to meet his daily needs.[1] Although he may be eligible for an occupational pension, he is currently unable to draw on the funds for unexplained reasons relating to his former company and/or previous debts. Peter's narrative also includes examples of volunteering at the local food bank, where he is also a recipient, and a local museum: "I'm always ready to help people because people help me. You know, it's very nice if you can share your happiness, or share … sometimes just a little word." He takes pride in helping others, living on a tight budget, and the improvements he has made since becoming ill.

Transitions

Peter's narrative reflects how a series of intersecting events resulted in him 'losing everything'. Peter begins the interview by outlining how he has arrived at his current state of being alone and impoverished through a series of misfortunes related to divorce, illness and impairment. He identifies four transitions in his life. The first concerned his divorce and the second the death of his parents. He discusses the combined impact of these two events: "Changed the whole thing, yeah, because, more pressure on me. I'd had trouble with my wife, plus my parents dying … I had more responsibility. And we had children." The third transition was an incident where Peter was involved in a train accident during the course of his work. The fourth, and most recent, was a period of hospitalisation lasting eight months and a long period of rehabilitation that resulted in his third wife leaving him. He describes his loneliness during this period, and how he managed to get through it, with the 'higher power keeping him to his sobriety'. The hospitalisation was difficult, and resulted in a divorce that left him 'penniless', ill and with expensive bills for medication: "I'm not an extravagant person. I don't eat steak every day because I know I can't … I had everything, but I lost everything." Although the details are unclear, Peter's story includes a long–standing connection with social service agencies, social workers and psychiatrists, who appear throughout his narrative:

> 'Well, with all this, me having everything and losing everything, and I didn't go on drinking or drugs and all that, I think I did pretty good....The social worker ... they can't believe how I am managing this without bothering or really doing anything wrong.'

What links each of Peter's transitions is a reflection on the multiple losses he has experienced, and the adjustments he has made.Throughout the difficult moments, Peter highlights how he manages, although he is aware of, and uncomfortable with, the position he finds himself in. He reflects on the sadness that his losses have caused:

> 'I was an engineer for 45 years....I've got a lot of certificates.... It was work and play.Those days are almost like day and night.... It's not the same. The happiness is not the same. Life is not the same.'

Contributions

Peter's narrative highlights how losses experienced throughout the lifecourse can affect the circumstances and interpretations of late life. In particular, his story highlights the effects of illness prior to retirement, the intersections of age and illness, and how circumstances can mean having to rely on food banks and to make difficult choices such as offering rent-free accommodation in exchange for care that may result in increased vulnerability. For example, he states that he does not approve of how his lodger has started 'drinking and getting into trouble'. Peter outlines how his expectations of ageing and late life have not been fulfilled in the way he had hoped, both in relation to his financial situation and his relationships with his children and spouse:

> 'To live a nice quiet life, have children that I could, or we could, say. respect them, they respect us. And lead a life, ah, as best as we can until the time came to depart. Not to be left, like, hand to mouth, and always tense, tense, tense.'

He discusses how difficult it was to be in hospital for eight months, and how hospitalisation made him increasingly aware of his own dependence and eventual mortality – something he refers to as the 'dangerous signs': "Not able to do what you want to do. Or take care of yourself as you would normally do if you were well ... that took everything out of me. Everything." Having survived this difficult experience, however, Peter highlights how he has regained a sense of independence. He reframes his renewed expectations around the concept of self-reliance:

> 'I'm just looking forward to being able to take care of myself as much as I can, not to depend on others.... I just have regrets that I have to do it by myself. And that's why I have these animals [Peter has three cats].'

Despite these challenges, he feels he has lived a good life, and relies on happy memories to 'keep his spirits up'.

Diverse social locations: rethinking age- and stage-based structures

Case seven: Elizabeth

Elizabeth is a 70-year-old never-married Caribbean woman, who, although reluctant to speak about her qualities, describes herself as 'ambitious, independent, determined, and busy'. Born in Barbados, Elizabeth emigrated to Canada at the age of 25 to pursue a nursing career.[2] Her story focuses on her determination, career and various volunteer and leisure activities. After she arrived in Canada, she trained as a nurse, completed a successful work placement and secured a full-time job. This professional security enabled her to bring several family members, including her younger sister, from Barbados to Canada. She is currently retired and living on a pension in her home in the suburbs of Montreal. Elizabeth leads an active life in retirement, volunteering and socialising with her six friends. She is involved with two community organisations, travels every chance she gets, reads, bowls on a weekly basis, and goes to the movies. Being retired means that she is still busy, but on her own terms. When asked how her life has changed in the past 10-15 years, she says: "Well, I'm older.... Fifty-five I was still working.... Now ... I am still busy.... The only difference is that I ... am not going to work....] I'm still busy but on my own, at my own speed." The themes of work and 'busyness' are central to Elizabeth's story. Elizabeth does not consider herself as old: "I don't know if I'm fooling myself, but I don't consider myself 'old', I consider myself a mature person who is retired from work."

Transitions

Elizabeth's turning points and transitions are related to immigration and her personal and professional goals. She begins her story with the following:

> 'I will start by telling you I was not born in this country. I came ... when I was 25 years old. All alone.... I had heard that Canada wanted people. I took my chance.... Not easily, but through that I became a nurse ... I worked ... until I retired in 2000.'

Elizabeth identifies three main transitions in her life, all of which relate to her immigration: pursuing education and a professional career; adapting to the climate and weather of Montreal; and her experiences of racism. Elizabeth's emigration to Canada was prompted by her mother's death, which occurred shortly after the birth of Elizabeth's youngest sibling. After this, Elizabeth applied for jobs as a nurse both in her hometown and abroad, a decision she would not have made if her mother had still been alive. At the age of 25, she went on holiday to Canada to visit a friend who had moved there as part of the domestic workers programme. While she was in Canada, she decided to make some enquiries about pursuing a nursing career there. She felt that this would be wise, given that there were very few places available on the nursing programme in Barbados. She succeeded in arranging a one-year intensive placement in a mental health hospital, where she studied while working there, and was eventually able to apply for immigration status. She describes her first few years as difficult, as a result of experiencing discrimination and having to adjust to a very different climate – challenges she believes she overcame through determination:

> 'That was [clears throat] that was tough. But I say, if I go back, people are going to say … "You can't cut your mother's … natal string?" I didn't want to be a failure [laughs], so I stuck it out.'

Although Elizabeth never uses the term 'racism', her narrative outlines the discrimination she experienced in Montreal. She highlights her first experience as scarring: "I did not feel accepted … it was an awakening." She recounts how, while living in the nurses' residence, her colleagues either ignored her or only engaged with her when it was absolutely necessary: "It's an experience that I will never forget…. It wasn't easy … but I survived it. You know, one learns very easily to adapt to [taps table] circumstances. And I did." When asked how things had changed over the years, she replied: "It hasn't passed … it's just that I learned to adjust to it and it doesn't have the same effect anymore." Throughout her account, she attributes her strength of survival to these difficult experiences. Although for years she was uncertain whether she would stay, she highlights the moments when she became aware that she could achieve a successful life in Canada:

> 'There's immigration. There was higher education…. I felt that even if I did not get my placement [at the hospital] I was going home with something that I could do: nursing…. I bought a house…. I learned French. I said, "Now, I'm on my way." … Accomplishment. I'm on my way…. And all the ambition that I came with, I could see it … going, moving in that direction.'

Contributions

Elizabeth's narrative makes three major contributions. First, it highlights the centrality that key events such as the death of a family member, and immigration in her case, can have on one's life and the interpretation of experience across the lifecourse. Rather than being segmented into ages or stages, Elizabeth's narrative is framed around opportunities afforded her through immigration, and measurements of her professional and personal success. Second, it highlights the strategy of 'busyness' or activity that is often cited in public policy documents. Yet, although she uses this strategy as a way of rationalising her success and providing a coping mechanism for loneliness, she also sees it as having produced negative consequences in terms of preventing her from having the time to invest in a relationship. In this sense, her narrative both draws on and challenges the discourse of activity and productivity. Third, her story is an example of drawing on personal qualities to overcome adversity. She describes how she has drawn on her strength of character to meet the challenges she has faced in late life. For example, she outlines how she was able to overcome a brain tumour, hospitalisation and rehabilitation – things that were very challenging for her as a mature woman. Although her life both did, and did not, develop along the lines she would have expected, she feels that she has led a fulfilling life: "I don't have any regrets.... It took a longer time, it was tough, but no regrets ... if I had to live my life again, I would do the same thing."

Case eight: Elaine

Background

Elaine is a 67-year-old divorced woman who moved to Montreal from the Gaspé region of Quebec with her parents when she was eight years old. She has a grade-nine education and four children, three of whom are still living; her son died at 36 years of age. Elaine had her first child at age 17, and by the time she was 25 years old she was divorced with four children. In order to support her family, she went to work as a chambermaid in a residential hotel. Her parents helped her by looking after the children while she was working the night shift (7pm to 3am): "My parents babysat the kids.... It was not bad.... Knew the kids were okay, eh?" Throughout her employment, she worked at a few different hotels, the most recent being the best. Finding the work physically demanding, she counted the days to her retirement. Now retired, she has a meagre income. However, she is pleased to have retired and does not dwell on her financial situation. She focuses on her independence and ability to manage – a strategy that seems to have served her well across the lifecourse. Elaine maintains close relationships with her family, including many grandchildren and great-grandchildren. For example, her 12-year-old granddaughter spends every weekend of the summer with her. Elaine is also a generous and active individual. The day of the interview, for example, she helped her landlord clear branches away from a tree at the front of her residence, an apartment building she has lived in for 22 years. She also runs a shelter for cats from her home, and currently looks after eight cats. Elaine's story provides an illustration from a location of the working poor and single parenthood, including the ways in which unskilled and poorly compensated employment can affect experiences across the lifecourse. At the same time, it is an account that demonstrates resilience, generosity and the importance of close relationships.

Transitions

Elaine begins her story with her divorce and single motherhood, which led her into hotel work and left her alone in late life: "A little bit about me? Well, I'm alone now." Following this trajectory, she outlines three major transitions in her life story. The first two focus on traumatic incidents, and the third on her experiences of ageing and retirement. First, she outlines the death of her son as a difficult moment in her life. While she does not discuss this event in detail, she alludes to violence and suspicious circumstances. Second, she refers to a trauma whereby a fellow chambermaid and friend was murdered while Elaine was working the same shift: "I was witness to that. We were talking to the guy. She went into his room, and I went in and did my room. And he killed her." The impact of this was devastating; she was unable to work for a year. Returning to work was a scary and difficult process for her: "I was off for a year.... Was watching every corner.... Never know if he's got friends around or not." This is not the only incidence of violence in Elaine's story; she also mentions another friend killed by her husband about 30 years ago, an incident that she believes was drug-related. The details of the interview demonstrate that life has, at times, been difficult for Elaine. Over the lifecourse, she has struggled with finances and physically demanding work, and been surrounded by violence. Elaine, however, presents herself as resilient. The description of the first part of her lifecourse outlines transitions relating to the experience of these traumatic events rather than to processes of ageing.

The third transition, however, focuses on retirement as freedom from difficult work, and the adjustments she has made in late life. For Elaine, retirement was a welcome change. She was pleased not to have to go into work: "Oh, it was nice! It was relaxing [laughs].... Just stay around the house, not get up at 4.30am." She describes retirement as something she and the other women at work were looking forward to: "First we were counting the years, and then we were counting the months [laughs] and then we count the weeks, and then the days!" Her job was a difficult one, as the hotel rooms were residential ones; she had to clean ovens and wash dishes every day as well as clean the rooms. Although Elaine is delighted not to be working any more, she discusses how she wishes she could live more comfortably. But, for Elaine, her limited income is balanced by her liberation from a difficult job; she enjoys her freedom. She does believe, however, that the physical injuries to her arms are due to repetitive motion and the heavy lifting she has done over the years in the course of her work: "I mean, I should have stopped working 10 years ago. Maybe I wouldn't have a sore arm. You know?... 'Cause all that scrubbin'."

Contributions

Elaine's narrative provides an insight into the lifelong effects of low-paid employment and exposure to social issues that can be associated with particular locations: "Yeah, when you work at a hotel, there's a lot of drug dealers, and all that.... They kept to themselves, and I, I mind my own business, you know?" It also demonstrates how this type of physical work can result in the onset of injury at earlier ages, and how low income makes it difficult to participate in certain activities. At the same time, it outlines a lifelong strategy of strength and coping. Elaine admits that her ageing has slowed her down and introduced a few new health-related concerns into her life, but nothing that is not currently being managed. Elaine is a diabetic, suffers from emphysema and has problems with the mobility of her shoulder. She has made changes in her life to accommodate her ageing body. For example, she used to enjoy biking and roller-skating, but is aware that she can no longer do these activities: "Well, I don't drive a bike now. I can't see that good. I don't have a decent one anyway.... Oh yeah, and roller-skated. I loved roller-skating." Elaine firmly believes in staying active, and takes the changes of ageing in her stride. She highlights her independence through activities such as shopping for groceries, and socialising with the friends she met at two local food banks. Highlighting the practical and social aspects of such services, she says: "Sometimes you get food. The things you want. And I see ... all the gang I know there, eh?" Overall, Elaine is satisfied with her retired life, friends and family support network. The question of her health and income, however, presents a worry for her future.

Case nine: Colin

Background

Colin is a 61-year-old, retired gay man from Montreal. The son of an Italian mother and a Spanish father, Colin grew up speaking English in Montreal. Colin had a strict upbringing, and learned that being gay was socially unacceptable. He 'came out' as gay at age 44, and has been living with his partner for seven years in an owned condo in Montreal. He says:

> 'Always hearing very negative things about homosexuality.... Well you know, you don't want to be like that ... I guess it was my cultural family and church, as I say it, made it [being gay] such a horrible thing at the time to contemplate. But like once I got over that, then the rest was quite easy. And, of course, society was a lot more open.'

Colin has recently retired from a management position in the travel industry and receives a pension. He has a social life with his partner and friends, is involved in the local church and community life, and cooks and travels. He has a number of friends that he has known for over 30 years, as well as more recent friends, and emphasises the importance of nurturing friendships prior to late life: "I mean people die ... often cancer or heart attack or whatever ... but if you haven't nourished friendship, then ... you can't be surprised if somehow, you know, you're starting from zero." As an older gay man, he is acutely aware of the need to address ageing in the gay community, and devotes a good deal of his time to advocacy for older gay men's issues. Colin agrees that older gay men tend to be marginalised in both the mainstream and gay communities. To address this, Colin is actively involved in coordinating social events, trips and activities for older gay men. In addition to this, he is an advocate for social issues, including combating isolation and loneliness, and the provision of long-term care.

Transitions

Colin's narrative centrally focuses on his identity as a gay man. He discusses three transitions in his life: 'coming out' at a late age; the death of his father; and his retirement. Central to his narrative is his 'realisation of being gay' and going through the process of 'coming out' at a late age. Colin was unsure of whether he would be able to find a life partner:

> 'I resigned myself to reaching old age and not really finding anyone to live with ... but then out of the blue, I did meet this man who is a wonderful man ... and I guess it was obviously reciprocated because, here we are, just about seven years later, and it's still holding strong.'

He was not always as confident and comfortable with his life, however. Colin speaks about his personal struggle to deal with his own misconceptions and relatively conservative views of the gay community, which he attributes to his upbringing and he social norms of the time. Among them was a fear of HIV: "I couldn't hear, talk of AIDS ... I'm ashamed that I didn't do much, volunteering and that. But, it was a very hard step for me." The transition of 'coming out' and becoming comfortable with his identity was a long and difficult process for Colin. He speaks in detail of addressing his own internalised homophobia and the need to confront that of the community and society around him.

The second transition in his life was the death of his father, which resulted in short-term depression. Colin describes how the death of his father was a major turning point in his life:

> 'Not that I was so close to him.... He was an old-school European father ... and all of a sudden out of almost the blue, my father ... passed away. So I had a lot of trouble accepting that.'

As a result of his father's death, Colin fell into a depression:

'I was very shocked that that could happen to me because I always thought, wrongly I thought, oh you know, depressions are for people that are weak.... So, I think, in a sense it made me afterwards, it made me a stronger person after going through that period'.

In his narrative, his father's death, his depression and his 'coming out' are linked. He discusses how the death of his father made him more aware of his own mortality. Just following his depression, he decided to be 'himself' and 'address his own stereotypes toward being gay'. His third transition was that of his early retirement, and the freedom this has brought him: "Well, there was a change when I stopped worked and I retired. You know, my life was different.... We used to work weird hours ... I didn't miss that."

Contributions

Colin's interview makes several contributions that challenge dominant age- and stage-based understandings of transitions. First, his narrative highlights how transitions such as 'coming out' and the process of accepting one's identity can represent an unrecognised form of transition. It also highlights the intersections that exist between ageing and sexual orientation. Second, as a result of his upbringing and a social cultural context perceived as hostile, his transition to a significant relationship occurred much later, or 'off time', than would be generally expected:

'I define, define myself today as a gay male but I didn't always. I made my coming out when I was 44, so that's quite late ... and, since I came out at age 44, I had never really met anybody ... these are things that I should have been finding out when I was 21.'

Third, his narrative highlights how personal interpretations take place within a shifting socio-cultural backdrop. In several instances, he highlights the differences between the closed context of his youth and the more open context of today's life in Montreal. The following quote that speaks of older men's needs for specialised services clearly highlights the links between personal experience and social contexts over time:

'You know, the police were very homophobic back then and so on and so forth. So they had to put up with all of this stuff and it was a fight. And so now they say, "Well, now that we're old and maybe a little feeble, do we have to go back into the closet?" ... People say no, and they're not willing to take that step back in time. You know, because they've known freedom.'

Fourth, he highlights how interpretations and decisions can also be linked to the life events of others, such as the death of his father. Fifth, his insights draw attention to the personal and emotional processes that can be involved in transitions, and the amount of time that can, as in Colin's case, be spent in identities that are 'in-between':

> 'I think I can do most things that I want to do, within reason.... So life is just, life is easier but I, you know, going back to it, I think it's just because society has changed. People have decided to make life easier.'

Conclusion

The nine illustrations provide various interpretations of transitions in late life. Presented according to typified constructs of healthy and successful ageing, impairment in late life and diversity, the three sets of cases draw attention to the socially constructed nature of the divisions themselves. They highlight how the experiences of older people in each of the constructs can vary, with experiences more fluid than dominant discourses and practices tend to depict. The diversity between these cases raise important challenges where understandings of continuity and change across the lifecourse are concerned. Questions of social structures, social locations, individual identities and coping mechanisms can be raised in each of the nine cases.

The forthcoming chapters draw heavily on these cases, supplemented by examples from older people in the larger sample, where appropriate. Themes to be explored in the coming chapters include passage, and how individuals move through life; liminality and being within and between; continuity and cumulative disadvantage; linked lives and the relational aspects of transitions; coping and adaptation; and questions of intersecting social locations and the polarisation of health and illness that are addressed in Chapters Eight and Nine.

Notes

[1] The GIS provides additional money, on top of the Old Age Security pension, to low-income seniors living in Canada. To be eligible for GIS, older people must be receiving the Old Age Security pension and must fall below the income threshold determined at taxation. As such, receipt of GIS is a fairly reliable measure of income-based poverty in old age.

[2] At the time, Canada was actively recruiting caregivers and nurses from the West Indies. Elizabeth's story can thus be placed within the wider context of the intersections between care policies and lived experiences.

SEVEN

Rethinking transition

This chapter identifies and discusses alternative and flexible interpretations of transition in late life. Rooted in the narratives presented in Chapter Six, it highlights themes that challenge suggested models of how older people 'ought' to experience the changes associated with growing old. It reconsiders the forms of transition that have become common place in social science approaches, including the idea that individuals move across a linear and stable backdrop as they age. In particular, this chapter draws attention to the challenges of fixed interpretations of age and stage, linear progression through the lifecourse, the tendency to focus on the individual, and the extent of control or choice that mark dominant understandings of continuity and change across the lifecourse. In order to reconsider transition in late life, material is presented according to five intersecting themes: passage and liminality; multiple and intersecting forms of transition; events, social locations and identity; linked lives and relational notions of transition; and continuity/adaptation in relation to lifelong disadvantage. Themes drawn from older people's experiences in the late life transitions project related to the accounts presented in Chapter Six point to the variations experienced in late life under contemporary conditions; that is, they provide evidence of just how the lifecourse may be more fluid or subjective than previously understood, and suggest fresh models for rethinking transition in late life. Bringing these themes together with current knowledge in the academic literature can help to better understand movement, continuity and change across the lifecourse. At the theoretical level, the themes also connect the approaches of critical gerontology with those of narrative and the lifecourse perspective. Questions that guide the analysis in this chapter include:

- How do older people define and understand their lifecourse transitions? What types of trend and innovation exist?
- How do the models used by older people correspond or conflict with those expressed in policy frameworks and the academic literature?

Table 7.1 highlights the challenges that older people's accounts raise in relation to dominant understandings of transition in late life. On the left, the table lists five dominant tendencies that characterise understandings of transition. On the right, it lists the concepts derived from older people's accounts. Material in the chapter is organised and discussed in relation to these challenges and insights.

Table 7.1: Challenges to dominant understandings of transition

Tendencies in dominant interpretations	Challenges from older people
• Linear passage, fixed moments of 'arrival' and exit points	• Liminal and/or fluid experiences across the lifecourse
• Transitions as single, marked events that take place in the lives of individuals	• Multiple and intersecting forms of transition across the lifecourse
• Age- and stage-based experiences	• Variations based on events, social locations • Importance of subjective interpretation and identity
• Events that happen to individuals in families and societies	• Transitions as linked experiences that occur in relationships with the self, family, society
• Control or choice over events • Adaptation as development	• Lived experience of constraints in relation to control or choice (for example, disadvantage) • Adaptation and resistance as a difficult emotional process

Passage and liminality

Older people's accounts challenge the idea of a linear passage between fixed age- or stage-based markers. However, the challenges to fixed notions are complex, with older people's stories containing messages that both correspond and conflict with dominant understandings. Yet, the nuances of their words carry greater weight when considered in relation to dominant constructs. Illustrations that correspond with age-based interpretations as a marker of change can be identified in the narratives. For example, Elaine says, "Suddenly I turned 80 and all my problems started, health-wise" and Edwin speaks about realising that "I wasn't a kid anymore – and that there were things I could no longer do, and will never be able to do." Such statements are consistent with age-based markers of the fourth age, set around aged 75 or 80. Yet, looking deeper into stories such as Dorothy's reveals how the actual experiences of impairment began before she reached the age she identifies as being the marker for 'when things changed' for her. In both cases mentioned, the use of age was not factual, but a representation of how each made meaning of the event. Dorothy and Edwin made sense of their experiences by establishing connections to the dominant narrative that impairment can be expected in advanced age. Their accounts thus demonstrate the importance of subjective perceptions that occur in relation to socio-cultural master narratives, and the relationships created between the two. Yet, while such accounts correspond with established markers, other interpretations directly challenge age- and stage-based understandings, drawing attention instead to the socially constructed and personal meanings of age. Sam's example, where he discusses the discrepancy between his actual age and his perceived age, is case in point. Emphasising his determination and attempts to stay active, he says: "My age is one thing and what I feel is something else." Also relevant is Peter's discussion of how others say 'he looks a young 76'. Together, these examples point to the discrepancy between chronological and perceived socio–cultural interpretations of age, and draw attention to a more fluid and relative process of movement than is articulated within dominant models of ageing. They highlight how fixed end points or boundaries of experience may not exist as previously understood.

Both the process-based elements of passage or becoming, and the liminal space of being between, that are evident in older people's accounts are important features that challenge dominant understandings of transitions in late life. A number of authors have drawn attention to the processes of becoming through ritual or identity. For example, Myerhoff (1984, 1992) explores meaning through ritual in relation to age, while in *Passages*, Sheehy (1974) distinguishes mid–life as a transitional phase of status passage from middle age. For the most part, understandings of passage and liminality are located in rereading the anthropological work on rites of passage and ritual proposed by van Gennep (1960 [1909]), Hertz (1960 [1907]) and Turner (1969), as explored in Chapter Three. However, while the 'rites of passage' were widely adopted in the social sciences, and influenced gerontology through the works of Cain (1964, 1967) and Neugarten (Neugarten et al, 1965; Neugarten, 1968), these approaches have been criticised for their narrow interpretations emphasising structural and normative aspects over the process-based elements of experience (Spencer, 1990; Hockey and James, 2003). However, process and ritual, as explored in anthropology (Myerhoff, 1984; Cohen, 1994; Hockey and James, 2003), draws attention to the fluidity in older people's accounts compared with dominant constructs of growing old.

In their discussion of lifecourse identities, Hockey and James (2003) outline the importance of process in the works of Hertz (1960 [1907]) and VanGennep (1960 [1909]) – readings that have been lost in understandings of transitions as structural locations that ensure stability within society, as tended to be the case in gerontology. Their interpretations of these works highlight the social constructionist aspects over structural-functionalist or biologically determined interpretations, leading them to the importance of identity across the lifecourse. They alert us to the possibility of viewing transitions as socially constructed passages, as well as to the relevance of liminality (Turner, 1969) defined as a space or zone that is located 'betwixt and between the fixed social positions' of van Gennep's three-stage model discussed in Chapter Three. Their analysis allows for a reading of transition as a process-oriented notion of liminal time spent in-between, rather than one focused on fixed points of exit and entry. Identities in late life, argue Hockey and James (2003), are based on rites of passage and 'becoming' rather than fixed stages such as roles or ages to which we have become accustomed. As such, the experiences of continuity and change that are highlighted in older people's accounts can be interpreted as transitional processes of becoming that occur through meaning making and identity reshaping. Such interpretations resonate with approaches based on socially negotiated identities and lifestyles whereby older people come to create their identities through reinterpreting or reinventing the self (Featherstone and Hepworth, 1991; Tulle-Winton, 1999; Gilleard and Higgs, 2000; Hurd Clarke, 2002). They also correspond with scholarship focused on the meaning of transitional events, whereby older people subjectively interpret existing 'rites of passage' such as retirement (Stokes and Maddox, 1967; Crawford, 1973; Myerhoff, 1984). Liminality is thus an important concept from which to challenge understandings of transition in relation to late life. The problem is, however, that while the notion of passage can render evident the fluidity in older people's accounts, the emphasis on 'becoming' is less helpful in relation to illness and impairment – events that in late life are often unexpected, unplanned and could be interpreted as lacking a point of exit other than death.

While the concept of liminality holds potential for rethinking transitions in late life, anthropological interpretations are somewhat restricted by the underlying assumption that the liminal period is temporary and is, at some point, exited for a new social status. Even interpretations of the process of becoming imply that there is a moment of arrival at the new identity. While there is a strong argument to be made in relation to identity, as Hockey and James (2003) have done, the implied temporary nature of liminality may be problematic for older people whose experiences may be more permanent and ongoing than such analysis would seem to allow. Taking the case of Dorothy as an example, older people may find themselves in a liminal space for an extended period of time. While options for 'exit' could include wellness, reminiscence or acceptance, the symbolic weight of the constructs of decline and death seem more prevalent in accounts of severe impairment and long-term illness. In her narrative, Dorothy reports reluctantly to having relinquished the continuous aspects of her life. She seems to find herself unable to integrate impairment or resist being defined by it. Unable to move to a point of adjustment, or to continue to fight against being defined by the impairment, her narrative exudes a strong sense of loss, and in particular the loss of her subjective self. Drawing on Kleinman (1988), her narrative becomes a type of 'illness narrative' in which her impairments become a central storyline and defining feature of her experience.

The issue of choice in relation to the duration of transitional events raises an important predicament that is left unaddressed in the focus on lifecourse identities. It is one, however, that is a central component of the lifecourse perspective. To what extent do individuals have the potential to shape their transitional experiences through identity choices, in cases of structured locations, lifelong disadvantage or illness/impairment? The locations and experiences of late life are not necessarily ones that can be exited. Further, the structural and psychological dynamics of being located in these spaces in-between are underemphasised in models focused on 'becoming'. Yet, a focus on the interpretive or phenomenological understandings of what it means to be located 'within and between' can advance the analysis, and challenge both fixed age- and stage-based interpretations. Herein lies an important potential for the reconsideration of transition: rethinking the conditions, experiences, assumptions, and subjective experiences of this liminal space.

Experiences located at the intersections of age and illness challenge the dominant interpretations of age through their liminal location. At the same time, they confront the usual interpretations of liminality as a temporary space. What is interesting in the examples of illness or impairment in late life is how thinking through the concept of liminality demonstrates the uncertainty and disruption that can occur. Dorothy's case points to the importance of subjective interpretations and the emotional consequences that occur in relation to late life. For example, she had expectations of ageing that included togetherness with her family, and in particular, spending her retirement with her husband. While widowhood is normally characterised as a transitional point with fixed exit points, Dorothy remains in the liminal space of adjustment, coping and grief that occur at the intersections of widowhood and decline. While she maintains what could be described as a 'mask' (see Biggs, 1997, 1999, 2004a) – a model suggested for coping with the set-backs of age – her discussion of her increasing physical impairments and declining social networks point to this period as likely to continue. The difference here is between her reality and the interpretation of her experience. Dorothy is not likely to improve in her health status, and her expectations of ageing and late life have not been met. Experiences such as Dorothy's raise several questions relating to transitions, including: Does the experience of illness/ impairment represent a transition or a liminal space of being 'between'? Why is staying in a liminal space problematic? What does it tell us about the relationship between psychological adjustment and existing within and between liminal spaces? Does coping or adjustment as an indication of success represent an exit point? And finally, what happens if and when older people cannot adjust as they are expected, and are unable to integrate these changes into their lives and identities?

Social location, identity and experience

Older people's experiences highlight how social locations and identity can affect the interpretation of transitions in late life. Illustrations from diverse social locations reveal the extent to which accounts may differ from age- or stage- based frames, constructed instead through alternative storylines based on structured locations, identity or experience. Take as an example the accounts of Elizabeth, Elaine and Colin, presented in Chapter Six. Elizabeth speaks from the standpoint of a woman of colour, Elaine from that of lifelong poverty and Colin from that as a gay man. Together, these illustrations demonstrate how storylines such as immigration, risks of particular work contexts and sexual orientation can, for example, shape and influence interpretations of ageing. In some cases, such experiences take precedence over expected storylines or themes of ageing. This is not to equate the experiences of all diverse social locations with a position outside of age, thereby relegating the accounts of older people from diverse social locations to that of 'other' or 'different'; rather, the point is to draw attention to the variability between accounts, and how meanings may be constructed along alternative lines to age or stage. Each of the three accounts pursues a unique interpretation of life that is related to the individual's experiences across the lifecourse, and in doing so challenges the assumption that narratives in late life are organised around age.

The collective contribution of these cases demonstrates how structured locations and particular identities may prove more powerful than age in the interpretation of transitions in late life. As such, they extend the relevance of the argument focused on liminality as a process of 'becoming' or 'being between' that may be used to characterise older people's interpretations of their experiences. Older people's accounts from diverse social locations establish links between the interpretive and structured experiences from differing vantage points in late life. In particular, they highlight the long-lasting impact of locations affected by discrimination related to racism, classism and homophobia in culture and society. Considering the combination of structured locations and the psychological or interpretive aspects of experiencing these locations can move the analysis forward. This can be achieved by drawing on recent interpretations of the complex experience of being both 'outsider' and existing between dominant spaces –an experience that older people at marginal social locations articulate clearly in their accounts (see Torres, 2006a,b; Hazan, 2009a). Two important strands used to reconsider the relationship between social locations, identity and the experiences of transitions are post-colonial interpretations of liminality and the psychological processes of what it means to occupy a marginal or colonised identity.

The intersections of diverse social locations and ageing challenge interpretations of the lifecourse based on age or stage, and draw attention to the need to reconsider the liminal spaces of being 'within and between'. Understandings of diverse social locations can be advanced by considering the process of 'becoming' that is involved in identity formation across the lifecourse, and the positioning that may occur in relation to needs and rights (see Fraser, 1987; Spivak, 1995). Yet, understandings of liminality that are based solely on 'becoming' can overlook how experiences at 'othered' locations represent continuous aspects of the lifecourse that cannot be exited. They overlook how such locations can cut across interpretations of ageing and late life, and ultimately shape experiences across the lifecourse. Intricately connected with power relations, locations of discrimination or disadvantage intersect to shape experiences across the lifecourse. In the interviews with older people conducted as part of the Late Life Transitions project, structured and social locations were found to shape their narratives and experiences of growing old. Just as the accounts of older people cannot be separated from age, the accounts of older people from diverse social locations cannot be separated from the structured and socio-cultural contexts that shape their experiences. Among the diverse locations described in the accounts in Chapter Six are minority ethnic status involving racism, sexual orientation resulting in marginalisation, and poverty leading to lifetime disadvantage and victimisation. Interpretations of transition and late life differ most markedly from age- and stage-based notions of transition when social location is taken into account. The accounts of Elizabeth, Elaine and Colin, for example, highlight how age is a part of their experience, but is not central to the definition of their lives or identities.

In these differing accounts, experience was often organised according to particular events, such as immigration, or identities, such as being a gay man. The cases of Elizabeth, Elaine and Colin all highlight how being considered 'other', existing in the liminal spaces characterised by marginalised identities, can challenge dominant interpretations of age-based transitions. For example, Colin's narrative is framed around his 'coming out' as a process of personal growth and development, and the strength he has gained from this process. His narrative clearly depicts how being gay affected his transitions in ways that meant he was 'out of synch' with expectations, while Elizabeth's account was held together by qualities of strength and perseverance expressed in relation to immigration and racism throughout the lifecourse. She clearly identifies how social location and identity can overshadow the importance of age and illness in late life, and, in doing so, contests a linear model of transition punctuated by age and stage. Her transitions are related to her identity as a woman of colour who immigrated to Canada and successfully made her way, overcoming obstacles and barriers throughout life. While such accounts could be interpreted in relation to identity and the making of self, they are also illustrations of the importance of considering structured social locations and the contexts within which people make sense of their experience. In the final illustration, we have Elaine, who as a result of lifelong poverty and low-level work as a chambermaid is repeatedly exposed to violence, which alters the trajectory of her lifecourse and affects her experience. The contrast between the three structured social locations of Elizabeth, Elaine and Colin raises challenges for understanding transitions and liminality in late life. These examples point to different pathways that can occur as a result of diverse social locations and illustrate how such locations are not often chosen and have lifelong consequences.

Although postcolonial theory will be discussed in greater detail in Chapter Eight, its insights on liminality are relevant to the discussion at hand. Rather than considering liminality as a temporary space in-between, post-colonial definitions of liminality refer to this space as one of negotiation – a 'space of symbolic interaction' (Ashcroft et al, 2007, p 117). Post-colonial interpretations of liminality address the shortcomings of anthropological interpretations mentioned in the previous section. They draw attention to the negotiation that occurs from within marginal locations, the intersections of structured locations of 'otherness', the centrality of identity claims and the psychological processes involved in making meaning of a marginalised or colonised identity. As such, post-colonial interpretations of liminality offer the means to understand experiences that take place in the context of discrimination or marginalisation, such as those of ageing from diverse social locations. Not only is this space negative, however, but it also holds the potential for resistance and reinvention. In their book of key concepts in post-colonial theory, Ashcroft and colleagues outline the following for liminality:

> The importance of the liminal for post-colonial theory is precisely
> its usefulness for describing an 'in-between' space in which cultural
> change may occur: the transcultural space in which strategies for

> personal or communal self-hood may be elaborated, a region in which
> there is a continual process of movement and interchange between
> different states. For instance, the colonized subject may dwell in the
> liminal space between a colonized discourse and the assumption of
> a new non-colonial identity. But such identification is never simply
> a movement from one identity to another, it is a constant process of
> engagement, contestation and appropriation. (Ashcroft et al, 2007,
> p 117)

The parallel to be made with the liminal space of ageing is clear, as is the way in
which post-colonial understandings of liminality highlight how 'outsider' status
of structured locations such as 'race', class, and sexual orientation can affect the
interpretation of experience. Although post-colonial thinking is rarely discussed
in social gerontology (for an exception, see Hazan, 2009a, 2009b), its insights have
much to offer a reconsideration of transitions as they relate to late life. In particular,
post-colonial analysis devotes attention to the insider/outside boundaries that are
created in discourses and practices, as well as the ways in which colonised and
marginalised people may claim voice and negotiate experience. These themes will
be examined more closely in Chapter Eight in the discussion of how scholarship
can more accurately take account of diverse locations of experience.

   While identities based on 'race' or sexual orientation cannot be relinquished in
the same way as class, the markers of class can also be seen to shape and impact
experience across the lifecourse. The similarities between the diversely situated
accounts in Chapter Six point to the impact of occupying marginalised locations
of 'other'. The differences between the accounts speak to the need to consider
elements of agency/choice, personality/motivation, and the extent to which an
individual can actually transcend structural and cultural barriers. The ways in
which diversity and structured social locations affect experience in late life will be
explored in greater detail in Chapter Eight. For the moment, what is important
is the challenge that each of these locations represents for age- and stage-based
understandings, and the questions that surface as a result.

Multiple and intersecting transitions

Older people's accounts in Chapter Six and the Late Life Transitions project
more generally, challenge how transitions are often approached as single and
separate events. Dominant understandings tend to highlight the most prominent
types of transition, such as retirement and widowhood, with little attention to
alternative experiences in late life, or how additional or intersecting transitions
may complicate adjustment. This is in part a result of the paths taken in sociology
and psychology, whereby the study of transition between roles, for example, is
considered separate from that of coping. Yet, in older people's narratives from the
LLT project and presented in Chapter Six, connections are made between events,
the psychological aspects of coping, and maintaining a consistent identity, for

example. Their accounts are more complex than simply addressing one loss at a time, as is implied in standard notions of transition or organisational practice that classify older people on the basis of one primary diagnosis or experience. The types of transition discussed by older people in Chapter Six, as illustrative of the themes found in the larger study, were broader than the generally cited list of personal success, widowhood, retirement, grandparenthood; they also included, for example, experiences related to impairment, social locations or identities, and interpersonal relationships, to name a few. What was most striking, however, was how events were rarely depicted as discrete. Instead, transitions were presented as embedded in other transitions or key events, relationships or notions of self, as articulated throughout the interviews. The accounts gave several examples of multiple and intersecting transitions experienced across the lifecourse. In doing so, they suggest that adjusting to transition is more pronounced and complicated at the intersection with other major life events, in particular when one of the events is unexpected or deemed to be outside the control of the individual (Neugarten, 1979a; Diehl, 1999).

Two of the cases presented in Chapter Six illustrate the multiple and intersecting nature of transitions. Elizabeth's major transition of immigration and ensuing professional success correlates with her mother's death:

> 'But I should say, if my mother was alive, I would have been home [in Barbados]. But when your mother is *not* there, and you are the oldest person, and, you know.... I had two brothers and my father, it's not the same as with a mother.'

In Elizabeth's case, the death of her mother was not only the impetus for her emigration to Canada, but was also connected to the perception of her independence and her rationale for staying in Canada. She comments: "That was [clears throat] that was tough. But I say, if I go back, people are going to say ... 'You can't cut your mother's ... natal string?' I didn't want to be a failure [laughs], so I stuck it out." Elizabeth's narrative of achieving personal and professional success through immigration was intricately linked with the transitional events of reaching adulthood, pursuing education, her mother's death and leaving Barbados. In her case, these transitional events culminated to provide the rationale for her emigration and lifelong residency in Montreal. They also, as discussed in the next section of this chapter, highlight the links between her life and that of her mother, and the emotional significance that prompted her to take a particular life path. Multiple and intersecting transitions can positively affect the interpretations of age and the lifecourse, as well as raise challenges that are difficult to overcome.

Dorothy's example, by contrast, describes how the connected experiences of widowhood and retirement resulted in a loss of purpose. The beginning of her interview reads as follows:

> 'What could I tell you? I was a very active ... working person ... took care of a sick husband; went to work to support the family.... My

husband, of course, had died in '98. … And I'm suddenly alone …
with no job, nothing to do.'

She elaborates on how the combined events of her husband's unexpected death
after a lengthy illness, and the subsequent loss of her caregiving role shortly after
her retirement, deeply affected her sense of self and purpose:

'He was sick for 30 years. That's why I had to support the whole
house.… It was becoming too much paying a girl working taking care
of the house … so I quit my job, I retired. And then my husband, six
weeks later, he died … I wouldn't have retired and gone away. I was
good at my job.… He died. And I didn't have a job, and I didn't have
a husband.'

The associations between these events speak to the impact of multiple and
intersecting losses, but also to Dorothy's sense of worth. Her words reveal anger
and disappointment relating to her husband's death, as well as the regret she
has for the loss of her meaningful roles of carer and worker. In this sense, the
multiple and intersecting forms of transitions reveal a compound experience of
loss. Her feelings of being useless and without a role become worse with the
onset of health problems in her early 80s. As a result, her narrative outlines how
the multiple and intersecting losses have left her in a weakened state where she
struggles to find a new purpose in life. Her story parallels notions of the role-less
role of retirement (see Burgess, 1950). Yet, in Dorothy's case, it was not simply
retirement, but the intersections of widowhood, retirement and impairment, that
caused her to feel unneeded.

Together, such accounts suggest a link between simultaneous events or
transitions, coping, and the interpretive meanings associated with these changes.
Where older people interviewed as part of the Late Life Transitions project
discuss drawing on their coping mechanisms to respond to single events, their
narratives reveal how drawing on these same strategies in the event of multiple
and intersecting transitions is more difficult. In many cases, what made experiences
of change challenging for the older people was the composite nature and the
timing of transitions. For example, many older people discussed how experiences
of retirement and illness occurring at roughly the same period were seen as
major challenges. This combination of transitions is perhaps characteristic of late
life, and in particular the period known as the fourth age. As such, the ways in
which multiple transitions can affect coping raises important questions where
experiences of continuity and change in late life are concerned. In most cases,
what seemed particularly difficult about the experience of multiple transitions
was that the changes occurred unexpectedly, such as Dorothy's husband's death
and Edwin's wife's illness. In considering these cases, three issues are of particular
concern with regard to multiple and intersecting transitions.

The first is how multiple and intersecting transitions can drain an individual of their capacity to cope (Baltes and Baltes, 1990; Carstensen, 1992; Baltes, 2003). On their own, these transitions may not have had the same impact, while as cumulative events they come to represent a difficult change in late life. The psychological literature has addressed this phenomenon through an identification of the types of coping mechanisms needed to cope with large changes. However, the mainstream literature on transitions has not adequately addressed the challenges that multiple and intersecting transitions raise for the interpretation of late life.

The second concern is the timing of events, and whether such events are expected or unexpected. Older people's ability to cope with, and adjust to, multiple losses appears to be affected by the timing of such events and whether or not they are expected. When the events are expected, older people seem to have the time to prepare and integrate such changes into their view of themselves and their lives. This is not to suggest that such experiences are not difficult, but that their accounts of these changes differ. When the events are unexpected, it seems more difficult for older people to adjust (Neugarten and Datan, 1973). This may relate to both the extent to which the event challenges their sense of self, the cumulative effects of multiple losses, and weakened social and personal resources required to initiate change.

The third concern relates to how multiple and intersecting transitions are bonded to the identity and sense of self that people hold throughout the lifecourse. Elizabeth's transitions and life events came to together to provide a strong rationale and driving force for her experience. Dorothy's experiences, however, resulted in a sense of loss, of both self and purpose. Here, connections have focused on how narratives may provide clues to the threat or rupture that may occur in relation to self, as well as the means to reconstruct experience (see Crossley, 2000). What seems important in the accounts of older people is the extent to which the experience is interpreted to reinforce a quality, such as determination in the case of Elizabeth, or seen to threaten the identity of the individual as, for example, a good worker and carer, as in the case of Dorothy. Yet, while the impact of multiple and intersecting transitions is considered in the psychological literature, it has not been clearly identified within the more broad social science scholarship on transition.

Linked lives and relational aspects of transition

The narratives of the older people in the current project challenge the understanding of transitions as events that happen to, and affect, individuals. In many cases, the transitions described referred to the influence of other people, or to events in other people's lives, rather than their own. The accounts point to the relevance of considering notions of linked lives and relational aspects of experience in a reassessment of transition in late life. The concept of 'linked lives', as presented in Chapter Two, highlights the interrelationships that influence experiences and events across the lifecourse (Elder, 1994; Elder and Pellerin, 1998).

This concept resonates with the ways in which the older people presented their lives as intricately connected to the lives of others (Lang and Carstensen, 1998). The concept of linked lives, however, points to the intersections of experience, and less to the relational and emotional significance within these relationships. Yet the older people's accounts highlight how the interpersonal and emotional relationships that occur between individuals deemed significant must also be considered – that is, they draw attention to how meaningful relationships and perceived links with others may also affect the interpretation of transitions across the lifecourse. Together, a focus on linked lives, and the relational and emotional significance of these connections, allows for a more complex interpretation of older people's narratives that challenge transition as an individually experienced event.

The clearest examples of linked lives and the relational aspects of experience were found in the discussions of the interviewees' parents and spouses. In these cases, events in the lives of others affected the older people's own trajectory and lifecourse. The accounts demonstrate that linked lives and relational aspects of experience are not separate from the challenges of multiple and intersecting transitions mentioned earlier. Instead, they are an expansion of their stories and sense of self that reveals how deeply relationships with others can affect the experience of one's own transitions and lifecourse. Edwin's account, for example, contains several examples of the connection between his life and that of his father and his wife. These examples draw attention to the meanings derived from linked lives and the relational aspects of transition. When asked about the key events in his life, Edwin identifies his father and the life lessons learned from him:

> 'One of the key events in my life was that my father was my father.... We had a real relationship.... By the time I was 13, 14 years of age, I knew that there was another world outside of the world we lived in.'

Later in his interview, he provides another example of linked lives and the relational aspects of experience. He identifies his wife's illness, which followed shortly after his retirement, as another major turning point. This time, it was an event that affected his expectations of ageing and late life. Her illness meant that he experienced a role change from husband to husband and primary caregiver, but in doing so altered his expectations and plans for late life:

> 'And then a very unfortunate thing ... happened early in our retirement ... she [his wife] had a ... heart attack ... my biggest resentment ... I saw retirement for a short period as endless time for myself – which is really selfish.... And my wife, as I said, got sick ... and I discovered that I have much less time for myself than I even had when I was working.'

Edwin's account is an illustration of the importance that linked lives can play in the interpretation of experience. Corresponding in part with the dominant success-based interpretations of 'growing old', Edwin's narrative is framed according to a success that is attributed to his upbringing, opportunities throughout life and the continuation of lifelong activities. Edwin's story, beginning with the knowledge his father instilled in him, corresponds with Erikson's (1982) notion of generativity, outlined in *The life cycle completed*. Edwin attributes his relationship with his father to the trajectory of his success. Later, he emphasises the reciprocal relationship with his wife, who delayed her education in order to work and support his career, and his current provision of care for her in late life. She thus also contributes significantly to this narrative of success. The onset of his wife's illness in late life, however, becomes a major turning point in his life story, and demonstrates the extent to which transitions can occur in the context of someone else's life rather than as an individual pathway. It also highlights how the continuous aspects of a storyline framed around success may be interpreted or 'ruptured' by a transition in a life other than one's own. Edwin's narrative reveals how such a moment altered his expectations and situation of his retirement, and emphasises how he makes sense of this through independent and relational aspects of care.

The importance of interpersonal relationships such as those identified in Edwin's account challenge the dominant models of transitions based on individual movements that occur across the life span. The older people's accounts presented in Chapter Six, and collected throughout the Late Life Transitions project, suggest that transitions are events and experiences in the lives of those they care about. In this sense, their stories not only suggest linked lives, but also alter the starting point from which to anchor experience throughout the lifecourse – that is, they shift the focus from the individual to the couple, family or community. As such, there is merit in more detailed exploration of transitions as experienced by the couple dyad (Henretta et al, 1993; Blau and Riphahn, 1999; Moen et al, 2001) or family unit (Kahn and Antonucci, 1980; Antonucci et al, 1996; Price et al, 2000). Together, the older people's narratives highlight the importance of an interpretive lens that draws attention to linked lives and how meaningful relationships affect transitions and experiences of ageing and late life.

Continuity and adaptation: illness and disadvantage

The accounts in Chapter Six and the Late Life Transitions project correspond and conflict with understandings and expectations of continuity, discontinuity and adaptation in relation to ageing and late life. Continuity and discontinuity represent an important tension in relation to ageing and late life and form an important backdrop for the interpretation of experience. Continuity carries a positive connotation, and has become clearly embedded in the success–based models of late life. Originally articulated to highlight how late life may be characterised by similar interests and activities pursued in earlier segments of the lifecourse (see Atchley, 1999), continuity has become central to resisting a narrative of decline through ongoing activities and involvement. Yet, while continuity in the lives of older people represents a challenge to the normative notions of the lifecourse, the accounts in Chapter Six demonstrate how continuity is more complex than it appears. These accounts reveal two situations where lived experiences confront the dominant expectations of continuity in late life: that of illness or impairment, and that of lifelong disadvantage. The accounts challenge dominant expectations of continuity in two ways.

First, illness or impairment may prevent continuity regardless of personal wishes, and even adaptation to new circumstances – perceived as the second-best strategy – may be difficult, and as discussed earlier, may result in an individual finding themselves in a liminal space between continuous and discontinuous experiences.

Second, although continuity in late life is considered to be a positive strategy, lifelong disadvantage may have negative rather than positive repercussions. In cases where marginalised older people experience poverty, violence and exclusion there is a need for change rather than continuity across the lifecourse.

Continuity is considered to link earlier and later parts of the lifecourse and is prominent in older people's experiences. In doing so, it challenges the dominant interpretations of late life as a separate developmental or life stage marked by change; opens possibilities for agency, choice and self-determination; and introduces fluidity and movement through individual interpretations such as identity. Illustrations of continuity were most prominent in the success-based narratives of Charles, Anna, Edwin, Elizabeth and Sam, each of whom constructed coherent and continuous narratives. Forming the core underlying assumption of the lifecourse perspective, the premise of continuity meshes well with positive interpretations of the lifecourse, and as a result has taken a prominent place within the dominant models of success. It also features in domains of scholarship such as identity and lifestyle, where these aspects are seen to remain central despite age. Consider as an example the work of Jones and colleagues (2008), which identifies and compares patterns of consumption between earlier and later periods of life, arguing that as people age, they will continue to engage in lifecourse patterns of consumption initiated in their youth. As emphasised in social-cultural contexts, public policies and older people's interpretations, continuity represents one of the positive means by which to successfully grow old. Yet, the accounts in Chapter Six highlight how achieving continuity is best suited to circumstances of health, activity and financial stability, and most difficult in relation to illness, impairment and disadvantage. Further, their accounts reveal a discursive shift into adaptation and coping that occurs when continuity is challenged, and how this distinction reinforces the symbolic difference between groups of older people who are healthy and those who are ill or impaired.

The power of continuity is clearly articulated in older people's accounts. In all cases the older people interviewed demonstrate a strong desire to achieve continuity in some aspect of their lives. The continuation of work, leisure and activity, for example, are central to their narratives. Yet, the decisions taken in relation to continuity vary between individuals and their circumstances. In some cases, ongoing involvement in work is an important expression of continuity, while for others a break from work is sought out in retirement. Consider the differences between Edwin or Sam, who emphasised how their work and work-like activities extended beyond the official retirement age of 65, and Elaine, who discussed how she and her co-workers counted down to retirement. Where ideas about continuity in relation to work can be understood as partially structured by social locations such as class and the circumstances of work, health and physical activity is an area where the discourse on continuity is particularly pronounced. So while Elaine expressed a desire to break the continuity provided by her work, she, like all the other older people in the study, wished to remain physically active and well. For Elaine, continuity in her employment would have meant ongoing injuries and most likely a decreased level of physical function and wellness.

In their interviews, many of the older people discussed their attempts to achieve continuity in relation to illness and impairments as they aged. This perception of achieving continuity, and therefore success in relation to health and wellness, was central. Yet, at the same time, the undercurrent of the interviews was that illness or injury may disrupt continuity, and the expectations that older people have for achieving continuity in late life. The accounts clearly articulate how experiences of illness or impairment challenge dominant understandings of continuity. In many cases, experiences of illness or impairment were seen to represent rupture or a threat to the self or identity (see Dittman Kohli, 1990; Biggs, 1997; Grenier, 2007). In their interviews, older people's responses to experiences of rupture vary from adapting by engaging in a similar activity that is less physically demanding, to making serious adaptations, to entering a liminal space of uncertainty. The older people's responses to illness or impairment ranged from making slight adaptations – for example, Sam's altering his exercise routine from skiing and running to water aerobics and stretching – through to more drastic measures – Dorothy baking a cake over several days. The change in activities, however, was only one component of achieving continuity; the subjective perceptions of such changes were also integral to individuals' ability to make sense of impairment or illness in late life.

Marked differences could be identified between the accounts whereby older people felt that they had achieved at least one aspect of continuity, and those where they either struggled with this continuity or felt that they had 'failed'. For those unable to achieve continuity, the framework for the discussion shifted to one of coping and adjustment. Yet, in setting a standard whereby decline is not considered to be a natural part of the lifecourse, older people who find it difficult to adjust to impairment are perceived as having failed. In this context, it is not surprising that those who are unable to achieve continuity across the lifecourse lament their circumstances when achieving continuity is no longer possible. Their accounts reveal how they struggle not only with the instrumental adjustments to impairment, but with the meaning this failure of continuity comes to represent. Activities they can no longer achieve become judged in a social-cultural context, and in turn, come to affect personal interpretations of success in relation to late life.

Discussions of continuity and success provide insight into the ways in which older people's lived experiences challenge dominant understandings of transition in late life. What is clear from the older people's narratives in this study is that people respond in a variety of ways, with some older people adapting wholeheartedly to the discourse of continuity and success, including expressing disappointment when they cannot achieve it, and others calling into question the very expectations of continuity. There are several examples of older people challenging continuity and whether or not it is actually possible. For example, some of the older people interviewed challenged the idea of a smooth adjustment into late life, and in particular the emphasis on managing and success. Their accounts draw attention to the subtle differences between coping, adjusting and managing, and outline how difficult it can be to achieve continuity or adapt to change in late life. In some cases, such as Dorothy's, they highlight how adaptation seems simply no longer possible.

What is striking is the extent to which discussions of coping and adaptation can dominate the stories of those with serious impairments. However, this was not always the case, with older people's perspectives differing greatly despite similar levels of impairment. While some older people characterised themselves through impairment and elaborated on the impact of illness on their sense of self, others with serious impairments, such as Sam, seemed to transcend the narrative of decline and cope well with change. The question of how some individuals adapt and cope while others do not remains (see George, 1996). What seems to emerge from these differences are variations in identity and outlook – although pursuing such arguments on their own would be tantamount to blaming individuals for failing to adjust. It would be more fruitful to recognise the subjective meanings of impairment, and identify what is deemed by older people to be 'acceptable' forms of adjustment that take account of their social locations, social environments, histories and accumulated life experience. One way of addressing these differences would be to analyse the constraints and opportunities available to the older person (see George, 1996). As such, achieving continuity through adaptation is not merely a question of whether the person can continue their activities, nor of the timing of such events, but whether they can make adjustments and in the way they want to. Here, resources, and the ways in which these intersect with a subjective interpretation of needs, play an important role. For example, Elaine speaks of not being able to afford to attend events due to the costs and Elizabeth also raises the question of finances and having to restrict her social activities. Together, the accounts demonstrate that it is the perception of continuity in some aspects of experience, rather than actual continuity, that plays a key role in successful negotiation of transitions and positive assessment in late life.

Other major challenges to continuity may be found in locations of vulnerability and lifelong disadvantage, where the continuity of circumstances such as poverty and marginalisation is negative rather than positive. Several interviews speak to the impact of cumulative disadvantage on the lifecourse. While the narratives of older people in these situations demonstrate strength and resilience, to focus on their ability to cope without drawing attention to continual lifelong disadvantage and its cumulative effects, especially when comparing them with those who seem to achieve the 'success-based model', would be to overlook important aspects of their experiences of transition in relation to late life. Consider Peter, for example, who grew up in poverty and continues to rely on social assistance and food banks to meet his daily needs. He lives on a meagre pension as a result of patchy employment history, life circumstances and illness prior to retirement. His poor financial situation has been exacerbated by a recent impairment that has forced him to hire an informal caretaker in exchange for rent-free accommodation. His ill health, reliance on help with day-to-day activities and dearth of resources have resulted in a situation where he is forced to make choices that place him at further risk of deterioration and vulnerability. He has been forced to take fewer meals and less medication, and hire an informal caregiver. As a result, even in late life, Peter is unable to break free of the poverty cycle. Elaine's narrative also provides insight into the impact of lifelong disadvantage. Her long-term employment as a chambermaid has resulted in insufficient income and long-term ill health. Although she does not have the severe physical limitations of Peter, her story is one of being surrounded by violence and victimisation. The continual aspects of disadvantage and poverty follow such individuals throughout the lifecourse and seriously affect their transitions and experiences. The situations of Peter and Elaine are supported by data that draw connections between poverty and ill health over the lifecourse and in late life (Hennessy and Walker, 2004; George, 2005; Walker, 2005a). There is also the increased risk of exposure to experiences such as victimisation that provide alternative explanations of the circumstances of older people such as Elaine who lives at the intersections of poverty and violence. The extent to which these individuals can make changes and have positive experiences of ageing in relation to their constraints is on ongoing challenge.

The multiple and ongoing impacts of lifelong disadvantage challenge notions of continuity as a series of flexible and autonomous choices made throughout the lifecourse. The emphasis that currently tends to be placed on the continuity of positive activities such as work life, citizen involvement and physical activities overlooks the continuity of cumulative disadvantage that may occur at particular times throughout the lifecourse. As a result, the continuity of cumulative disadvantage, whereby negative experiences such as impoverishment begin early in the lifecourse and are reinforced through structures and practices, gets lost in dominant interpretations. However, illustrations such as those provided by Peter and Elaine draw attention to how power and structural aspects of experience affect late life. In doing so, they highlight the similarities and differences that exist between individual cases, as well as pathways that maintain or interrupt cycles of exclusion, such as employment, health benefits and financial resources. Several cases presented throughout the Late Life Transitions project highlight how continual disadvantage has a negative impact on the lifecourse. The lesson to be learned is to draw attention to the differences between those aspects and experiences of the lifecourse that older people wish to retain and those from which they wish to disengage or change. A number of questions emerge from this analysis: How can understandings of transitions take into account the distinctions between positive and negative forms of continuity that do not negatively affect those at the margins? Further, does a social location of cumulative disadvantage such as poverty preclude one from definitions of 'successful ageing'? What changes can be made? What are the best means of addressing disadvantage across the lifecourse and in late life? How can policy better respond to the situations of marginalised older people?

Conclusion

The older people's narratives in this study challenge dominant interpretations in several ways. They highlight the disjuncture that can exist between suggested models and older people's experiences of transitions in late life. First, they highlight the process and liminal spaces that exist within and between age- and stage-based interpretations. Second, they draw attention to the multiple and intersecting forms of transitions. Third, they highlight the importance of social locations and identities with regard to interpretations of ageing and late life. Fourth, they emphasise the linked and relational nature of lives. Fifth, they question accepted notions of continuity, including the difference in expectations of late life between those who are healthy and those who are ill, and the negative impacts of continuity rooted in disadvantage. Together, the accounts challenge existing frameworks and point to lesser-known interpretations of transitions. They illustrate the complex ways in which experience may correspond or contrast with dominant models and thus present complex challenges for rethinking transitions in late life. In particular, the accounts highlight how the locations of diversity and illness in late life require more detailed attention. Yet, aside from identity and lifestyle claims, there are few models from which to interpret these types of experience. The following two chapters focus on a detailed consideration of the impact of social location and diversity on experiences of transition in late life, and rethink the transition between health and impairment as one that has not previously been considered within this discourse.

EIGHT

Social location and 'othered' constructs of age

This chapter explores how difference[1] rooted in social locations can affect the lives and accounts of older people across the lifecourse and in late life. Older people's experiences of late life, seen from the perspective of varying social locations, serve to accentuate the lack of attention paid to diversity in social gerontology and studies of transition. Linking the narratives of older people from diverse social locations with the conceptual and theoretical debates on age and diversity provides a foundation from which to reconsider what is known about transitions in relation to late life. Reflecting specifically on diversity reveals the extent to which accounts from diverse social locations correspond to and conflict with the existing knowledge and expectations of transition and late life. Drawing on notions of the 'other' and 'liminality' articulated in post-colonial theory, for example, extends the challenges to understandings of transition raised in Chapter Seven, revealing how diverse social locations can contribute to experiences that exist within and between dominant and alternative models of late life transitions. The analysis put forward in this chapter renews the focus on 'difference' in relation to transition in ways that take account of the alternate frames of experience and negotiation.

The case illustrations of older people from diverse social locations that were presented in Chapter Six are the main focus of this chapter, supplemented by additional stories from older people in the Late Life Transitions project. The narratives of Elaine, Elizabeth and Colin, reveal similarities in how older people negotiate their experiences in a cultural context where they are defined as 'other', albeit from varying social locations. The illustrations in this chapter demonstrate how older people from diverse social locations can articulate their experiences through a lens informed by 'difference', emphasising the importance of considering diversity in relation to continuity and change in late life. The cases draw attention to the structural and culturally constructed aspects of the specific locations of experience. The accounts expose the tensions between personal and socio-cultural discourses on ageing, taken-for-granted assumptions, and the lived experiences of older people at diverse social locations. As such, they challenge normative and homogenous interpretations of age. They demonstrate how power, marginalisation and internalised notions may affect experiences and interpretations of ageing and late life. The lessons learned from Elaine, Elizabeth and Colin move the analysis towards a more complex consideration of diversity, transitions and the relations of age.

The interviews from the Late Life Transitions project suggest that experiences related to 'difference' are central to the accounts both in subject matter and in the way the story is told. The accounts of older people from diverse social locations often emphasised particular types of experiences or performed identities over standard age- or stage-based frameworks for transitions. Two fundamental differences were evident. The first was the presence of discrimination or disadvantage in the accounts, and often its centrality in relation to an identity or strategy taken throughout the lifecourse. While presented differently depending on the person and situation involved, discussions ranged from direct statements about discrimination, to reliance on an identity, to understatement or reference to discourses of lifelong independence or coping. In the latter, the discourse was often linked in some way to the experience of discrimination through proximity or actor, for example. The second defining feature was that when asked to identify transitions, turning points or key events, the types of transition presented by older people from diverse social locations seemed to adhere to a slightly different range of topics or emphasis. For example, stories from older people at diverse social locations contained storylines such as immigration or emphasised particular dominant identities such as strength or independence, with a notable avoidance of any direct reference to age. Although such variation is often attributed to 'cultural differences', in the context of policymaking, the accounts of older people from diverse social locations reflect a more meaningful interpretation that remains unaddressed in understandings of transitions as they relate to ageing and late life. The post-colonial understandings presented in this chapter demonstrate how responses from older people from diverse social locations must be considered in relation to the socio-historical and cultural context within which they are offered, with locations of 'otherness' or 'difference' central features of the analysis. This chapter considers the following questions:

- How is difference understood or accommodated in the dominant approaches to transition and the lifecourse? How do older people's narratives from diverse social locations correspond or conflict with dominant models, discourses and practices?
- How do older people at various social locations experience continuity and change across the lifecourse? Do diversity or social location alter the storylines of ageing and late life? What do accounts from diverse social locations reveal about social and cultural practices in relation to age?
- How can post-colonial understandings of performance and 'otherness' inform the analysis of older people's accounts? Does separate attention to accounts from diverse social locations sustain difference based on 'otherness'?

Trends in the study of diversity and ageing

The conceptual and theoretical study of diversity in relation to continuity and change remains relatively underdeveloped in social gerontology (see Dannefer, 1988; Calasanti, 1996, 2010; McMullin, 2000, 2004, 2010), with broad studies of transitions neglecting the impact of diverse social locations in later life. Instead, transitions in late life have been assumed to refer to age- and stage-based changes that occur against a stable backdrop. While older people's accounts from diverse social locations suggest that the structured and social locations they occupy shape their lifecourse trajectories, there is little available material that connects their experiences to transitions and late life. The available literature on diversity and transition tends to focus on transitions experienced early in the lifecourse, in particular in relation to adulthood (Foner and Kertzer, 1978; Clausen, 1991; Irwin, 1995; Shanahan, 2000). In most cases, when the concept of diversity is used in relation to transition, it refers to diversions from generalised or normative patterns rather than the consideration of social locations such as age, ability, gender, 'race', sexual orientation, socioeconomic status and so forth. An analysis of trends within and outside social gerontology underscores the shortcomings of diversity research in relation to late-life transitions. The following section outlines key developments in the study of diversity and ageing.

Heterogeneity and additive oppressions

The study of diversity in social gerontology was prompted in the 1980s by a criticism of the presumed homogeneity of the ageing population (see Dannefer, 1988; Blakemore and Boneham, 1994) and questions about its relevancy for people from diverse social locations. Often stemming from groups of people with disabilities, people of colour and women, these questions sparked debate in the social sciences, and provoked a growing awareness of diversity in gerontology. The approach initially used to combat the invisibility of these groups in social gerontology was known as 'double jeopardy', popular in social sciences throughout the 1980s and 1990s in the United States. Originating in the studies of the National Urban League, double jeopardy suggested that older Blacks in the United States experienced a twofold handicap of age and race discrimination, particularly in relation to poverty and ill health (National Urban League, 1964; Anthias and Yuval-Davis, 1992). This in turn focused attention on the multiple oppressions of older people in relations to age, gender, disability and class, resulting in notions of triple jeopardy. Together, these approaches established a precedent for addressing structural inequality. However, in these models, discrimination was additive and focused on only one group at a time. The resulting argument was an essentialist one, whereby older people of similar backgrounds were assumed to experience discrimination in exactly the same way. Research focused on the differing experiences of Black Caribbean elders, South Asian elders and Japanese or Chinese elders, for example, led to misunderstandings of homogeneity within ethno-cultural and minority groups. Although conceptual thinking has moved from the 'double-jeopardy' perspective, the tendency to treat oppression as additive or to focus on a particular cultural or minority ethnic group continues in research and practice (see Dannefer, 1988; Brotman, 2003; Grenier and Brotman, 2010).

Intersecting power relations

The next phase in the study of diversity and ageing focused on intersecting power relations. Responding to the weaknesses of additive oppressions and the essentialism implicit in the double–jeopardy approach, scholars working largely from critical and feminist perspectives averred ideas of disadvantage as intersecting sets of oppression. Drawing on the centrality of power and its practices, attention turned to an analysis of the 'interlocking structural positions within a society' (Calasanti, 1996, p 148). Sometimes labelled 'intersectionality' (see Fraser, 1997; Yuval-Davis, 2006), this approach focused on the interaction between powerful and less powerful structured groups in society (Calasanti, 2009). As McMullin (2000) has outlined, 'addressing diversity in this way, took account of how class, age, gender and ethnicity/"race" act as interlocking sets of power relations that structure social life' (p 517). In social gerontology, the focus on intersecting oppressions called attention to problematic relations between older people of various social locations and society.

Still relevant to social gerontology, a focus on intersecting power relations contributes to understanding how practices create and sustain the oppression of marginalised groups. It focuses on the intersections between structured forms of oppression over the lifecourse and in late life. Yet, while this approach has made significant contributions to the study of age and diversity, three key limitations impede its relevance in a contemporary context. First is the tendency to privilege age in a field where interlocking oppressions are assumed to occur in relation to age. Second is the uncertainty about how to practically integrate the theoretical claims for 'intersectionality'. Third is the tendency to address one form of diversity at a time in a research context. This last issue relates to the difficulties in designing samples and methods that account for diversity in a context where generalisation continues to exert influence. Integrating diversity that addresses the intersecting forms of disadvantage across the lifecourse remains a challenge.

Interpretive understandings and negotiated identities

The study of diversity has also been approached via subjective interpretations and identity claims. Although more widely developed outside gerontology,[2] this perspective started to take hold in the late 1990s in relation to age. Though not always linked to the study of diversity, identity became an important anchor for the expression of 'difference'. Consider, for example, perspectives focused on the importance of voice, challenging oppression, seeking justice, rights and making claims. The ways in which individuals select and present their identities were seen as integral to the politics of needs interpretation (Fraser, 1997) where an individual drew on identity-based platforms to challenge dominant interpretations, advocate for rights or gain access to claims or services. Identity came to form a powerful platform from which to challenge oppression or discrimination, either in the more traditional sense of collective resistance or through more personal processes of negotiation. One weakness of the identity perspective, however, in particular when articulated through group claims, was its reliance on relatively fixed locations such as 'disabled' or 'older woman of colour' that complicated allegiances in the sense of multiple oppressions, or did not always accurately depict the complexity of an individual's locations.

The study and use of identity shifted over time, and was combined with ideas of 'intersectionality' – that an individual was recognised to simultaneously occupy several identities that could be selected and adhered to. Strategies and negotiation became key concepts. In gerontology, scholars outlined the strategies used to challenge static understandings of age through understandings of identity (Biggs, 1997), positioning (Jones, 2006) performance (Woodward, 1995) and discourse (Coupland and Coupland, 1988; Coupland, 2000). For example, in a social-cultural context infused with ageism, older people negotiated age-based classifications through such statements as 'I am not old' that distinguished them from negative discourses. Three interrelated concepts informed the analysis of identity: first, performance, whereby an older person could act out a particular role or identity deemed relevant for the context (see Mead, 1934; Goffman, 1959; Butler, 1990); second, positioning, whereby the older person may strategically use a construct or role on a more temporary basis (see Searle 1995; Harré and Moghaddam, 2003); and third, negotiation, whereby an identity may be used or performed in various ways, including as voice, or in claims for rights or needs, and in relation to perceptions and social constructs (see Fraser, 1997; Jones, 2006). Perspectives focused on identity as a negotiated terrain demonstrate how identity is at least in part performed (Hurd Clarke, 2002), and performed differently across contexts (Kaufman, 1986; Gubrium, 2001, 2005; Grenier, 2005, 2007a). However, while identity and negotiation have gained acceptance as an important means by which to challenge dominant claims, the most popular interpretations tend to articulate these claims at the individual level, and may overstate the extent to which individuals exercise choice and agency. To do so would be to run the risk of losing track of the similarities between structured locations and the intersecting social relationships of power that are central to sustaining these differences.

On its own, identity remains insufficient to understand transition in relation to the multiple and intersecting social locations of late life. Considering transitions in late life requires taking account of identity, but also moving beyond subjective standpoints or claims making into the various ways older people from diverse social locations make sense of continuity and change across the lifecourse. What is needed is an approach to diversity in late life that is capable of considering identity in relation to cumulative disadvantage, socio-cultural practices and psychological dimensions of experience. The next section considers the merits of post-colonial understandings that merge an analysis of history, structures, culture and subjective interpretation. Focused on an analysis of 'other' and 'difference', post-colonial analysis provides insight into the implications of marginalisation. Understanding how identities are constructed and performed in the context of powerful socio-cultural constructs such as those of discrimination or colonisation may help move the debate beyond identity claims understood as individual choices into a more complex analysis of constraints and processes of negotiation.

Post-colonial analysis: 'difference' and 'othered' accounts

Developed in order to understand and confront the social and psychological effects of colonialism and colonisation, post-colonial theory's attention to the impacts of power relations in a social, historical and cultural context make it a relevant analysis from which to consider the case of older people at diverse social locations. Post-colonial notions of the 'other' and 'liminality', for example, have much to offer an analysis of 'difference' in late life. Post-colonial theorists argue that identities are created and performed in social and cultural contexts characterised by historical and contemporary relations of power and control that can affect interpretations and psychological states, and as a result, shape and reshape cultural spaces. Although rarely discussed in social gerontology (see Torres, 2006b; Hazan, 2009a,b for exceptions), post-colonial theory provides a strong analysis of the current and historical relationships that exist between the binaries that are relevant to age and 'difference' in society. Hazan (2009a), for example, has drawn on post-colonial analysis in order to demonstrate how the very condition of being 'old' that is 'constructed as essentially different, situates older people outside culture' (p 60). It is this idea of 'othering' that can offer an insight into the accounts of older people from varying locations of ageing and late life.

The post-colonial attention to the process of 'othering' (see Fanon, 1967 [1952]; Said, 1978; Bhabha, 1994) provides a starting point from which to understand the experiences of older people from diverse social locations. In the post-colonial context, 'othering' is the process by which individual and groups are set aside as different. In articulating this concept, Bhabha (1994) highlights how even the mainstream focus on 'diversity' is itself an act of 'othering'. He distinguishes between the concept of 'cultural difference' rooted in 'otherness' and 'cultural diversity' as a token neoliberal recognition of difference grounded in multiculturalism (pp 49-53). His distinction reveals that the first focuses on recognising and understanding 'difference', while the second represents an act of accommodation or tolerance. Bhabha (1994) takes the position that one must argue for an understanding of 'cultural difference' as indicative of the powerful processes of 'othering'. In doing so, Bhabha (1994) demonstrates how identities and stories of 'othered' groups are often immediately interpreted as 'racialised' discourse within cultural discourse. Drawing parallels with ageing, then, analysis should not only focus on a critique of older people being assigned an automatic status of 'other' based on age or stage, but should also recognise the various ways in which they are automatically 'othered'. As such, their accounts can be read in relation to social, cultural and historical processes of negotiating the 'othered' constructs they occupy – such as such as age, class or 'race', for example. Recognising how the process of 'othering' takes place, and how particular relations come to be, are important first steps in understanding experience from locations of 'difference'.

Identifying what exists 'outside' or as 'other' destabilises the certainty of age and stage that is deeply embedded in transition. At the same time, it also exposes the inherent trappings of the study of diversity and age, in the extent to which groups of diverse older people from varying backgrounds have been considered as 'other' older people. Post-colonial understandings of 'liminality' draw attention to how marginalised groups such as older people from varying social locations are located on the outside of culture – in some cases, even farther outside the space of an already marginal group. They also highlight how presentations of self in such contexts are negotiated in a liminal space that exists 'within and between' culture. Offering a strong critique, the post-colonial interpretation of the concept of 'liminality' forms the basis from which to transgress existing socio-cultural boundaries anchored in fixed interpretations and lifecourse identities. In *The location of culture*, Bhabha (1994) outlines how the negotiation of identity takes place in liminal spaces:

> The move away from the singularities of 'class' or 'gender' as primary conceptual and organizational categories, has resulted in an awareness of the subject positions – of race, gender, generation, institutional location, geopolitical locale, sexual orientation – that inhabit any claim to identity in the modern world. What is theoretically innovative, and politically crucial, is the need to think beyond narratives of originary and initial subjectivities and to focus on those moments or processes that are produced in the articulation of cultural differences. These 'in between' spaces provide terrain for elaborating strategies of selfhood – singular or communal – that initiate new signs of identity, and innovative sites of collaboration, and contestation in the act of defining the idea of society itself. (Bhabha, 1994, p 2)

Several post-colonial theorists have focused on the negotiation of experience that takes place from within 'othered' or marginalised locations. In *Black skin, white masks*, Fanon (1967 [1952]) discusses how the 'racialised' identity is a colonised identity that is required to adapt, perform and act. He outlines how a 'hybrid identity' is constantly negotiated in relation to cultural constructs and practices related to 'race' and colonialism (Fanon 1967 [1952]). It is on this basis that scholars such as Spivak (1995) have developed concepts of 'strategic essentialism', whereby 'others' may draw on a racialised or essentialised identity in order to react, resist or make claims in a particular socio-cultural context. Such interpretations are helpful in reconsidering fixed forms such as those in late life. Instead of having to choose between affiliations, as fixed forms of identity would require, individuals may purposefully select an identity on a temporary basis without having to relinquish another identity important to them. They may as such perform or position themselves in relation to larger socio-cultural constructs or social relations. For example, as elaborated elsewhere, Grenier and Hanley (2007) demonstrate how essentialist notions such as the identity claim of being a 'strong Black woman' have been used by 'women of colour' in order to negotiate the negative constructs of 'frailty' in public home care services (also see Grenier, 2005). What is most poignant about strategic essentialism is the ways in which it renders binary divisions, fixed identities and dominant expectations obvious – challenging these through temporary and fluid choices. Interpretations focused on the performative nature of identities are thus very useful to link understandings of social structures with socio-cultural notions and experiences. Post-colonial analysis also draws attention to the psychological impact of a colonised identity, whereby the social and cultural relations of oppression related to colonisation are considered to have long-standing and inter-generational effects on colonised peoples (see Fanon, 1967 [1952]). Fanon, a psychologist by trade, outlined how colonised peoples must assert traditions and revive histories related to 'racialised' locations, class conflicts and the psychological impact of colonised experience. He drew attention to how the colonised identity contained, in part, wounds to the 'psyche' that could result in particular responses such as anger or aggression (Fanon 1967 [1952]). Bhabha (1994) asserts that while expected forms of identity negotiation tend to focus on anger and direct confrontation, there are also more subtle forms where the colonial context has been internalised. His insights on these differences and the way that they are heard in mainstream culture are important to understanding the variations in accounts from older people discussed later in this chapter. Such understandings make it possible to draw parallels between the colonised identity, 'othered' locations of difference and psychological processes related to marginality and powerlessness possible. The psychological wounds of particular locations have also been explored in relation to gender (Walkerdine et al, 2001) and class (Sayer, 2005). In *The moral significance of class*, for example, Sayer (2005) articulates how class can profoundly affect relationships, life chances and achievements across the lifecourse – an insight that, like post-colonial analysis, becomes important to understanding the emotional effects of 'othered' locations in late life.

Post-colonial interpretations of liminality provide a standpoint from which to better understand diverse older people's experiences of transition in late life. Bhabha's (1994) articulation of the liminal spaces 'in-between' as both the production of 'cultural difference' and sites of performance is helpful for understanding older people's accounts. His version moves away from fixed understandings of identity and towards experiences that are created and performed in liminal spaces. The liminal locale within which this occurs for Bhabha (1994) is at one and the same time considered to be 'outside' dominant spaces and characterised by a potential for cultural redefinition. The post-colonial understandings of liminality thus draw attention to the reality that identities and experiences can be organised as 'other' through social and cultural processes, and also provide an opportunity for negotiation and new cultural spaces. There are, however, differences in thinking. While Fanon (1967 [1952]) discusses this liminality as a more permanent and unending state, for Bhabha (1994), performance allows one to move in and out of this state on a temporary basis. Insights from post-colonial theory, especially when the socio-cultural and historical aspects of a colonised identity (Fanon) are combined with the fluidity of redefinition (Bhabha), challenge the social gerontological emphasis on the structural or timed aspects of age- and stage-based transitions (Neugarten and Datan, 1973; Neugarten, 1976; Hagestad and Neugarten, 1985), as well as interpretations of identity as a process related to claims-making or subjective experience (Hockey and James, 2003). Post-colonial interpretations of liminality emphasise 'being between' in ways that link the study of culture with that of identity. The strength of this analysis lies in recognising the process of 'othering' and the negotiations that are performed from within liminal spaces.

Reinterpreted concepts of the 'other' and 'liminality' can open debates related to ageing and late life. Understanding the process of 'being between', for example, brings us closer to understanding how 'difference' can alter experiences of continuity and change across the lifecourse. These concepts can also serve to challenge standard binary categories and expectations of age. Rather than sustaining current approaches that focus on diversity in age as a neoliberal concept rooted in accepting different cultures, post-colonial analysis can help to consider how 'difference' or 'otherness' is created, produced and negotiated in contemporary society. A perspective that considers accounts from locations such as (dis)ability, 'race', class and sexual orientation can therefore bring 'difference' to the fore rather than assigning it to the realm of additive or secondary analysis. In doing so, older people's accounts from diverse locations are viewed not as alternative models that exist outside the approach to ageing, but as exemplars where 'otherness' becomes a lens through which to approach and understand experience. As such, analysis can focus on how the differences produced and sustained in social and cultural relations affect the interpretation of late-life transitions. In doing so, the approach can incorporate more fluid experiences that occur within and between expected frames of age and difference. This includes the psychodynamic elements of the 'colonised psyche' and the ongoing processes of negotiation. The analysis can thus account for 'difference' as taking place in a 'liminal' space within and between dominant and alternate interpretations of late life.

A reconsideration of 'difference' that is rooted in being 'other' suggests that current approaches to diversity in social gerontology are flawed. In their continued approaches to either add diversity on to the analysis of late-life transitions, or focus on subjective interpretations of identity, current approaches neglect how socio-cultural and historical processes shape understandings of continuity and change across the lifecourse – a theme that is also expressed in the intentions of the lifecourse perspective. As such, post-colonial analysis reveals how any recognition of 'difference' that fails to account for the context within which the identity is performed, or creates an automatic 'othered' account of diverse experiences, reflects a liberal ideology of tokenistic culture and experience. So, while the individual is permitted to 'feel' and 'act' differently, they are given no access to rights based on their identity or the systemic, symbolic or psychological barriers that may exist in relation to this location. In this sense, the post-colonial analysis resonates with the roots of a critical perspective in ageing that argues that an awareness of the social problems of ageing is not enough, but requires a connection with recognition, power and change (see Phillipson and Walker, 1987; Estes et al, 2003; Bernard and Scharf, 2007). Taking account of the arguments of 'other', 'difference' and 'liminality' from post-colonial thinking moves the analysis towards an understanding that ideas are formed and negotiated from within colonised and marginal spaces in the modern context. This shift in thinking can break down binaries and expose models that are not only 'alternative' or 'different' but fundamentally challenge dominant age- and stage-based transitions.

Illustrations of 'difference': challenging dominant assumptions

The following illustrations explore transitions from three locations: 'race', class and sexual orientation. The three examples were chosen for the way in which they challenge standard age- and stage-based interpretations of ageing and late life. The intersections of structured locations and socio-cultural practices are crucial here. Similarly 'othered' in relation to ageing and late life, the illustrations are accompanied by differing social and structured locations and processes of marginalisation and discrimination. The first is a 'racialised' location that is 'othered' in terms of a white/non-white, majority/minority or coloniser/colonised binary. The second is the location of class and socioeconomic status that is 'othered' in terms of the relationship with the economy and the market, best represented in the binaries of rich/poor, included/excluded. The third is the location of sexual orientation that is 'othered' in terms of 'compulsory heterosexuality', to use a phrase coined by Butler (1990), and expressed through the straight/gay binary. Although the examples of 'race' and 'sexual orientation' are somewhat different from 'class' in that class can technically be 'exited' through social mobility,[3] each of the locations is structurally as well as socially and culturally defined as 'different'. However, the embedded process of 'othering' that exists within and between these assumptions is rarely explored. This section considers the narratives of Elaine, Elizabeth and Colin as examples of experiences that exist 'within and between' dominant constructs and expectations of age. In each of these cases, the reader will remark how these presentations from diverse social locations extend beyond identity claims and into accounts that reflect the post-colonial emphasis on the negotiation of social-cultural contexts and experiences across the lifecourse. Together, the accounts respond to the tendencies either to ignore difference between diverse social locations or consider them as 'different', and therefore separate, from the experiences of ageing. The following analysis represents an attempt to consider how varying locations of 'difference' challenge dominant interpretations of ageing and late life.

Location one: 'racialised' accounts

Narratives from 'racialised' locations of age reveal tensions between the use of an identity for the purposes of claims making (see Spivak, 1995) and the extent to which accounts adhere to dominant models such as successful ageing, highlighted in Chapter Five. These narratives demonstrate the use of strategies and models that are more complex than they appear, with older people moving fluidly between strategies of resistance and acceptance of expected models. The presentation of strategies of resistance and adherence in the narratives of older people from diverse social locations are noteworthy. Located on a continuum between 'racially' rooted identities such as that of the 'strong Black woman', the accounts of older people from diverse locations, in particular 'racialised' locations, are illustrative of how older people negotiate the liminal spaces of 'otherness'. Following post-colonial analysis, it is not surprising that older people's accounts move fluidly between various constructions, and as a result, are not solely based on age- or stage-based models. Accounts from individuals at 'othered' locations must carefully negotiate the various constructions imposed on them, including discrimination, oppression or exclusion. These include, for example, 'racist' interpretations of experience as well as age-based assumptions.

Narratives from diverse social locations reflect complex strategies for negotiating discrimination. For example, consider the way Elizabeth organises her story along the lines of a successful immigration, and her achievements in her vocation of nursing. Her narrative makes evident an emphasis on a 'successful' storyline of productivity and lifelong work contributions. She highlights her accomplishments of a successful career, the purchase of a home and various community contributions, and carries this coherent story of 'success' into her experiences of ageing. In doing so, she draws on dominant discourses of success to demonstrate her pride in her accomplishments. In part, however, drawing on the discourse of success also seems to be an attempt to confront racial stereotypes such as greediness, laziness and welfare dependency that have been associated with first-generation immigrants and women of colour (see Fraser and Gordon, 1994 for a critique of the discourse of dependency). Although the link is not as explicit as this in Elizabeth's narrative, her themes echo interviews with 'women of colour' who specifically contrast their strength with the discriminatory discourses of laziness. One woman interviewed stated: "I worked hard, I didn't sit around in no rocking chair" (see Grenier, 2003). Elizabeth's direct discussions of racism are, however, accompanied by illustrations of her strength, determinism and perseverance, thereby highlighting the associations she seems to be making between the strategy of success and negotiating discrimination. In giving this subtle but coherent account, Elizabeth outlines how racism is part of her story, but it does not define her or her responses. Elizabeth chooses to be defined by a strong and independent identity and her lifelong contributions to work and the community. Yet, the organisation and content of her narrative are intricately linked to her experiences of racism, and the ways in which she is accustomed to having her stories interpreted within a 'racialised' framework. It can be read, therefore, as an act of resisting the racism that could be contained in the interview context. Using the discourses of strength and independence, she simultaneously addresses questions of racism and ageism.

A different approach is evident in the case of Errol (not presented in Chapter Six), who utilises a strong identity based on resistance to shape his experience.[4] Errol's account is one of anger and overt resistance to racism and discrimination. His narrative corresponds with the arguments of post-colonial writers such as Fanon (1967 [1952]), who spoke of outrage at a system that has marginalised, oppressed and colonised his people. Writing in the context of French-colonised Martinique in the 1940s, Fanon (1967 [1952]) advocated violence as the only means to achieve national independence (see the chapter entitled 'Concerning violence' in *The wretched of the Earth* [Fanon 1965]). Similar to the message advocated by Fanon (1967 [1952]), Errol's narrative references violence against the systematic oppressive context and practices of employment, and includes several examples of speaking out and acting against discrimination he experienced as an English-speaking Black man living in Montreal in the 1950s. Errol describes experiences with racism in school, employment and in general life. In each case, he draws on confrontation and resistance – naming injustice and reclaiming power through direct means.

One of his first experiences of racism happened at school. He says:

> 'I'll tell you ... the first day that... the kids started calling me names at school. That will get you. Well, I says, "Well, you can't call me that" and went and got them. Two or three of them jumped me.... I fought like an SOB. I come home all messed up.... It took me a year-and-a-half to get enough within me to get even.'

Later in the interview, Errol discusses the inequalities for Black children in school:

> 'Let's be honest ... I never seen a Black teacher in my life. Not even one. And I went to school until sixth grade.... And there's been action taken by certain individuals who collectively said, "Wait a minute, where's the justice?"'

Drawing on his own experience with teachers, Errol highlights how his experiences of racism resulted in his decision to leave school at 12:

> 'When the school and me did not agree because of some White teacher ... who decided to batter into me what he believed to be right, I said "no", and I defended myself by making sure that we had a battle. There wasn't a way. I've never believed in that.'

His narrative then highlights how he built a strong and defensive stance against this oppression through fighting and aggression: "You can't work for 46-and-a-half years in the context of what I worked in unless you were aggressive.[5] You'd be out in a coffin in two days." In addition to citing direct strategies of confrontation, Errol draws on his self-education, citizenry and success as products of his resistance: "Never been in jail, didn't kill nobody. I ain't rob nobody, and I don't tell no lies, but I can fight." Errol's account is one that demonstrates speaking out against oppression through violence and aggression and differs from that of Elizabeth, which draws more subtly on discourses of strength, independence and success to confront racist practices.

The accounts of Elizabeth and Errol can be seen as illustrative of voices and responses of older people from 'racialised' backgrounds, and in Elizabeth's case, a migrant background as well. Although some may see the accounts of Elizabeth and Errol as immediately separated by gender, narrative accounts from the author's various research projects include examples from men more closely situated to Elizabeth and her approach, and women closer to Errol and his stance. Gender alone cannot explain the ways in which 'racialised' accounts differ from normative understandings of transitions in late life. While different in their approach, these two accounts are evocative of the ways older people negotiate and challenge the status of 'other' that they have been assigned. Drawing on post-colonial theory, the differences between these two accounts point to the permanence of liminal locations based on 'race' and minority status. They also contribute to rethinking unitary approaches that align social locations such as 'race' with expectations such as the acceptance of oppression, or speaking out against a racist and discriminatory structure through direct forms of resistance, as in the case of Errol. Post-colonial theory draws attention to how more subtle narratives demonstrative of ongoing forms of negotiation are not always understood as resistance (see Grenier and Hanley, 2007).

Seen through a post-colonial lens, the accounts of Elizabeth and Errol highlight how interpretations rooted in 'difference' require greater attention as complex accounts of negotiation and resistance. Constructed as the 'other', dominant interpretations make it difficult for accounts of older people to be seen as anything but polarised voices of resistance or integration. Yet, insights from post-colonial theory point to the powerful socio-cultural discourses and practices and the accompanying psychological implications that are helpful in understanding these accounts. So, while accounts such as Elizabeth's can be difficult to understand within models that expect direct confrontation and resistance, and could be interpreted as 'success' or 'integration',[6] post-colonial theory draws attention to the way in which subtle references to dominant discourses are also a strategy. Elizabeth successfully defies the racism and 'otherness' that is thrust on her in social, cultural and interpersonal relations, such as those of being ignored by professionals and colleagues – and she negotiates these experiences through success rooted in professional achievement. The accounts of Elizabeth and Errol provide evidence of Bhabha's (1994) notion of the 'hybrid identity' that stresses the ongoing negotiation that takes place within a racially defined culture, and how the use of discourses such as 'success' may themselves be acts of negotiating racism. Without post-colonial analysis, Elizabeth's account may be rendered invisible – adapting to the dominant model of growing older, she may be seen to fit into the accepted models for ageing. Yet, understood as 'other', post-colonial analysis points to how her narrative must also be considered for the way it exists both outside the normative models and as such, how drawing on 'success' is in part a strategy for negotiating the 'othered' identities of age and 'race'. When considered from a colonial context, the narratives of Elizabeth, an immigrant from Barbados, and Errol, the descendant of slaves from the Caribbean islands, cannot be considered otherwise. However, in drawing attention to the colonised and 'racialised' aspects of their experiences, questions must be raised about the extent to which the practice of exploring their accounts as strategies for resisting 'race' reinforces the 'other' status that both Elizabeth and Errol have successfully negotiated. The post-colonial analysis draws attention to unrelenting negotiation that occurs in the activities and responses of older people from diverse social locations, in particular the psychological aspects that affect interpretation of experience in relation to transitions and late life.

The experiences related from 'racialised' locations of 'other' challenge dominant age- and stage-based understandings of transitions in late life. As highlighted by post-colonial theory, constructions of 'other' are central to the experiences and interpretations of older people from diverse social locations such as Elizabeth and Errol. Automatically designated as 'other', they are met with the challenge of negotiating a socially liminal space that is related to a 'racialised' identity. Their negotiations across the lifecourse thus come to inform negotiations of yet another 'othered' location of age in late life. As such, the accounts challenge dominant models in two key ways, first, through the direct confrontation in the insistence of an identity rather than the age- and stage-based notions of age, and second, through aligning themselves with a dominant perspective such as success that is used to transcend age- and stage-based models. Questions may be raised about how strategies that have originated in response to discrimination early in the lifecourse may be maintained or changed across time, when presented with additional experiences and constructs such as age.

Location two: class, socioeconomic status and poverty

Narratives from older people at marginalised locations in respect to class and socioeconomic status reveal tensions between the lifelong impacts of disadvantage and the strategies used to negotiate late life. The illustrations of older people from impoverished locations challenge the dominant models of age. In particular, they undermine the notion that life unfolds against a stable backdrop. The accounts of Peter and Elaine, presented in Chapter Six, can be seen as examples of financial impoverishment through the lifecourse. Their narratives reveal that the lifecourse experienced from these locations is anything but stable. Both accounts include reference to vulnerability and violence. Elaine's narrative is heavily influenced by a trauma where a fellow chambermaid was murdered as well as other violent events. Peter's account is one of increased vulnerability in late life because of illness, poverty and the resulting constraints on his choices. For example, without the resources to hire a professional home care worker, he provides room and board in exchange for care – a decision that places him at increased risk of victimisation.

Both Elaine and Peter speak of being good citizens, taking honest paths and being satisfied with their lives; however, their stories are also filled with obstacles and struggles absent in the accounts of older people with greater financial resources. In both accounts, the reader becomes acutely aware of the difficult events both have experienced throughout the lifecourse. While social gerontology has made a significant contribution to understanding stratification of society, disadvantage and exclusion (Riley, 1987; 1972, 1971; Scharf et al, 2004, 2007; Walker, 1982), it has focused less on the strategies and emotional consequences that may accompany such locations.

Peter and Elaine recount their experiences of marginalisation in different ways. As a result of poor health, Peter has meagre financial resources, and this aspect of his experience plays a large part in his storyline. Elaine only mentions her poverty in relation to not being able to pursue the leisure pursuits she desires in her retirement. However, the violence that marks Elaine's account, and the repetitive strain injuries she suffers cannot be separated from her employment experiences. In her case, vulnerability to violence and workplace injury are a direct result of her location in the stratified society. Peter and Elaine similarly draw on charity services for food, and both recount how they manage to survive on income from low-paid employment (Elaine) or welfare (Peter). There are differences, however, in the presentation of the stories, and the extent to which each is able to draw on resilience and stability, or to experience difficulties in late life. Both describe themselves as 'managing the best they can' and getting through life by drawing on their strengths. In Peter's case, however, illness and impairment challenge his ability to cope, and seem to deplete his strength. Nevertheless, resilience is a feature of his story. Elaine presents her case very differently. She does not self-identify as poor, but the implications of living on a low income are embedded in her account; her story is punctuated by having limited resources. The prominent message of her story is her relief from work, and her pride in having made it to a long-desired retirement. She emphasises that she is thankful to be living on the state pension, which gives her a stable, albeit low, income that does not involve physical labour. Elaine offsets her difficult experiences, at least in her interview, with examples of her energy, community involvement and generosity. The difference between the accounts may be explained in part by the fact that Elaine's retirement brings her long-desired stability, while Peter's life continues to be overshadowed by instability as a result of chronic illness – a theme that will be further explored in Chapter Nine.

The disadvantage that can occur across the lifecourse highlights how difficult it can be for older people from marginalised and impoverished groups to achieve the success outlined in dominant models of ageing and late life. Drawing on post-colonial interpretations, poverty and exclusion can be understood as 'othered' locations that exist outside of expected transitions of successful development across the lifecourse. Experiences such as those of Elaine and Peter challenge the expectations of success and enjoyment that have come to dominate interpretations of late life and in particular, the third age. They demonstrate the extent to which the socio-cultural constructs of modern life associate poverty in late life with failure or at the very least a feeling of sadness. It is this generalised expectation of success linked to choice and financial resources that makes this a difficult location for older people with lower socioeconomic resources to negotiate. As Elaine and Peter clearly articulate in their narratives, the reality of their financial situation means that they have less choice when it comes to taking part in leisure activities, accessing care or meeting their everyday needs. Yet, what is less clear is how the expectations of 'success' may be differently interpreted at such locations as lower socioeconomic status. Elaine considers her life as successful and sees her retirement as a reward for many difficult years of contributing to the workplace. Yet, she is unlikely to be associated with success in terms of socio-cultural constructs because of her poverty. Peter's case is somewhat different, as he portrays his illness and strained relationships as challenges to his success and expectations of late life. Yet, his achievements – albeit limited through illness – are located in his ongoing community and volunteering activities. Both accounts demonstrate how 'what counts as success' may differ from dominant expectations and be challenged by circumstances such as impairment, poverty and illness.

What tends to be overlooked in understandings of transitions in late life are the psychological effects that accompany 'otherness' or the injustices of a stratified society. Although those older people who are located at positions of lower socioeconomic status and class may have adapted coping strategies such as resilience, their material limitations are ever present in their narrative, regardless of whether this is intentional. Here, an analysis that takes account of the long-lasting psychological implications of class put forward by Sayer (2005) seems relevant. Sayer (2005) outlines how class can mark and affect opportunities and experiences across the lifecourse. Elaine and Peter's accounts contain a tension between lifelong disadvantage on the one hand and resilience on the other. As such, similar to Elizabeth and Errol and their 'racialised' locations, Elaine and Peter exist within and between the liminal spaces of 'otherness'. The accounts are located between material realities, lifelong disadvantage and the desire to achieve success across the lifecourse and in late life. It is important to draw attention to the interwoven nature of the reality of their situation, and the subjective interpretations that take place in a socio-cultural context. This is especially the case where relationships to discourses of success and productivity are concerned. It simply does not feel right to focus on identity claims or negotiation strategies that intentionally gloss over the sometimes unstated difficulties of their situations, as these strategies are located in deeply set power relations, practices and assumptions. Their accounts disclose intricate lifelong strategies used to move across the lifecourse with meagre financial resources in ways that are deemed acceptable to themselves and others.

Accounts such as those of Elaine and Peter demonstrate how socioeconomic status, poverty and class challenge fixed age- and stage-based transitions and the accompanying expectations of success. Drawing on understandings of disadvantage and impoverishment from critical gerontology (Townsend, 1981; Walker, 1982; Scharf et al, 2004, 2007) and post-colonial interpretations of liminality (Bhabha,

1994), the reader can begin to better understand the complexity of accounts from liminal spaces such as poverty and marginalisation. Their stories draw attention to how the strategies used take place from locations that may contain symbolic meanings or 'emotional injury' related to class. In doing so, their accounts highlight how a social and psychological understanding of the locations related to class and socioeconomic status can lead to a better understanding of late-life transitions from these complex positions. In their cases, it seems naive to assert that older people can change their experiences through rhetorical devices, adapting a positive outlook or making meaning through a negotiated identity. Focusing only on the subjective interpretations of coping or identity claims would overlook the realities of their struggle, and how material realities limit activities in late life, as well as the psychological and physical wounds of class. A focus on the structured aspects of their lives, however, would neglect the emotional injuries that may underlie older people's strategies and interpretations of age. The cases of Elaine and Peter are difficult to read because they point to inequality and its effects in late life. They effectively portray the lifelong effects of being located at the margins of society and raise critical questions about the dominant notions of activity, success and enjoyment that are promoted in policy discourse. An analysis that does not address the underlying inequities in situations such as those of Peter and Elaine may result in a failure to generate policies to tackle such inequity and lead to continued exclusion, marginalisation and disadvantage across the lifecourse and into late life.

Location three: sexual orientation

Narratives from 'othered' locations based on sexual orientation also challenge understandings of lifecourse transitions. Constructed in relation to what Butler (1990) calls 'compulsory heterosexuality', gay, lesbian and transgendered people are positioned outside normative locations of heterosexuality and ageing, and are often invisible in dominant interpretations of ageing. The binary location of straight/gay creates an ordering whereby any sexual orientation not deemed 'straight' is automatically considered 'other' and frequently associated with invisibility and/or discrimination. Sexual orientation remains relatively underdeveloped in social gerontology (see Rosenfeld, 1999; Brotman et al, 2003; Heaphy, 2007; Brotman and Levy, 2008 for exceptions) and the study of transitions and the lifecourse. Yet, in many ways, the socio-cultural and personal experiences associated with a gay, lesbian, bisexual or transgendered identity, and the implications of this 'othered' location, represent noteworthy challenges across the lifecourse. In regards to transitions, the location of an 'othered' sexual orientation can reorganise social relationships, alter family forms, and the timing of expected events in the lifecourse. Structured as 'other', this location can impact lived experience and identity, and the extent to which one's life can be seen to correspond with or challenge dominant models of ageing. Analysis focused on liminal status of sexual orientation as an 'othered' location has much to offer an analysis of transitions in late life. Although experiences from 'othered' locations based on sexual orientation may correspond with dominant notions such as 'successful ageing' through work and work-like activity, they may also call into question the assumptions based on standard lifecourse transitions relating to ageing, family support, and the timing of normalised stages.

The narratives where sexual orientation was present, either explicitly or implicitly, challenged dominant age- and stage-based models of growing old. There are three key issues that emerge from these accounts. The first is the magnitude of 'coming out' as a personal process, in the context of a rigid society or an unsupportive family unit. The event of 'coming out' was a major turning point in many of the stories. This is not to say that all 'coming out' stories were negative, but that discrimination was often a feature of those accounts that related to a time when homosexuality was less accepted. Take, for example, Colin, whose interview was presented in Chapter Six. He highlights the closed socio-cultural context of his situation and his fears that his own family would regard his homosexuality as unthinkable. Of course, the absence of 'coming-out' stories in accounts where older people keep their sexual orientation a secret is also significant. Although their accounts would not contain a 'coming-out' story, they were marked by a secret, as in the case of one participant (Ian, aged 82, Late Life Transitions project), who did not self-identify as gay. Ian's relationship with his live-in friend of 25 years was ambiguous, although the couple's closeness and the role played by his friend in his story seemed to suggest a gay relationship. Although this friend played a significant role in Ian's life, to many, Ian would have been considered a single heterosexual man living with a flatmate. If, indeed, Ian's friend was his partner, the decision to conceal their relationship would have had implications for their rights as a couple for official purposes. A failure to openly declare their status would, for example, affect their eligibility for social services and benefits such as public pension. It also has important implications in relation to the formal recognition of meaningful roles and transitions.

The second notable issue in those interviews pertaining to sexual orientation was the existence of alternative family-like support networks of friends and communities where the individual concerned was estranged from their family of origin as a result of their sexual orientation. This phenomenon represents a serious challenge to the constructs of family, stability and development implied in understandings of transitions and the lifecourse. A prominent theme in the research is how older gay, lesbian, bisexual, two-spirited and transgendered people may be marginalised as a result of their sexual orientation (Brotman et al, 2003). Communities of friends replace close familial networks where families reject the individual's sexual orientation. Given the importance of family in the normative conceptualisation of transitions, having a community of friends rather than a supportive family network automatically alters transitions and trajectories throughout the lifecourse. It also possibly contributes to the perception that older gay, lesbian, bisexual or transgendered people have fewer traditional supports in times of transition. This is particularly the case when one considers the ways in which family roles and separation from family affect experiences of the lifecourse, and the extent to which one's life is seen to correspond to, or contest, dominant stage-based models.

The third issue is that sexual orientation, and in particular the experience of 'coming out' as a turning point, may alter the timing of events experienced in the lifecourse. For example, Colin's reluctance to admit his sexual orientation to himself and others meant that he entered into his first relationship only later in life. His transition to a relationship is thus marked as 'different' because it was with a man, but also because it occurred late in life.

Colin's account demonstrates how experiences rooted in an 'othered' or liminal location based on sexual orientation challenges dominant forms of transition in late life. Speaking as an older gay man, Colin describes the discrimination he has experienced in society throughout his life, as well as the discrimination he has experienced from the gay community in later life. He thus exists in multiple liminal spaces outside the norms of heterosexuality, timed transitions and the perceived youth of the gay community. His narrative at the intersections of age and sexual orientation challenges the dominant storyline of transitions in late life. His story is one of personal development amid a context of invisibility, discrimination, marginalisation and guilt. What becomes evident is the extent to which his storyline of development differs from the typical models and stages. It thus simultaneously reinforces his status as 'other', and provides the cultural space for a negotiation based on identity. He draws this experience together through the 'gay identity' he discovers in late life, emphasises the importance of 'coming out', and uses his experience as the foundation for advocacy for older gay men.

Colin's account delineates how his lifecourse has differed from the standard normative model based on age- and stage-based transitions. He defines how his background and identity have shaped his experience in ways that tend to conflict with dominant interpretations of age. Occupying a place 'in-between' dominant and alternate forms of growing old, Colin reveals how his experience is not fixed into movement across age and stage based forms as suggested in dominant models. He did not enter into a relationship until late life. On the other hand, the account of his life is not entirely resistant either. A successful former businessman, he describes a life that corresponds to notions of success achieved through work-like activity. Yet in relation to his transitions throughout life, his pathway differs from normative accounts organised along age- and stage-based transitions in substantial ways. While ageing forms a backdrop against which Colin judges his experiences, most of Colin's transitions have occurred 'off-time' and in ways that are atypical to the 'norm' (see Neugarten and Datan, 1973; Neugarten, 1976; Hagestad and Neugarten, 1985). As he did not 'come out' until he was in his 40s, like many gay men of his generation, he did not have a relationship with a man until later in life. Colin's experience of a significant relationship happened much later than the transitional norms would suggest. On the other hand, his retirement happened early, as a result of his business success. His narrative thus challenges in many ways, the underlying 'timing' of transitions across the lifecourse.

Colin's account, and in particular the 'coming-out' story, confronts the dominant notions of ageing in several ways. First, the 'coming-out' story represents a major transition that is not recognised in standard transition types that include, for example, work, marriage, parenthood, grandparenthood, widowhood and so forth. Second, this 'coming-out' story is so central to the interpretation of his life that it shapes most of his transitional experience. Although he mentions some of the more typical transitions of work, relationships and so forth, what is more central to his narrative is 'coming out' and using his experience to highlight the invisibility of older gay men and advocate for the gay community. The emphasis of the 'coming-out' story parallels the prominence Elizabeth gives to her narrative of immigration – both were significant storylines that shaped their accounts and experiences across the lifecourse, but that do not appear in dominant understandings of the lifecourse.

Colin's account also clearly articulates how family and community views affected his decisions – demonstrating the powerful presence of the socio-cultural context, expected models, interpersonal/familial relations and emotions. For example, Colin's account of 'coming out' contains a reference to waiting until after his parents' death. While this demonstrates the interconnectedness of lives highlighted by Elder (1994), it also represents the role played by what was, at the time, perceived to be a closed socio-cultural context. It also demonstrates how the standard models of transition emphasising independence on entry to work and the centrality of the family unit shifted in Colin's case. Colin's narrative reveals that he only truly felt independent once he 'came out'. Rather than being linked to ages or stages, therefore, Colin's moment of achieving personal development or maturity was linked to the centrality of his identity as a gay man and not to reaching adulthood through integration into a work context. His story also highlights the emotional impact of socio-cultural and interpersonal relations that are addressed within post-colonial theory as 'wounds to the psyche' – in particular, the ways in which decisions and strategies are related to the location of being 'other' or 'outside' dominant social locations. Similar to the two contested locations of 'race' and class, Colin's case, rooted in the location of sexual orientation, demonstrates how the identity-based claims of 'being gay', for example, are only one aspect of his experience. His narrative reveals how living in this location – as in many 'othered' liminal locations that exist within and between socio-cultural norms and expectations, interpersonal relationships and developmental processes – challenges understandings of transitions and presents alternative interpretations of continuity and change across the lifecourse.

Conclusion

Illustrations from 'othered' locations of 'difference' link the narratives of older people with understandings of the lifecourse, and draw attention to the intersections between structured conditions, cumulative disadvantage and lived experience. Accounts from diverse social locations provide important insights into the complexities experienced across the lifecourse and ultimately challenge fixed concepts of transitions and the lifecourse. While there is little known about diversity and transition, the illustrations in this chapter suggest that 'difference' can alter the presentation of accounts, the experiences throughout the lifecourse, and, subsequently, interpretations of late life. The illustrations explored in this chapter highlight similarities and differences that can exist between dominant and 'othered' accounts, and expose how 'otherness' can alter interpretations of late life. The accounts demonstrate that while narratives of 'difference' at times correspond to dominant models, the reasons for doing so are often more complex than assumed. Drawing on post-colonial analysis reveals how the perspectives adopted often represent strategies used to adapt to lifelong experiences of discrimination or marginalisation that, if unrecognised, can be sustained in socio-cultural relations. Further, the illustrations explored in this chapter demonstrate that identity plays an important role in the interpretation and negotiation of experience, but is not enough to fully understand the implications of 'otherness' across the lifecourse. This includes understanding the emotional or psychic impact of occupying locations considered as 'other'. Nor is identity enough to advocate change in relation to the lifelong effects of vulnerability, marginalisation and exclusion.

Insights from post-colonial theory draw attention to how accounts located in liminal spaces may be informed by difficult and sometimes traumatic events, and may result in identities or strategies used to address experiences such as racism, classism or homophobia. When the unexamined effects of culture or the significance of such locations are considered, notions of fitting in, adapting and achieving success take on new meanings for those occupying 'othered' positions. Thought must be given to how accounts may correspond to or differ from dominant expectations in age, as well as from the accounts of diverse social locations at earlier periods in the lifecourse. The intersections of various socio-cultural locations and resulting liminal spaces alter experiences of being in the world, and affect strategies formed to deal with continuity and change across the lifecourse. As a result, understandings of success and failure that have come to be fixed in the dominant interpretations of ageing and the lifecourse must be reconsidered. Adherence to particular frameworks may, in fact, represent strategies that are temporarily taken on by older people at differing social locations, and may represent ways of resisting forms of discriminatory discourse and practice.

Locations of difference such as those illustrated throughout this chapter call into question taken-for-granted notions of success, achievement and disadvantage as they are understood and addressed across the lifecourse. In particular, they demonstrate how strategies that appear to correspond with successful models may indeed do so, but may also originate from liminal spaces whereby older people draw on dominant frameworks in order to negotiate experiences of age and 'othered' locations. Combining the insights of post-colonial interpretations of liminality with Sayer's (2005) work on the emotional injuries of class demonstrates that, whether experienced from dominant or 'othered' locations, age is not only structured and constructed, but also intertwined within social, cultural and emotional experiences. Drawing on dominant models may therefore, in part, represent an attempt to heal the wounds of cultural 'otherness'. As such, the accounts from social locations of 'difference' are not only alternatives to dominant models but examples that call to question the assumptions that exist at the very depth of the dominant models. Locations of 'difference' emphasise the importance of the intersections between socio-cultural and psychological understandings of change that often remain separate in social gerontological approaches, diversity and the study of the lifecourse.

Although preliminary in scope, the analysis set out in this chapter – that of linking an understanding of social locations with post-colonial thinking on 'otherness', liminality and emotion – has produced several questions:

- How do diverse social locations affect the interpretation of late life and the lifecourse?
- Can identities and experiences based in social locations be used to construct forms of stability that help older people negotiate the conditions and experiences of late life? Are these related to lifestyle, identity and/or cumulative experience across the lifecourse?
- How do the strategies adapted across the lifecourse differ from or correspond with those of older people that are developed in later life? Are strategies used in late life any different from earlier models of continuity and change?
- How can understandings of transitions be broadened so that they better include the variety of experience of older people from diverse social locations?

Interview results suggest that the literature on transitions in late life should be bridged with that focused on 'difference', in particular, the postcolonial literature focused on 'otherness', liminality and psychological impact or emotion. Further exploration of 'othered' accounts would contribute to current debates on how to better incorporate diversity and 'difference' into studies of continuity and change across the lifecourse.

Notes

[1] Bhabha (1994) refers to difference in the following way: 'Terms of cultural engagement, whether antagonistic or affiliative, are produced performatively. The representation of difference must not be hastily read as the reflection of pre-given ethnic or cultural traits set in the fixed tablet of tradition. The social articulation of difference, from the minority perspective, is a complex, on-going negotiation that seeks to authorize cultural hybridities that emerge in moments of historical transformation' (p 3). Although post-colonial writers such as Bhabha prefer the term 'difference' to diversity, I use diversity in some cases throughout the book, as this, despite its weaknesses, is the current term used in social gerontology.

[2] Fields of study range from those of queer theory (Butler, 1990; Cerulo, 1997; Halberstam, 2005) to critical race (Crenshaw et al, 1995; Delgado and Stefancic, 2000; Hutchinson,

2002), postcolonial studies (Mohanty, 1993; Radhakrishnan, 1993) and the social model of disability (Shakespeare, 1996; Oldman, 2002; Riddell and Watson, 2003)

[3] There is, however, an argument that while exit through social mobility may be achieved, the wounds of class remain (see Sayer, 2005). Such understandings are consistent with Fanon's interpretations of the wounded, colonised psyche.

[4] The interview with Errol was conducted by a male research assistant, also from a visible minority ethnic group. The communication between Errol and the researcher is thus based on a shared sense of connection important to the results produced. Errol's discussion of his experience would have been significantly different had I conducted the interview. What is produced across locations of 'difference' requires more detailed attention (see Grenier, 2007a).

[5] Errol pursued two simultaneous career paths. He was a boxer, and also worked in manufacturing and groceries. He attributes his work in menial labour to the racist context that made it difficult for English-speaking persons of colour, men in particular, to find employment in Quebec. Through his work, however, Errol became a powerful union organiser and defender of worker rights. He later came to be elected to several prominent positions within the Black community. In contrast, women of colour at the time tended to be employed primarily as domestic workers, although some, like Elizabeth, were able to pursue training programmes through immigration policy initiatives and eventually gain full-time work within the nursing profession. Men of colour had more difficulty securing stable employment (see Grenier et al, 2010).

[6] The concept of integration is the official discourse on multiculturalism in Canada.

NINE

The fourth age: impairment in late life

This chapter explores the period of fourth age that is characterised by the transition to impairment and advanced age. With much of the gerontological literature addressing the earlier part of late life, the attempt here is to understand the transition into later periods of the lifecourse. The chapter begins by outlining ongoing attempts to establish what is meant by the fourth age, and points to mounting tensions from social and psychological perspectives. Rather than focusing on the dominant interpretations based on age or stage, it draws on the significance of this change and the associated socio-cultural meanings and processes involved. It considers how, while structured by biophysical notions of advanced age and impairment, this period is marked by a decline-based discourse that is significant as far as interpretations of continuity and change are concerned. What is important from a social perspective is that for older people, the period conceptualised as the 'fourth age' is a highly significant social construction involving personal experiences of making meaning of impairment in late life.

This chapter draws on older people's experiences in order to confront the knowledge on transitions and late life. The accounts given challenge how impairment in late life is unrecognised as a transition, as well how dominant understandings depict late life as a period of illness and decline. The stories from older people draw attention to the socio-cultural constructs and the personal interpretations of such change. Specifically, these stories highlight the importance of the assigned identity; the tension between achieving continuity amid change; liminality and the uncertainty of 'being between'; and the structured and interpretive nature of vulnerability across the lifecourse. Through these issues, older people with impairments in late life become located within and between dominant and alternative models of late life transitions. The accounts highlight the importance of considering the socio-cultural context within which experiences are interpreted, the emotional significance of impairment, and the cumulative nature of disadvantage. Questions explored in this chapter include:

- What approaches have been used to understand age and impairment in late life? What trends can be found within the social, biological and psychological literature?
- How can the relationships between age and impairment in late life be explained? What characterises this experience?
- Can the fourth age, or the acquisition of impairment in late life, be considered to represent a major transition in late life? What elements of continuity and change are experienced? What role does cumulative disadvantage play?

- What is the relationship between socio-cultural constructs and lived experience? How does the polarisation of health and illness in late life affect social relations with older people? Why have the social sciences and socio-critical perspectives remained silent?
- Can a broader consideration of liminality, uncertainty and anxiety shed light on the expectations and experiences of impairment in late life?

Approaches to ageing and late life

The polarisation of the third and fourth age sustains the distinction between a period of health in advanced age, and that of illness or impairment in late life. As mentioned in Part One of this book, most anthropological, sociological and psychological examinations of transition have overlooked late life. Yet, understandings of the fourth age are based on the idea of change or movement into a period marked by illness, impairment and decline. While the term the 'fourth age' is not always used outside gerontological scholarship, inquiry into this period takes place through research related to constructs of risk, frailty and longevity (see Bortz, 1993, 1997, 2002; Rockwood et al, 1994, 1996; Fried et al, 2001). Studies in this area seem to be at their apogee, with attention to 'frailty' a dominant theme in geriatric research (Rockwood et al, 1996; Strawbridge et al, 1998; Fried and Watson, 1999; Hamerman, 1999; Fried et al, 2001; Rockwood, 2005; Bergman et al, 2007; Rockwood and Mitnitski, 2007). Scholars in biomedical and clinical research on late life are concerned with identifying how 'frailty' in late life might be similar or different from the preceding stage (the third age) and the rest of the lifecourse. Practices focus on setting age- and stage-based criteria, most often through functional criteria. Age, incidence of disease, impairment and co-morbidity are the prime means used to explain the period of the 'fourth age'. The studies on frailty are thus highly relevant to considering the transition into later life.

Although the relationship between the fourth age and frailty is often implicit, there remains uncertainty in the medical community as to whether the concept of frailty is synonymous with the fourth age (see Boyd et al, 2005; Fried et al, 2001). However, from a social perspective, the characteristics of frailty that are being researched in biomedical studies closely correspond with definitions of the fourth age – making frailty an analytic category that represents the period characterised by impairment and decline (see Gadow, 1983; Kaufman, 1994; Grenier, 2007b, 2009b). For example, both frailty and the fourth age refer to the physical decline, impairment and weakness that are considered to occur in late life – judged roughly to begin after age 80 (Baltes and Smith, 2003). The fourth ago captures experiences that are located at the intersection of age and impairment and result from medical classifications, organisational practices and socio-cultural constructs rooted in decline.

Biomedical debates on frailty and the fourth age

Most debates on the fourth age have taken place in biomedical research and clinical practice, significantly affecting approaches to late life.[1] Rooted in a disease-based model, this literature is replete with studies of probability, causation and prediction. It contains several attempts to isolate the condition of frailty in order to predict longevity, target risk and shape successful medical interventions, and, as such, can be read as an attempt to attribute the conditions of late life to a distinct period. Much of the research in this field points to additive models whereby the greater number of medical issues contributes to the condition of frailty. Assessments of function and impairment are pivotal to classifications, and have heavily influenced even social care practices (see Grenier, 2007b). There are four prominent debates relevant for understanding late-life transitions.

The first is whether the fourth age is related to age or illness. Although the criterion for frailty has, in many cases, been set at the advanced age of 85, the direct link between frailty and old age is contentious. Frailty is generally understood to connote a sense of physical weakness resulting from a particular medical, physical or social limitation (Rockwood et al, 1994, 1996), as well as an increased risk of morbidity, mortality or loss of autonomy (Morley et al, 2002; Schmaltz et al, 2005). Although, linguistically, the fourth age implies an age-based concept, the way in which it is articulated is more in line with impairment or illness in advanced age rather than age alone. This may partially explain the medical community's decision to use the term 'frailty' over 'fourth age'. However, what remains important for this discussion is that the concept in question is one that occurs at the intersection of illness, impairment and age. This leads to the second related debate, of whether the fourth age – classified through conditions such as frailty – is specific to late life, or whether it can occur in earlier periods of the lifecourse. At present, most research has focused on such conditions in late life, rather than throughout the lifecourse, thereby consolidating the construct around age and impairment.

The third debate in the biomedical literature, albeit less prominent, is whether the fourth age is a condition or a result of cumulative disadvantage. For example, frailty has been defined as an age-related inability to respond adequately to stress (Bowsher et al, 1993; Rockwood et al, 1994; Campbell and Buchner, 1997); a result of natural decline, such as the ageing process or disease (Bortz, 1993, 2002; Michel, 2001); and a multidimensional construct comprising two or more medical/functional problems (Rockwood et al, 1996; Stawbridge et al, 1998; Fried and Watson, 1999; Hamerman, 1999; Fried et al, 2001). Yet, medical researchers have also raised questions related to lifestyle (Bortz, 2002) and the balance between health and impairment (Rockwood et al, 1994; Raphael et al, 1995). Some practitioners have extended their analytic scope to social influences such as family support, income and education (Rockwood et al, 1994, 1996), environmental factors (Raphael et al, 1995) and experiential variables (Bowsher et al, 1993; Michel, 2001). Although the articulation of frailty remains firmly rooted in biomedical research, these interpretations coincide with social scientists in saying that vulnerability and cumulative disadvantage may be more aligned with frailty than age. A focus on vulnerability also corresponds with older people's narratives from disadvantaged locations whereby old age may occur without frailty, but where frailty may be the result of lifelong processes rather than the onset of impairment in late life. There is a strong social gerontological literature focused on cumulative disadvantage (Ferraro and Kelley-Moore, 2001; Ferraro and Shippee, 2009) and exclusion (Scharf et al, 2004, 2007; Townsend, 1957, 2007 ; Walker, 1982), although links with the fourth age are rarely articulated. Views of frailty and the fourth age as a result of lifelong disadvantage challenge dominant age- and stage-based interpretations and affirm the need to consider impairment in late life more carefully.

The fourth debate, located primarily in psychological scholarship, focuses on the extent to which the fourth age represents new developmental tasks of coping and adaptation. As with the biomedical approach, the psychological literature has attempted to distinguish the specificities of the oldest old from other periods of the lifecourse. As discussed in Chapter Three, Baltes and colleagues (Baltes, 1987a, 1987b; Baltes and Smith, 1999; Baltes et al, 1999) have drawn attention to the neglect of the oldest old in psychological thinking, and outlined the need for support, maintenance and compensation in the fourth age that result from increased biological deterioration. They highlight the age- and stage-based changes that occur in late life, and depict the fourth age as a time of psychological morbidity. Baltes and Smith (1999) suggest that with decreasing social contact and psychological resources, the fourth age can be likened to a gradual period of decline – depicting a diagram of this slope over time. This work corresponds with the social-cultural interpretations of the fourth age that can be found in Laslett's (1989) construct. Yet, building on the suggestion that the oldest old face different developmental tasks characterised by coping, the works of Baltes and colleagues point to the psychological and emotional transitions that accompany functional change. As mentioned in Chapter Three, Baltes and colleagues' later work suggests a model of selection, optimisation and compensation that outlines how older people psychologically compensate for these losses (Baltes and Baltes, 1990; Baltes and Smith, 2003). The thinking in 'lifecourse psychology' clearly locates impairment in late life in a stage-based construct. At the same time, however, it moves the debate forward by suggesting that the developmental tasks are dealt with differently, and require both a different set of skills than in previous parts of the lifecourse and an emotional adjustment.

Frailty and the fourth age as socio-cultural constructs

In the social sciences, the fourth age is articulated as a social construct that takes place at the intersections of advanced age, illness, impairment and decline. The best representation, and one that typifies the polarisation of health and illness in late life, is Laslett's (1989) notion of the fourth age. The response to this construct, however, is divided in the social science literature – with both a common usage of the term, and implied acceptance, and a critique based on age and impairment (Gilleard and Higgs, 2002; Baltes and Smith, 2003; Wray, 2003; Wiggins et al, 2004). Gilleard and Higgs (2010) refer to the fourth age as a social imaginary that is based on decline. Yet, while social science perspectives have started to devote attention to the socially constructed nature of the concept of frailty and the fourth age (Gadow, 1983; Kaufman, 1994; Grenier, 2007b), its existence as a key transition or turning point has been overlooked. The fourth age is not included in the standard list of transitions said to occur in late life. Instead, understandings of the intersection of illness and impairment run parallel to the consideration of age and transition. Yet, the social science literature is beginning to take note as reflected in the following three responses.

First, social science literature draws attention to the problematic socio-cultural discourses and practices that are created in regards to advanced age and impairment. There is a small body of literature on the socio-cultural associations between advanced age, decline, dependency and devalue (Gullette, 1997, 2004), in particular, how frailty has become constructed as socially and culturally burdensome location (Grenier, 2007b, 2009b). This literature highlights the extent to which decline in late life is assumed, and questions the associations made between ageing, decline and death (Myerhoff, 1979, 1984; Gullette, 1997, 2004). It also highlights how such assumptions shape social relations and practices (Kaufman, 1994; Grenier, 2007b). While not directly applied to the fourth age, Calasanti and Slevin's (2001) concept of 'age relations', for example, can be used to demonstrate the extent to which social relations are structured and shaped by age. This includes assumptions of decline and stigma that sustain a separation between younger and older people based on judgements of health and functional status.

Second, the social science literature exposes the dominance of the biomedical interpretations of body size, weakness and illness that characterise frailty and the fourth age, in particular, the extent to which care practices have adopted biomedical notions of functional impairment. For example, the literature highlights how the construct of the fourth age becomes instrumental in setting eligibility for services, and in doing so, sets apart these older more physically vulnerable seniors from those in earlier periods of late life (Grenier, 2009a). As such, practices conducted in relation to frailty and the fourth age reveal how the long-standing divisions of age are no longer only focused on biological age-based segregation, discrimination or ageism (see Butler, 1969, 1975, 1980; Bytheway, 1994), but also on a more complicated construct rooted in the intersection of age, poor health, the body and the accompanying social stigma of dependency and decline. The polarised locations of the third and the fourth age reinforce the separation of healthy older bodies from declining older bodies. Practices taken up in relation to these classifications solidify health and activity as the gold standard in age, with frailty and decline as negative conditions to be avoided. As a result, notions of the fourth age, and the accompanying practices based on conditions of frailty as functional impairment, create an internal rift within the cohort of older people that is based on binary distinctions between 'health' and illness, and the physical condition of the body (Grenier, 2009a).

Third, more recent approaches link social and psychological understandings of transition to the fourth age. A few authors have drawn attention to the emotional processes of adjustment in later life (Baltes and Smith, 2003; Grenier, 2006a,b). The literature on loss and coping is one such area. In these accounts, authors demonstrate how the binary classification between health and illness breaks down at the experiential level. Although the literature has long existed in relation to the emotional processes of transition into illness, these insights are rarely applied to late-life transitions or the acquisition of impairment in late life. Yet, narrative perspectives hold great potential for elaborating on the emotional transition into this period of late life, and the ways in which impairment in late life may affect life trajectories. The challenge at present is that the fourth age is solely characterised by illness, impairment and decline, and consequently is offered few other meaningful roles, especially where the links to care systems are concerned.[2] Regardless of the root cause or specific conditions of impairment in late life, movement into this period can be critically read as a transition that occurs on a physical, socio-cultural, interpersonal and emotional level.

The question of advanced age and impairment requires more detailed attention both as a construct and process of transition. Scholarship critiquing 'frailty' and the fourth age from a social science perspective began with an exploration of the concept and practice, as articulated by professionals and older people (Kaufman, 1994; Grenier, 2005, 2007b). More recently, Gilleard and Higgs (2010) have attempted to articulate a conceptual model of the fourth age from a sociological perspective, linking powerful discourses of healthy or successful ageing, biotechnology and longevity, and suggesting that the fourth age is a 'black hole'. While differing somewhat in approach, and in the question of the extent to which redefinition is possible, the discussions taking place around the fourth age challenge the invisibility of the 'old old' in a field that tends to focus on third-age issues. It also draws attention to practices whereby the fourth age is used to mark cohort distinctions between 'younger' and 'older' groups in research and practice (Grenier, 2009a).

A reconsideration of the intersection of age and impairment as 'something different', however, contains several challenges. Gilleard and Higgs' (2010) concept of the 'black hole' confronts the invisibility of the fourth age and the void of cultural space allocated to this group. The problem in doing so, however, is that the concept sustains the distinction between the third age as one of freedom, choice and health, and the fourth as one of decline and dependency – a complex configuration that Gilleard and Higgs (2000) noted in their earlier work. The concern is that in recognising the fourth age as characterised solely by impairment, older people in this category become socially and culturally 'othered' – both from society and within groups of older people. This is especially the case if the 'accepted' construct privileges social and cultural notions of decline and devalue over subjective meanings, and the emotional significance of this change. It is here that the liminality and potential of post-colonial interpretations discussed in Chapter Eight may be relevant. Rather than sustaining the binary of age, the fourth age can be approached as a socio–historical and cultural practice whereby the 'other' is created, maintained and experienced in relation to constructs of impairment and decline. However, for the moment, thinking about the fourth age from a social science perspective provides an important step in reconsidering the implications of polarising health and illness, as well as the ways in which older people's experiences of continuity and change may differ in this period. What seems crucial in relation to the question at hand is how experiences of impairment in advanced age may be understood as a symbolic and meaningful transition.

Accounts from older people

Illustrations from older people highlight tensions that take place at the intersection of age and impairment in late life. Ideas explored in this chapter build on the case illustrations of Dorothy, Peter and Sam, presented in Chapter Six. All three experienced impairment in late life, but only Dorothy and Sam had reached the advanced age that is often seen to constitute the fourth age. Yet, their responses to impairment differed significantly, with Dorothy's everyday experience described as a difficult struggle and Sam's met with the same positive outlook he appears have taken throughout his life. Peter is significantly younger, but has experienced impairment at a similar level to Dorothy. His case highlights the effects of lifelong disadvantage, and how acquired impairments affect the ageing process. Dorothy's case most typically corresponds with dominant interpretations of the fourth age, including the extent to which it is characterised by a narrative of decline. Conversely, Sam is nearly the oldest person in the sample and has a serious visual impairment. Yet, his story provides the greatest contrast where constructs of the fourth age are concerned. Sam maintains a positive outlook that overshadows the storyline of impairment. Together, these examples challenge standard interpretations of the fourth age as a period of functional decline. They also move the analysis into a complex reconsideration of age and impairment and highlight the need to more carefully consider the significance of the fourth age as a process of making meaning of continuity and change.

The narrative accounts correspond and conflict with age- and stage-based interpretations of impairment in late life. As mentioned in Chapter Four, the sample from which the illustrations were drawn contained two groups that typified the constructs of the third and fourth age – a healthy group of adults involved in a late-life education programme and a group of adults with physical and visual impairments in late life. Accounts depicted in the two groups differed in subject matter, level of impairment, life trajectory and response, with the main dividing line being that of serious impairment. In fact, the distinctions commonly made with regards to health and illness that underlie the construct of the fourth age became apparent in the different stories of the two groups. While moments of transgressing these lines were visible, the structured divisions between typified groups were for the most part relatively clear. For example, the stories of Dorothy, Sam and Peter were a stark contrast to the third-age illustrations of Charles, Anna and Edwin. However, the stories from the two locations defied a strict division based on the presence or absence of impairment – a finding that challenges the dominant constructs of frailty, the fourth age and understandings of the lifecourse.

Older people's attention to the meanings and processes of impairment in late life contrast with the expectations of research and practice. Research on transitions in gerontology emphasises the timing of events and how they correspond with normative lifecourse expectations (see Neugarten, 1968, 1979a,b; Neugarten and Datan, 1973). However, the accounts illustrated the importance of process and meaning. This included the extent to which experiences may be interpreted as on- or off-time in relation to personal frames of meanings or expectations (see Gubrium and Holstein, 1994, 1998, 1999) rather than against standard sets. The accounts extended beyond simply accepting or rejecting normative expectations, with the older people actually relating to and employing these frames to shape their lives and experiences. For example, both Dorothy and Edwin make reference to an age-based marker of change in their lives. Dorothy says, "And suddenly I turned 80 and all of my problems started," and Edwin says, "It was only around maybe my seventieth birthday that I became aware of the fact that I wasn't a kid anymore ... the things that I could do, I could no longer do, will never be able to do." While both draw on age-based discourses to make sense of the changes in their circumstances, their narratives reveal how, in actuality, these changes started to occur much before the identified age-frame. Dorothy's health became impaired while she was a full time caregiver, but she does not assign any significance to her impairments until later in her life (around age 80). Peter, on the other hand, notes how the onset of illness 15 years earlier (around age 60) was the starting point for the decline that has led to his current situation. Age-based criteria are used in these cases to link personal experience with powerful discourses and expectations, making meaning of their lives and experiences in a larger socio-cultural context.

Close examination of older people's stories from the fourth-age group, however, reveals a complexity related to the subjectivity by which this period may be declared, and a fluidity that exists within and between situations. What emerges from the cases, and in contrast with the third-age accounts, is evidence of a symbolic or interpretive threshold related to impairment in late life. The accounts reveal how impairment represents a marked change in the lives of the individuals concerned. For example, Peter says: "Those days are almost like day and night. It's not the same. The happiness is not the same. Life is not the same." Similarly, Dorothy acknowledges this change by emphasising the difficulties she now has with coping. She says: "Life was never easy but when you're younger you're able to cope" She later states: "It's hard! It's hard on the people helping you. It's hard on you; it's hard on the family." Such complexities highlight a distinction between the onset of illness or impairment and the impact of such change. In other words, the turning point identified was not about the onset of impairment, but about recognising the permanence of impairment and the impact it has on late life. This appears in many narratives, as statements along the lines of 'this isn't going to get better' or 'I may as well get used to it' (see Grenier, 2007b). Older people do not define their experiences in relation to a fixed and objectively available moment, as dominant interpretations of the fourth age would imply, but to a more permanent state of uncertainty that is distinct from earlier periods of their lives. The accounts of Dorothy, Peter and Sam outline how the presence of illness or impairment has changed everyday experience in ways that were not predictable or predetermined along the lines of a biological clock (see Kirkwood and Holliday, 1979; Kirkwood, 2002).

The accounts of Dorothy, Peter and Sam draw attention to the complex connections made to discourses and expectations of decline, dependency and mortality. At times, their interpretations suggested that frailty or impairment was a late-life marker that represented the penultimate period of the lifecourse, with only death remaining. It was therefore the power of the proximity of decline and death that spoke to its significance as a moment of change, and one that required a fairly substantial level of adaptation. For example, Dorothy poignantly says: "I don't like to talk about the death thing, but it is something that automatically comes up." She discusses the difficult adjustment to late life, stating "My eyes have gone, my bones are pretty much shot." In her case, the timeline of past, present and future highlights how change brought on by impairment takes on a different meaning in late life: "I can't get about. I can't do the things I did before." Her statement reflects before and after distinctions created through narrative structures of the past, present and future (Dittmann-Kohli, 1990; Grenier, 2006b). It is this from this location of more permanent change that negotiation and visions for the future may become more difficult, especially when strategies from earlier parts of the lifecourse can no longer be enacted (see Grenier and Hanley, 2007). In Peter's account, understandings of impairment are portrayed through statements such as "I'm not as brisk as I was" that are closely aligned with emphasising his remaining independence and personal strengths, while Sam's account highlights how he has made adjustments to some activities, such as painting: "I still paint today ... it takes a hell of a lot longer than when I used to do it." In this sense, while Sam would technically be classified as someone in the fourth age, his outlook corresponds with successful models of late life, raising questions about differences in coping mechanisms and interpretation of experience. All three examples relate to the discourses and realities brought about by age and impairment, the meaning this has had in each individual's life, and the changes that person has made.

In this sense, the older people's accounts of impairment in late life are layered with complexity – deeply connected to an identity or sense of self that takes shape in a particular social and cultural context. Yet, similar to the discussions of diversity in Chapter Eight, the strategies of negotiating impairment in late life are more complicated than understandings of identity claims or resistance would imply. In psychology, making sense of impairment in late life can be considered a developmental task (Baltes and Smith, 2003), while from a social constructionist or identity-based perspective, it may be seen as a deeply personal process in relation to life as a whole (Gubrium and Holstein, 2000, 2009; Holstein and Gubrium, 2000). Yet, the accounts demonstrate that combining the insights of psychology and social constructionist perspectives, for example, would allow for better understanding of the developmental and personal processes that occur in relation to continuity and change. Consider, for example, Sam's statements that "ageing has never really been a problem for me" and that his hip fracture is "no big deal", expressed in accordance with his personal beliefs and the socio–cultural discourse on independence, strength and activity. Comparing and contrasting accounts located in the fourth age demonstrates the different pathways that may occur, including how illness and impairment may represent a major rupture, how poverty may affect experience, and how the interpretation of events may differ significantly.

Older people's accounts located at the intersection of age and impairment draw attention to the challenges of understanding continuity and change in late life. In particular, they focus on the tensions that exist between the desire to maintain continuity and the challenges of adapting to change over time (Dittmann-Kohli 1990; Grenier, 2006a). In the accounts of older people in what is known as the fourth age, the notions of continuity and change become somewhat fused. In most cases, the accounts demonstrate a struggle to make sense of their experiences in light of their lives. Although threads of continuity remain, there is a growing realisation of change and of movement into a period that is more permanently characterised by – or at least interpreted through the lens of – an impairment that is distinct from other patterns experienced across the lifecourse. Rather than demonstrating straightforward illustrations of continuity reflective of the productive and successful discourse, accounts located in the fourth age may begin to reference uncertainty, a more permanent state of decline, and in some cases, proximity to the final transition of death. But this is not always the case – some accounts highlight lifelong identities, strategies and activities. Together, they depict the breadth of experience located between the finite points of continuity and change, and, as such, resound with revisited interpretations of liminality pursued in the second half of this book.

Rethinking transitions: the intersection of age and impairment

When considered in relation to existing debates and challenges, the older people's accounts suggest three pathways towards a better understanding of transitions in relation to age and impairment:

- The first pathway is to consider the fourth age as a period located in a liminal space between health and illness at the end of life.
- The second pathway is to draw on understandings of cumulative disadvantage and impairment that exist in critical gerontology and the literature on disability and critical geography.
- The third pathway is to more deeply explore the significance of the fourth age, including the underlying assumptions and emotional relationships that shape practices and subjective interpretations.

Although they represent divergent paths, these steps can help us reconsider how impairment affects continuity and change in the lives of older people.

The liminality of the fourth age

Older people's accounts point to the processes and symbolic meanings of impairment in late life. The accounts contrast dominant interpretations of the fourth age as a period characterised by advanced age, functional impairment and decline and emphasise the meaning of this transition. In doing so, they highlight the relevance of reconsidering the concept of liminality in relation to lifecourse transitions such as the fourth age (also see Hockey and James, 2003). In particular, the accounts highlight the symbolic weight of the fourth age that is uniquely located in relation to illness, dependency and the proximity to death (Grenier, 2009a). With old age closer to the end of the lifecourse, it is not surprising that this location, with no formal exit other than death, has such an imposing presence. It is perhaps for these reasons that Gilleard and colleagues (Higgs and Jones, 2008; Gilleard and Higgs, 2010) suggest that the fourth age is a metaphorical 'black hole'. Yet, rather than a presence, the 'black hole' alludes to a lacuna and/ or uncertainty related to frailty and impairment in late life (see Grenier, 2006b, 2007b, 2009a). However, defining this period as a void is problematic. Bhabha's (1994) view is that liminal spaces from 'othered' locations can also contain space for redefinition. A crucial aspect to understanding this period is the way in which older people in the fourth age shift from being considered as consumers of culture and lifestyle to consumers of public services (see Gilleard and Higgs, 2000; Grenier, 2007b, 2009a). The permanency of impairment, dependency and finitude of life as a whole (mortality), however, are not the only interpretations older people offer. They also offer an analysis of the dominant associations made about ageing and impairment, and active attempts to negotiate the meanings of this period. Perhaps there is a distinction to be made between the concept of a 'black hole' as a socio-cultural construct, and a process by which older people are categorised by socio-cultural notions and organisational practices into a location considered devoid of agency (Grenier, 2009a). The linkage whereby the dependency of the fourth age sustains the potential of the third remains relevant (see Gilleard and Higgs, 2000). However, a nuanced understanding of this period as enacted through processes and practices may permit meanings and alternative models to emerge (Grenier, 2006a,b, 2007b). The challenge at this point is to develop a model that, while drawing attention to the polarisation of health and illness in late life, and inherent socio-cultural notions that accompany these constructs, does not sustain and replicate this period as a devalued location of existence. Attention to the emotions and symbolic processes that 'deny' and experience dependency may thus be useful to the analysis (see Lloyd, 2004).

Drawing on post-colonial interpretations that view liminality from an 'othered' space that has room for redefinition, allows for a reconsideration of impairment in late life. In Turner's (1969) classic anthropological approach, this period of the fourth age could be considered a liminal period of being 'betwixt and between' that is temporary in nature (also see Hockey and James, 2003). Lawton (2000), for example, has argued that those who are dying exist in an extended period of liminality. Yet, older people's narratives from the fourth age reveal how impairment in late life is a more permanent state or marker of being located 'in-between'. Considering the fourth age as liminal corresponds in part with the liminality of the dying, but also of those assigned marginal or 'othered' locations, and the possibility of creating alternative perspectives or experiences. When the complexity of the accounts of older people are considered, they can be seen to resonate more closely with post-colonial interpretations of liminality as a 'continual process of movement and interchange between different states' (Ashcroft et al, 2007 p 117). On a socio-cultural level, the older person becomes located between discourses of health/productivity, impairment/decline and the significance these experiences hold in their lives. Their narratives reveal fluid and uncertain interpretations of impairment in late life; acts of creating distance from impairment and the negative associations of burden and dependency (distancing themselves from friends with impairments); and a heightened awareness of mortality expressed through a sense of 'time left'. Together, these sentiments speak to the liminality experienced with regard to impairment and late life.

Yet, while this period is significant to older people, there are few suggested models within which to understand and plan for this transition. The realities of impairment and illness can mean that older people no longer 'fit' the productive model of late life, yet do not wish to adhere to a model of decline that is associated with failure. Models used to think through the challenges of late life include the fourth age as a period characterised by new developmental tasks of adjustment (Baltes et al, 1999); late life as a period characterised by a need to draw on strong identity-based claims constructed and maintained throughout the lifecourse (Hockey and James, 2003); and the consideration of the fourth age as an alternative space from which to make sense of this existential experience (Tornstam, 2005). Yet the more permanent state of liminality that is brought on by impairment in late life suggests that these models in isolation are not enough to explain this period of change. Each suggestion has limitations. For example, the developmental tasks set out in lifecycle psychology are defined in relation to an assumption of bodily decline as negative, with coping and adaptation the available tasks. While the more positive and ongoing aspects of older people's personalities may be accounted for through identity-based frameworks (Hockey and James, 2003), such claims can become limited or unconvincing in the face of serious decline (see Grenier and Hanley, 2007). At present, it seems that liminality offers the greatest potential for understanding this transition – a liminality that accounts for being 'othered' or outside by means of age, as well as within and between the uncertainties brought about by impairment in late life.

Liminality, defined as 'an "in-between" space in which cultural change can occur' (Ashcroft et al, 2007 p 117), holds potential for rethinking this period. Liminality in the fourth age may thus leave a space from which older people can negotiate change as a symbolic process. It may, however, also reinforce socio-cultural distance from older people in the fourth age. To date, what the literature on the fourth age has failed to articulate is that living within this space in-between can have serious emotional implications on an individual and social level. What is it like to occupy this space? How does one make meaning of this being 'in-between'? Is socio-cultural change possible, and to what extent does current thinking leave this defined on an individual level? Likening the experiences of impairment in late life to a symbolic and meaningful space of being more permanently 'in-between' more closely aligns the analysis with a consideration of the intersections between the socio-cultural context, internalised processes, and subjective experiences of impairment in late life. Additionally, linking this with the elements that remain continuous despite change may shed further light on late-life transitions. However, identifying the features of change and continuity represents an ongoing challenge for rethinking the transition into the fourth age.

Continuity despite change?

Older people's accounts demonstrate that experiencing impairment in late life creates a tension between continuity and change as a more permanent issue that requires different personal and psychological strategies from those used across the lifecourse. When confronted by change, older people emphasise a desire to maintain the continuous aspects of their experience over change brought on by illness or physical impairment. On the one hand, these efforts may be read as attempts to fix the continuous aspects of their experience across time, possibly to protect or maintain their sense of self. On the other hand, they reveal the extent to which their efforts take place in a socio-cultural space defined by expectations of continuity, health, productivity and success. Older people's interpretations of continuity take place amid powerful biomedical assessments of function, powerful 'age relations', socio-cultural discourses of decline and the complicated personal processes of adapting to change.

With continuity interpreted as more difficult to achieve in the case of impairment in late life, older people seem to respond in one of three overlapping ways. These strategies can be identified in the accounts of Sam, Dorothy and Peter. First, they may modify their activities and efforts, reducing the level of physical exertion. Second, they may create distance between themselves and the notions of weakness and vulnerability. Third, they may focus on coping, managing and adaptation – often citing how these are difficult to achieve. Together, these three strategies reflect a process of making meaning of changes brought about by impairment in late life. What is difficult is identifying the reasons why some individuals present storylines of adjusting to severe impairment, while others with more minor impairments may find this extremely challenging. What is clear in the accounts is how continuity can provide the means to negotiate impairment in a context where the fourth age holds consequences of stigma, exclusion, dependency and decline (see Laslett, 1989; Kaufman, 1994; Grenier, 2007b). Yet, continuity is only one aspect of the coping process – making meaning is also important.

Considering the difference between accounts describing earlier and later periods of the lifecourse is relevant to understanding continuity and change. In the case of impairment, discussions of change experienced earlier in the lifecourse differed from those experienced in late life. Earlier periods of impairment or illness were often depicted as temporary experiences from which they recovered, whereas in late life, the experiences of illness and impairment tended to represent a significant transition that became more permanent. While both were told as retrospective accounts, earlier experiences were framed in the past, whereas later experiences considered more permanent were discussed in relation to present attempts to cope. The meanings individuals made of impairment provided important paths from which to consider their experiences. For example, the desire and efforts to achieve continuity become a more prominent aspect of the storyline. Where change was interpreted as more permanent (even if it ended up being only temporary), the older people focused on maintaining their bodies and selves in spite of these changes. Negotiating the line between continuity and change became a pressing need in a socio-cultural context that emphasised success, activity and independence.

Yet, expectations of continuity that are embedded in understandings of transitions as positive events experienced across the lifecourse overlook the psychological and emotional aspects of older people's experience. With the dominant transition of work to retirement portrayed as one involving freedom, activity and leisure, and continuity predominantly focused on individual choices and lifestyles, more difficult transitions – such as the acquisition of impairment in late life – remain unacknowledged. There is no space attributed to the more difficult transitional experiences; older people are left on their own to negotiate these changes. As such, attempts to integrate change become individualised attempts that echo the psychological literature on adaptation. In the case of impairment in late life, the desire to achieve continuity can become contradictory – providing both the potential for a unifying thread, but also the indicator that socio-cultural and personal expectations are not being reached. This is particularly the case once older people feel that they have moved past the threshold of temporary impairment into a more permanent state. While interpretations of continuity based on fluid notions of desired identity across the lifecourse can be used to challenge age- and stage-based expectations, they may result in an additional sense of failure when interpreted as yet another marker that is difficult to achieve. When considered unsuccessful, the emotional consequences are serious. For example, in Dorothy's narrative, she matched her lack of continuity with a dislike for herself, saying 'she doesn't like what [she has] become'. In this sense, the emphasis on continuity in policy interpretations, academic research and the minds of older people themselves may, in fact, reinforce dominant interpretations whereby activity and functionality are sought after, and changes brought on by impairment in late life are considered undesirable.

There are few models that discuss how older people may maintain continuity despite change, when continuity – a dominant expectation of the lifecourse perspective and of older people – is desired. Older people's accounts highlight how the transition into late life can represent a process that is fraught with socio-cultural and emotional consequences, and, in particular, the finality that late life represents. While the work of Baltes (Baltes, 1997; Baltes and Smith, 2003) points to late life as a period of coping and adjustment, such challenges remain underexplored from a social perspective. Psychological models point to individual level tasks, raising questions about the extent to which new social roles or cultural redefinitions, as suggested in post-colonial literature or geography, are possible (also see Rowles, 1978, 2008). At present, it seems that the only available model for positive change is that of gerotranscendance, mentioned earlier, whereby older people may shift their awareness through a philosophical redefinition of themselves and their life world in order to deal with these challenges. Yet, such a model may pose problems if the idea of transcendence is one that rejects or denies the body and its impairments (see Wendell, 1996). What becomes most clear, both from personal accounts and notions such as gerotranscendance, is the importance of personal and symbolic processes that take place amid a socio-cultural context, and as a result affect understandings of continuity and change in late life. Older people's accounts provide insight into these processes, but more importantly highlight the extent to which late life may or may not represent the possibility of redefinition suggested by Tornstam (2005), as well as the process by which developmental goals may be reached (Baltes, 1997). Understanding continuity and change in late life involves a complex process that takes into account bodily changes, as well as socio-cultural, emotional, interpersonal and subjective interpretations of these experiences.

Intersections of age, impairment, disadvantage and vulnerability

Older people's accounts demonstrated that when combined with impairment, lifetime inequities and cumulative disadvantage had more serious consequences in late life. These accounts echo the literature on social disadvantage and more recent biomedical interpretations where conditions such as 'frailty', previously considered physical in nature, are seen to have a strong aspect of disadvantage carried from earlier parts of the lifecourse. While there were few examples of severe deprivation in the Late Life Transitions project, those that described material disadvantage stood out. Two major themes were prevalent in these accounts. First, the narratives of older people who had experienced economic disadvantage across the lifecourse seemed to recount earlier onset of impairment than those with modest or privileged means. While the reasons for this vary, the literature indicates that such discrepancies may be a result of lifelong issues of disadvantage such as nutrition or labour conditions (Ben-Schlomo and Kuh, 2002; Gluckman and Hanson, 2006; Ferraro and Shippee, 2009; McMullin, 2010). Second, older people affected by early illness and without the financial resources had more difficulty meeting basic needs such as food and shelter. The two themes were also intricately connected, with the inability to meet needs contributing to an increased severity of illness or more permanent impairment. While the link between meagre financial resources and impairment in late life cannot be seen to determine their accounts, the intersections of these locations clearly marked their experiences.

Accounts located at the intersections of age, impairment and disadvantage differed from the expected situations and norms of ageing and late life. The stories of Elaine, who acquired workplace injuries and has a low income in retirement, and Peter, whose illness resulted in increased impoverishment as a result of hopsitalisation and costly medications, are examples of the intersection of late life and cumulative disadvantage. Such trends are documented in the literature and represent serious challenges to changes in policy such as increasing the retirement age in line with changing expectations of late life. As previously discussed, the combination of illness and impairment takes on a different meaning when experienced early or late in the lifecourse, and especially when the older person has meagre resources to address them. In relation to his expectations of late life, Peter describes how he would have hoped to have more stability in late life rather than, as he says, 'living hand to mouth'. While the literature has tended to focus on understandings of 'on- or off-time' transitions set against age- and stage-based expectations (see Neugarten, 1968, 1979a; Neugarten and Datan, 1973), it has overlooked how locations such as cumulative disadvantage may affect the very achievement of lifecourse norms, or personal and socio-cultural expectations such as independence and financial stability. Understanding the link between lifelong disadvantage from locations such as poverty or disability, impairment in late life, and the relationship between socio-cultural discourses and personal meaning-making processes requires greater attention.

Compounding material need is that older people with meagre financial resources could be forced to make choices between basic needs such as food, medication and housing. Consider Peter and Elaine, both of whom use food banks to meet their needs. While Elaine is generally in good health, Peter has more serious impairments that make his life more difficult. Peter is already affected by the intersection of poverty and impairment in late life, while Elaine would no doubt experience similar struggles were she to experience ill health – especially considering that she is already a user of foodbank services. Despite feeling liberated from a lifetime of difficult work, Elaine wishes she had additional revenue and greater mobility in order to better enjoy her retirement. It is not surprising that Elaine and Peter's experiences of illness and impairment are more complicated as a result of not having the resources to meet their needs. An individual's financial situation can seriously affect late-life transitions – with older people of limited means less able to access non-medical type services found in the private rather than public domain, such as meal preparation or cleaning and rehabilitative services, that may ease their experiences of impairment or illness (see Grenier and Guberman, 2009; Neysmith, 1999, 2000). Yet, discussions of the functional issues of the fourth age, obscure the disadvantage that can differentially affect older people in late life.

What is missing is an understanding of how intersections of impairment and age are intertwined with lifelong experiences. Accumulated disadvantage remains relatively unacknowledged within the academic literature on frailty and the fourth age. Yet, in contrast, the experience of disadvantage is very prevalent in the accounts of older people considered to be in the fourth age. Struggles are related to material resources and the psychological adjustment, with some older people not knowing how to meet their material needs in ways they deem acceptable.

Older people's accounts of impairment and meagre resources outline how disadvantage could create a level of vulnerability that is rarely discussed in the literature. For example, precarious employment, the lack of financial resources, and dangerous work conditions across the lifecourse can create conditions of vulnerability in late life. Consider Peter, who, as a result of poverty, has taken in a lodger that places him at risk of victimisation and abuse, and Elaine, whose work exposed her to increased levels of violence across the lifecourse that have affected her sense of security and wellbeing. Such vulnerability and victimisation are often overlooked in studies of both the fourth age and exclusion, and yet, the accounts suggest that feelings of vulnerability could cause one to feel the impact of ageing and impairment in late life more intensely. The earlier discussion of liminality, continuity and change becomes increasingly complex where cumulative disadvantage and impairment in late life are concerned. The impact of lifetime inequities that become more prominent in the fourth age prompts a more careful consideration of the intersections between social structures and experiences of disadvantage across the lifecourse, including how older people may experience these events in relation to socio-cultural and personal expectations of growing old.

The socio-cultural 'denial of dependency'

Finally, older people's accounts provide an insight into the underlying fears and anxieties related to decline and dependency that can influence personal and socio-cultural responses to the fourth age. While such feelings and processes are rarely articulated in policy and practice, older people's narratives illustrate how the emotional significance of change may inform decisions and strategies, whether consciously or not. In fact, the emotional associations related to impairment, decline and death may in part explain why this period has for the most part been overlooked in social gerontology. Yet, outside gerontology there is a burgeoning literature on the culture of denial, experiences of illness, and the merits of integrating emotion into sociological perspectives (see Frank, 1995; Charmaz, 1999; Sayer, 2005). For example, a focus on how emotional responses are expressed in social relations – through, for example, distance from difficult issues – or how internalised subjective perceptions are expressed in policies and practices is relevant to understanding the responses to and interpretations of the fourth age (see Lloyd, 2004; Hoggett, 2008).

Thinking about impairment in late life can trigger a number of underlying fears and anxieties in individuals of all ages. Underlying the idea of the fourth age – a period characterised by infirmity and suffering that leads eventually to death– are emotional issues of ambivalence, uncertainty and denial. Such associations have always been present, and were clearly articulated in Laslett's initial list of anxieties that accompanied the fourth age.[3] Laslett's (1989) 'anticipatory anxieties' of ageing render visible the assumptions that can operate in the minds of individuals:

> The uncertainty about possible length of life is of considerable symbolic importance for elderly people, who live in a state of perpetual doubt. They never know how much time they have: whether to begin this, or to promise that; whether to plan for several years hence, or at most for a month or two....They can never be confident that a particular relative or associate near them in age will be present at all at any point in the future. In such direction as these the lives of all the elderly go forward in a state of hesitation and incertitude, however active and satisfying those lives may be whilst the Third Age itself continues. (Laslett, 1989, p 13)

Although such interpretations represent a negative portrayal of late life that may be likened to stereotypical links between ageing and death, they also point to the uncertainty that is present in the minds of many people, older and not. Writing from a cultural studies perspective, Gullette (1997, 2004) articulates the symbolic connections of decline that are linked with late life. She uses concepts such as 'ageing as death rehearsal' and the process of resisting this by 'declining to decline' that outline how powerful connections between ageing and death shape cultural interpretations of ageing (see also Woodward, 1991, 1999). Her analysis moves critiques organised around ageism and age-based stereotypes into accounting for social and cultural notions (see Bytheway and Johnson, 1990; Bytheway, 1994). In doing so, her analysis draws attention to the emotional associations of fear and denial that are apparent in cultural interpretations of late life, and how these may be consciously available as well as unconsciously present in social and cultural relations.

Considering how both older people and the literature poignantly outline the emotional challenges and associations of the fourth age, why then has this period received relatively little attention from social gerontology so far? Part of the answer lies in the very charged emotional issues that older people have discussed. Their accounts bring us closer to the realisation that both conscious and unconscious processes affect our perceptions and responses to ageing. Literature from the psycho-social perspective, an application of psycho-dynamic work in a socio-cultural context, can help to articulate more clearly how emotions shape social responses to groups such as older people of the fourth age (see Evans and Garner, 2004; Davenhill, 2007). This perspective links social relations with internal and potentially unconscious motivations (Frosh and Baraitser, 2008; Hook, 2008;

Walkerdine, 2008). The psycho-dynamic literature, when applied to the cases of public policy, for example, demonstrates how psycho-dynamic concepts such as denial and projection and the accompanying unconscious motivations may play out in social systems such as public welfare (see Clarke et al, 2006; Hoggett, 2000, 2001, 2006, 2008). Insights from this perspective can thus be used to suggest that it is in part our feelings and emotions towards frailty and decline that affect our interpersonal and socio-cultural responses and practices with older people.

Considering these ideas reveals how anxieties can be internalised by older people themselves or projected on to them in social relations and cultural practices. For example, the emotional significance expressed in Laslett's (1989) impressions of the fourth age can produce an internalised discourse of devalue or burden. Yet, Laslett (1989) clearly outlines the paradox that exists when he says: 'To dislike the old is hatred of the self, rejection of what you yourself must inevitably become ... in despising the old they are despising themselves' (p 97). He follows this assertion with a call to 'face our fears of growing old, lest we find ourselves content to take descriptions of the final years or months of decrepitude as covering the permanent condition of all elderly people' (Laslett, 1989, p 102). While Laslett clearly states the underlying fears that may exist in relation to ageing, he does so in a way that sustains the rift between the third and fourth age, where the dependency of the fourth age as a time to be avoided in fact creates the opportunities and freedom of the third (see Gilleard and Higgs, 2000). As such, he fails to address the social and cultural implications of the polarisation of the fourth age. Although reflecting the scholarship of the 1980s focused on stereotypes, when revisited, Laslett's distinctions between the third and the fourth age draws attention to the unspoken aspects of decline and dependency, and, with insights from the psycho-social perspective, can now be read to speak to the psychological defences that may operate in policies and practices against the more feared and intolerable issues of late life. What remains is the challenge of understanding the fourth age, and indentifying spaces of the fourth age that are not characterised as a 'void'.

Applying the insights of emotion in the current context of ageing can highlight the social and cultural ideas that operate invisibly in policies and practices. A particularly useful concept is the 'denial of dependency', which suggests that various political efforts to make individuals self-reliant, productive and independent represent a cultural discomfort or hatred of dependency (Hoggett, 1998, 2000; Lloyd, 2004). Although dependency is typically used to refer to an economic dependence on the welfare system (see Walker, 1982), the symbolic associations with burden and reliance on others is more pronounced in the case of impairment in late life. This 'denial of dependency' can therefore be used to make sense of the unconscious motivation for the polarisation of the fourth age (Lloyd, 2004; Grenier, 2009a). Emotions and unconscious feelings may be projected on to the bodies and experiences of older people, creating a distance from older people with impairments, a denial of issues such as vulnerability, and a construct that contains only threatening, intolerable or unbearable conditions. At the same time, however, older people's accounts draw attention to the subtle and often unarticulated ways in which decline may actually be experienced as disruptive and disturbing. This leads to questions about the extent to which the cultural, social and psychological distance from the intersections of ageing and impairment is a product of one's own negative feelings; whether such emotions hinder commitment to improvement and change; and to what extent social practices create and sustain distance from situations such as the decline or the death of loved ones or ourselves (Grenier, 2009a). An examination of the underlying themes in the present socio-cultural context demonstrates that taking account of the emotional responses relating to dependency and decline can add a crucial dimension to the understandings and responses to impairment in late life. Older people's accounts underline the need for a reconsideration of the malaise that seems to exist in the psyche of the culture or society – that is, in the feelings and unspoken associations relating to experiences of impairment in late life.

Conclusion: reconsidering impairment in advanced age

A consideration of the narratives of older people reveals the emotional significance that characterises their experiences of transition to the fourth age. Older people's accounts suggest that experiences of making meaning of this period take place in liminal spaces between the realities of impairment, socio-cultural discourses and subjective interpretations. While the various literatures reviewed early in this chapter address questions of frailty and the fourth age differently, each points to the existence of potentially significant facets of this period that require future exploration. Yet, the majority of the literature has focused on identifying the objective conditions of frailty, or fixed ages or stages of life, and, as such, has overlooked the meaning and significance that older people attribute to this change. Older people's accounts draw these aspects together, demonstrating how interpretations of late life are made in relation to the fourth age as a symbolic final period of the lifecourse, and the expectations of successful, healthy and active lifestyles carried over from the third age. When contrasted with academic debates, older people's accounts expose the extent to which dominant understandings of this period are informed by functional assessments and objective measures that overlook the subjectivity and emotional significance experienced. A more careful consideration of liminality, socio-cultural forms of denial and cumulative disadvantage are required in order to better address the needs of older people in the fourth age.

Set against the dominant understandings of age- and stage-based change, older people's accounts detail the problems that underlie the polarised locations of health and illness that separate the third and fourth ages. What becomes evident through this analysis is how practices create a distance from both the structured conditions and lived realities that affect late life. Older people's accounts highlight the extent to which the fourth age restructures social relations in accordance with the normative biological models based on body performance and the avoidance of its converse – decline. They also reveal how such models become integrated into socio-cultural practices, personal accounts and experiences. Dominant conceptualisations of the fourth age are also problematic in relation to the ways in which they fail to consider aspects such as disadvantage or diversity that may more profoundly affect continuity and change across the lifecourse. Already located in a liminal space between personal desires and socio-cultural interpretations and expectations, locations such as impairment, disadvantage and diversity may offer opportunities or present additional challenges that affect continuity and change across the lifecourse, yet they receive little to no attention in discussions of the fourth age. Older people's accounts demonstrate the need to reconsider socio-cultural relations and practices concerning impairment in advanced age, including practices in critical gerontology.

The differences between academic, professional and older people's interpretations of impairment in advanced age demonstrate the need for a perspective that takes into account the intersections of social or 'age relations', cultural practices (including those of organisations and agencies that categorise their bodies and needs) and lived experiences. The emotional significance of the transitions that take place at the intersections of advanced age and impairment require consideration, including how these may be experienced differently depending on social location. Older people's insights suggest the need for a model that is capable of recognising the challenges associated with this period. Such a stance, derived from the experiences of older people, strongly counters the dominant tendencies focused on functional impairment. It draws attention to the symbolic associations between the fourth age and mortality that give rise to emotional issues, as well as the ways in which underlying assumptions – whether stated or not – operate in scholarship and planning. A reconsideration of the fourth age would create an opportunity to examine this period in its own right. It would go beyond understanding of the fourth age as a practical concern – as is often articulated in relation to longevity and frailty – in order to explore the meanings and relationships on a symbolic, personal and social level. It would also highlight how the transition to impairment in late life, or the fourth age, occupies a significant, but liminal, space between maturation, ageing and death that is characterised by negotiating continuity and change. The four main areas that warrant more detailed investigation and better understanding are as follows:

- the way in which the fourth age is defined, and older people's interpretations of this transition;
- the powerful ways in which constructs, discourses and expectations shape policy, practice and experience by creating and maintaining different expectations for the third and fourth age;
- the social locations that cut across experiences of impairment in late life, in particular those of disadvantage and diversity, and the differences that each presents in the interpretation and response to change;
- the role that ascribed and internalised socio-cultural notions and emotional associations plays in the response to older people and the interpretation of

experience, in particular, the avoidance of the fourth age, and the associated question of public commitment for resources.

Notes

[1] In the social sciences, the distinction between the third and fourth age was articulated by Laslett in 1989.

[2] Separating groups of older people on the basis of health as a valued condition and illness as burdensome has profound implications for care practices where questions of ethics, citizenship and solidarity between generations are concerned (see Sevenhuijsen, 1998; Tronto, 1998; White and Tronto, 2004; Hollway, 2006; Grenier, 2009a).

[3] 'These anxieties include fear of death; fear of senile decay related to Alzheimer's disease; fear of life-destroying, bed-enforcing diseases such as cancer; fear of less life-threatening but grave afflictions which come mainly to the old (blindness, deafness, lameness, incontinence and so forth); fear of physical disability, mental decline or illness and the dependence they bring with them; fear of losing beauty, attractiveness, fertility and potency; fear of the inability to recall names, events, people and experiences; fear of losing keenness/senses and enjoyment; fear of losing mobility and being confined indoors as well as having less choice in terms of places to go and things to do; fear of losing earning power because of age; fear of falling status, public or private—political, social as well as economic—solely as a result of chronological age' (Laslett, 1989, p 14).

TEN

Future directions

This chapter draws together arguments used throughout the book to provide ideas for further development in the study of ageing and late life. It restates how current dominant age- and stage-based understandings of transitions overlook contemporary interpretations of ageing and late life. As demonstrated throughout the book, dominant models are often unable to address the tensions between structured and lived experience, the 'fit' between suggested models and subjective interpretations, the fluid nature of continuity and change, the experiences of older people at diverse social locations, and the intersection between advanced age and impairment. This concluding chapter reiterates the diversity and fluidity that can exist within and between structures, expectations and experiences and offers critical questions that have emerged throughout the reviews of academic sources, social and cultural discourses, and personal and social understandings of lifecourse transitions. It points to the fluid processes of continuity and change that may be experienced differently as a result of social location, life history, relationships and subjective interpretations over the lifecourse. It draws on the insights of older people from diverse social locations to reconsider transitions, challenge dominant perspectives and suggest new ways to approach ageing and late life in a contemporary context.

Contributions

Challenging fixed normative patterns

This book has confronted the normative patterns of the lifecourse as articulated in relation to late life. Exploring the intersections of policy, organisational practice and lived experience, it draws attention to the problems created in approaching ageing through a set of normative patterns or binary assumptions. Dominant socio-cultural constructions and expectations of ageing are set against interpretations of ageing from the academic literature and older people's accounts, resulting in the identification of contradictions and tensions that exist between normative constructs and lived experience. Consider, for example, how the new success-based models sustain the polarisation of health and illness in late life, thereby failing to provide a framework other than decline to impaired older people in the fourth age. The frame of transition has been incredibly illustrative in this regard. It has shown that while ideas and frameworks organised around change in age are deeply established in the mindsets of individuals and societies, and reinforced through policies, practices and socio-cultural constructs, the rigid boundaries suggested in understandings of transitions do not always correspond with older people's experience.

Older people's interpretations of dominant constructs and the ways they use these notions as frameworks to negotiate their experiences vary from case to case. The analysis of fixed constructs compared with narrated accounts points to power differentials that restructure relationships across the lifecourse, shaping expectations and experiences of late life. As such, experiences of ageing cannot be neatly constructed into age- or stage- related boundaries. Even the most 'typified' ideas that correspond with notions of the third and fourth age contain variation and challenges where transitions and late life are concerned. The critical analysis carried out through this book reveals how notions of transition used to structure and make sense of life experience must be considered as contested models rather than fixed and normative standards for ageing. Specifically, it has demonstrated how understandings of transitions as fixed structures, specific role types or psychological processes have failed to address fluid movement between transitions; intersecting social, cultural and psychological processes; and divergent pathways taken across the period of one's life. Take, for example, the non-linear paths that older people may choose, the ways in which experiences such as immigration may be more meaningful than age, and the extent to which linked lives can influence subjective interpretation.

The examples outlined throughout the book reveal that in many cases, older people live and exist between fixed points and processes in ageing and late life, rather than within the fixed age- and stage-based structures of the lifecourse. Older people appear to take pathways and trajectories that simultaneously represent both continuity and change rather than living in space characterised by movement between defined periods. This is not to say that an understanding of the dominant frameworks of ageing and late life is not valid. Such frameworks provide crucial signposts for understanding social responses to age, and how older people make meaning of their experiences in relation to late life. A distinction must be made, however, between such constructs as representations of older people's lives and the consideration of such models as fixed frameworks that set expectations and interpretations of ageing and late life. A critical perspective on transition in late life allows the space to consider how older people may draw on frameworks to negotiate or position themselves and their experiences in a particular social and cultural context.

Reconsidering process and pathways of continuity and change

The detailed exploration of transitions as articulated at the sites of policy, academic research and lived experience highlights the relevance of adapting nuanced views of continuity and change across the lifecourse. As outlined in early sociological work on transitions (Hareven and Adams, 1982; Cohen, 1987), the concepts of continuity and change hold enormous potential for the study of the lifecourse – a potential that has yet to be realised, especially where questions of late life are concerned. In this study continuity and change were themes that resonated in many ways with the lived experiences of older people. Many of the standard types of transition such as retirement and widowhood were discussed in the interviews with older people. At the same time, the older people interviewed tended to have many more transitions than those listed in standard models. Their accounts pointed to experiences outside the dominant models and age-based expectations of late life, and included, as discussed in Chapter Seven, transitions that occurred in the lives and experiences of others, and meanings incurred in particular social and cultural contexts and as a result of diverse lifecourse trajectories that differed from existing developmental models. The accounts demonstrated that, although the forms of transition may be contested, the desire for continuity featured prominently in their accounts.

Older people's accounts demonstrated the importance of integrating process, flexibility and diverse pathways into academic and policy understandings of transitions in late life. What becomes clear is that older people approach and understand transitions in unique ways that may be difficult to predict. Two specific issues addressed in the accounts point to the importance of integrating diverse pathways with subjective interpretations. The first is the question of powerful transitions that are used to frame life experience, such as identity claims or experiences of immigration. These locations provide examples that challenge the primacy assigned to age, suggesting that the frames by which people make sense of their experiences in late life may only be partially related to age. Second is the process of making meaning of the personal frames used to construct the lifecourse. For example, the accounts reveal that it is not impairment itself that is the problem, as classifications may lead one to believe, but, as demonstrated in Chapter Nine, the significance that this impairment comes to represent in one's life. From this perspective, it is not surprising that responses differ. Where one person with severe impairment may adjust to change in a manner that corresponds with notions of coping, another person with less impairment may cope less well. In such examples, what seems to play a key role is the locus of control, or choice, and the ease with which this may be integrated into the view of self, identity and/or ongoing activity.

Older people's challenges to the accepted age- and stage-based transitions raise a number of questions where models of approaching and explaining ageing and late life are concerned. These include:

- How are continuity and change experienced at a local level?
- How can diverse social locations such as those associated with strong identity claims, lifestyles or cumulative disadvantage alter understandings of continuity and change across the lifecourse?
- How might strengths and resilience developed in earlier periods of crisis or transition help older people in late life?
- How can motivations and/or choice alter the subjective interpretation of change in late life?

- Is choice or control central to a positive interpretation of late life?
- How might such expectations of control be problematic where impairment and the body are concerned?

Although choice, identity and lifestyle are currently promoted in the academic and policy literature as the means by which older people may negotiate late-life transitions, such interpretations may be limited where diversity and impairment are concerned. As explored in Chapters Six and Eight, diversity seems to alter the types of transition experienced and the subjective interpretations of these transitions across the lifecourse and in late life. While making choices about care, identity and lifestyle may provide the means for positioning oneself in relation to socio-cultural expectations, drawing on such methods can be problematic on a number of levels. First, they are often consumer-based choices that may only be available to those with the financial resources. Second, they are rational choices that imply full cognition and decision-making capacity that may not account for mental decline or cognitive impairment. Third, such choices tend to rely on a denial of the body and the difficult processes of change that can accompany ageing. In making such choices, older people may inadvertently reinforce the ongoing distinction drawn between health and illness in late life. Fourth, older people suggest that there is a threshold at which point it is no longer possible to draw on strategies of negotiation. At a particular juncture, efforts to make choices or draw on particular lifestyles are interpreted as inauthentic or deceitful. For example, older people discuss the point where they can no longer 'pass' as young, healthy or active (see Grenier and Hanley, 2007). There is a moment when they and those around them realise that the fourth age and other such socio-cultural assumptions are upon them, and are being used to classify their experiences. For such reasons, the claims of drawing on choice, identity, and lifestyle may be limited, especially in relation to locations that become permanent. These include structured locations such as 'race', lifecourse markers such as poverty in early life and impairment in late life. It is for this reason that understandings of the boundaries of experience and the liminality of ageing and transition require greater attention.

Innovative concepts

Process, fluidity and time

Older people's accounts draw attention to the importance of process in the experience of transitions and late life. Where traditional understandings of transition and the lifecourse have tended to assume a structured understanding based on age- and stage-based divisions, older people's accounts draw attention to continuity and change as processes that occur throughout the lifecourse. They outline the fluidity or difficulty with which older people move through life. Drawing on their insights, the lifecourse can be reinterpreted in relation to processes, turning points and significant experiences. Such insights offer a fresh perspective that could bring the suggested models for ageing and transition in late life closer to the lived experiences and subjective interpretations of older people. Models that focus on social location, accumulation of experience and subjective meaning, for example, can provide ways of addressing contemporary challenges such as variations related to disadvantage, diversity and the intersections between impairment and advanced age.

The themes discussed throughout the book centre on continuity, change and transition in late life. While concepts such as on- and off-time were central to early understandings of transitions in social gerontology (Neugarten, 1969, 1976, 1979a), the critical analysis of time has received less attention where transitions and late life are concerned. One of the problems is that much of the literature on transitions has been concerned with practical measurements of movement between ages, stages and/or coping. Dominant understandings have approached change in relation to timing rather than the philosophical and conceptual questions on how time and timing can inform subjective interpretations and pathways of experience, for example (see Baars, 1997). Although the literature on time tends to remain separate from that on transition, older people's accounts demonstrate that the questions of time and timing are extremely pertinent to this analysis. Discussions of time are becoming more central in the humanities and in narrative interpretations of ageing (Carr, 1986; Ricoeur, 1988; Gubrium and Holstein, 2000; Holstein and Gubrium, 2000; Randall and Kenyon, 2004), and thus seem integral to understanding transitions as fluid and dynamic processes. The notion of time may be approached in a variety of different ways: it may denote the timing of events, the significance of the timing of events, the social–historical time within which interpretations takes place, or an overall challenge to the linear and productive aspects that are assumed in policy and practice discourses for older people. Further elaboration of the concept of time may provide a link with notions such as 'liminality' or being 'between' that were discussed throughout the book. The concept of time, therefore, while left implicit in the analysis, holds great potential for the reconsideration of transitions as they apply to ageing and late life. Focusing on time may bring about fresh insights to the relationship between subjective assessments of time, continuity and change that more closely align with older people's experiences (see Baars, 2010).

Liminality and being between

The findings throughout this book have pointed to the increased relevance of considering late-life transitions as processes that occur in liminal spaces. As argued throughout, older peoples experiences are located within and between policy guidelines, socio-cultural discourses and organisational practices. Yet, considering these experiences of continuity and change as liminal spaces adds a layer of complexity whereby older people may be depicted as existing between ideas and expectations. A focus on liminality shifts the emphasis from experiences made meaningful in the age- or stage-based period to a more fluid process of creating meaning that takes place across the lifecourse and in relation to social and cultural contexts. While an analysis focused on liminality is appealing in its fluidity and attention to what occurs at the boundaries of local-level processes, the suggestion of being located in liminal cultural spaces requires greater appraisal. The idea of liminality can itself carry both negative and positive connotations. Understood as a temporary space in-between, as is the most popular interpretation in anthropology, liminality can represent a time of reflection, meaning and change on a social and cultural level (Hockey and James, 2003). Similarly, read from a critical or post-colonial perspective, liminal spaces may be used to negotiate terrain, hybrid identities and a powerful reformulation of self, identity and culture (Bhabha, 1994). Liminality can represent a space in which redefinition can occur – a space with potential for reinvention.

Yet, at the same time, interpretations of liminality can position the individual or group outside dominant culture, with the temporary space representing a negative or excluded location. Where liminal spaces become permanent, as could be the case in relation to older people, this liminal status may become problematic in relation to marginalisation. The challenge is that while liminality is currently being advanced as a conceptual means from which to understand older people's experiences, on a practical level, it may relegate older people to a marginal space, thereby creating problems where intergenerational conflict or resources are concerned. In this sense, liminality may perpetuate negative age relations between youthful healthy groups, and older people who are ill or in decline (see Grenier, 2009a,b). The varying interpretations and possibilities that exist in drawing on the concept of liminality thus raise questions in relation to older people. How might drawing on interpretations of liminality contribute to positive change for older people, and how might it reinforce problematic separations and boundaries that already exist between youth and age or health and illness in late life? While these questions are recognised as valid, liminality and the ideas of being in-between do offer a useful means from which to interpret older people's locations in a socio-cultural context. If linked with psychological understandings, liminality may also offer the potential to explore what it is actually like to live in such liminal spaces. A direction forward is thus to consider liminality from a critical perspective that draws on multidisciplinary approaches linking structures, practices and subjective interpretations of late life.

Illness, impairment and decline in advanced age

Older people's accounts highlight how the transition of the fourth age must be considered from a social perspective. As discussed in Chapter Nine, the fourth age presents numerous challenges for critical gerontologists and older people alike. When linked with socio-cultural discourses and public policy, older people's narratives reveal that the fourth age is a contested construct as well as a material reality. At the same time as older people position themselves against notions of decline, they speak to how impairment, especially when it becomes permanent, is a significant experience. Although the fourth age is taken for granted in dominant understandings and organisational practices as an experience of illness or impairment in late life, older people's accounts demonstrate the complexity of this construct and experience. The accounts reveal that although the fourth age is linked with the body, it is more than simply the acquisition of impairment in advanced age. They reveal how impairment in late life, and the accompanying socio-cultural assumptions play a major role in the subjective interpretation of experience and the overall reflection on one's life. First, older people's discussions reference a threshold where experiences of impairment became more permanent and/or more significant in later life. That is, they speak to a moment where change becomes more permanent than temporary and provides a contrast with experiences in earlier parts of the lifecourse. Second, older people's accounts refer to this time of change as a significant transition, albeit one that can only be identified in retrospect. Older people who are not yet in this period can consider what it might be like, particularly if they fear becoming dependent on others, but only those already located within can 'know' or speak of what it means in relation to their lives and identities. It is in this sense that the descriptions in older people's accounts differ widely from the established discourse. Older people's accounts highlight how transition to the fourth age carries an emotional significance that defines the period, and possibly the distance that is created from it in earlier periods of the lifecourse. Emotions ranging from fear to loss, and the distinction between health and decline in late life, would seem to have implications for social relations, particularly where questions of intergenerational support and public care provision are concerned (see Grenier 2009a).

Older people's accounts suggest that the fourth age be considered as both a socio-cultural construct and a lived experience. Here, a critical approach focused on policies and organisational practices has much to offer, especially as the construct of the fourth age becomes increasingly polarised from the discourses of success and productivity in late life. Yet, as services focus on those who need care, questions must be raised about the differential messages and targets that are established according to health or illness in late life. This includes the extent to which constructs reinforce notions of dependency as separate from independence, and whether the services available for this group adequately meet older people's needs. The strongest theme emanating from the interviews with older people is the importance of making meaning of change that is characterised by illness or impairment in late life. Here, the interdisciplinary links between social processes, cultural contexts and personal interpretations are emphasised. Areas that warrant further attention include the intersection between physical health, embodiment, and the interpretation of experience, making meaning of illness or impairment in late life, the connections between emotional processes and social relationships, and questions of integrating change into older people's lifelong identities. With much of social gerontology focused until now on what has been referred to as third-age issues, older people's accounts, especially when considered in relation to policy and practice, demonstrate the urgency of reconsidering the significance of the fourth age. Furthermore, they demonstrate how questions of impairment and age must also be considered as they intersect with cumulative disadvantage and diversity. Approaching the fourth age as a major life transition from a critical perspective is one way to better understand the experiences that affect older people's sense of continuity and change in late life.

Reconsidering transition in research and policy

Bridging scholarship: from multidisciplinary to interdisciplinary work

By exploring transitions from varying perspectives, this book demonstrates how moving from multiple and separate disciplinary approaches to an interdisciplinary perspective could enhance current understandings of ageing and late life. As demonstrated in Chapter Three, on their own, each of the academic approaches to the study of transitions has strengths and limitations where the study of transitions in late life is concerned. Each isolates changes in relation to structures, roles and developmental tasks – changes that in the lives and accounts of older people are intricately linked. As such, drawing on the insights of these disciplines in unison could provide the means to link social and cultural understandings of continuity and change in late life with psychological and emotional processes of meaning making. Such interdisciplinary linkages foster understandings of fluid movement between notions currently constructed as age- and stage-based – for instance, questions that arise in relation to the fourth age. An interdisciplinary approach could, for example, provide pathways from which to explore the emotional processes that accompany physical impairment or role changes in late life. Rather than looking to the extreme end points of the transition, exploration of events that exist within and between the boundaries may more accurately capture how older people experience late life. Topics that could be explored from such a perspective include how transitions may be understood as celebrations, met with ambivalence, or represent a disruption in the identity or self. Although gerontology has tended to cross disciplinary boundaries, explorations focusing on transition, such as this book, demonstrate the importance of fostering links between social studies in anthropology, sociology and psychology as they relate to the study of age.

Linking policy, practice and experience

The analysis of transition carried out in this book demonstrates the relevance of policy as a site from which to more carefully consider the intersection of structure, practice and experience. This approach expands on a long-standing tradition in critical gerontology discussed in Chapter Two, whereby culture and interpretation are added to the framework within which late life can be understood. Developing this perspective at the intersection of policy and experience as outlined in Chapter Four has helped to identify the connections between structures, socio-cultural discourses and model expectations for late life, in combination with biographies of lived experience. As such, the discourses and shapes of ageing that are promoted in public policy can be analysed as a type of institution that influences interpretations and responses to late life, with older people's experiences best understood within such complex locations.

An approach linking policy, practice and experience calls into question the taken-for-granted constructs and assumptions that have come to dominate knowledge, research and practice concerning older people. In particular, this approach draws attention to dominant interpretations of age, power differentials, and 'age relations' that take place in the shifting notions of transitions in late life. On the social level, for example, analysis calls into question the dominance of success-based frameworks, and the problematic social relations that may result from a polarisation of health and illness in late life. Stemming from this, a critical analysis of policy and experience can also be used to understand how public discourse may be internalised in both the consciousness of society and the minds of individuals living within it. For example, decisions taken in relation to policy structures such as retirement or health can affect the ways in which older people are perceived as well as alter their self-perception. As such, the messages in policy are constructs that not only exist in language and discourse, but also represent powerful frameworks used to make sense of change across the lifecourse. What remains to be seen is how older people utilise competing discourses on ageing, and how these mediate public policy and personal experience (Katz, 1995). This is especially the case when powerful interpretations relating to the uncertainties or anxieties of adult ageing are concerned. For example, age-based understandings of transitions may break down when productivity and health are no longer obtainable or when diversity is considered (Calasanti, 1996; Torres, 2006a). Detailed attention to the models suggested in policy, the constructs used in practice and the subjective interpretation of experience can help to better understand how older people may position themselves in these larger discourses and practices that are organised around age.

On a practical level, exploring policy and experience at the same time provides a new point of departure from which to understand contemporary issues in ageing. Research that links suggested models in policy with socio-cultural contexts and lived experience may prove relevant to Canadian policymakers who are in the process of developing statements and guidelines for older people's services. Exploring existing debates and suggested frameworks for late life can help to situate Canada and Quebec in the larger approach to ageing. On a practical level, the narratives examined in this book have challenged existing models and suggested pathways for exploration. They have prompted a reconsideration of the way ageing and transitions are organised and responded to in society, as well as the everyday relationships and practices with older people. Rather than creating policy as fixed accounts, the older people in this study have emphasised the connections that exist between social and emotional processes, and the importance of drawing on 'acceptable' models in order to negotiate the challenges of ageing, whether physical, psychological or social. The accounts here, for example, have exposed as problematic the growing trend in defining late life merely as a time of health, productivity and success. They have also drawn attention to the problem of separating late life from understandings of the lifecourse. Practical directions for policy consideration thus include the timing of social benefits across the lifecourse and in old age; the degree to which policies create, sustain or resist dominant interpretations of age; the extent of overlap between policy visions and personal experiences; the challenge of recognising and responding to diverse social locations and experiences; and the possible mounting conflict between generations.

Theoretical practice: what does this mean for critical gerontology?

This book's exploration of transitions highlights the importance of advancing critical perspectives that reconsider knowledge and practice in relation to late life. The analysis renews the mandate to render taken-for-granted processes and assumptions visible, to better understand how we approach critical practice, and to challenge or change practices and conditions (Bernard and Scharf, 2007; Phillipson and Walker, 1987). By adopting a critical approach, the book has highlighted the dominant assumptions and expectations that operate in relation to transitions, ageing and late life. The book's focus on the intersection between policy discourse, socio-cultural discourses and older people's accounts has brought tensions and contradictions to the surface. It has demonstrated how a critical perspective on gerontology can contribute to better understanding the links between normative classifications such as those organised along the lines of the third and fourth age, the socio-cultural interpretations and expectations related to productivity and decline, and the subjective interpretations of these experiences. In particular, the book's critical approach to the study of transition and the lifecourse has made apparent the challenges that exist in relation to linking structures, processes and experiences, especially where the unexplored issues such as diversity and the fourth age are concerned.

What becomes clear from this analysis is how the strands of critical gerontology that have focused on either structures or experience have greater potential when combined. Developing a more fluid account of transitions in late life, however, requires that studies of ageing on the macro level be merged with subjective experiences at the micro level. On an academic level, drawing on insights of critical gerontology from both structural and humanistic strands could result in an analysis that better addresses the issues older people experience in late life, especially where sites of public policy and practice are concerned. This is not simply a case of additive models, but of a more substantial effort that addresses what occurs at the intersection of society, culture and experience. Linking the long-standing, more structural, understandings of disadvantage in critical gerontology with interpretive or constructivist strands may provide a more comprehensive way of thinking within and across age. A focus on policy models and expectations may provide a locale from which to test and strengthen this approach. For example, more detailed attention to policy and practice could reveal the clash between models, expectations and experiences, and more accurately depict how structures and practices can shape older people's experiences. This is especially the case in relation to understanding how structures of disadvantage in late life may unfold on an everyday level.

Understandings of policy, practice and lived experience have long been considered central to approaches that highlight the political economy of ageing, to critical gerontology (Townsend, 1981; Phillipson, 1982, 1998; Estes, 1991, 1993; Walker, 2006a) and to biographical experiences of ageing (Gubium and Holstein, 1998, 2000; Bornat, 1999; Neysmith et al, 2005). Yet, bringing these strands together in a clear manner could help to address the shortcomings of each, and the pitfalls that exist in contemporary approaches to the study of ageing and the lifecourse. Linking these approaches could help to move beyond the binary treatment of structure or experience, or early and late life, that have so far characterised the study of ageing. As such, a critical approach could contextualise ageing and late life as part of the overall lifecourse, with late life becoming an integral and normal part of continuity and change. While this could be a difficult challenge on a conceptual level, the practical questions raised by older people located at the intersections of structures and experiences suggest that it is relevant. At the same time, the accounts here speak to the importance of understanding ageing within a socio-cultural context where ageing and decline are devalued. Several challenges remain in addressing ageing and transitions in contemporary conditions. Linking these levels through an expanded critical approach provides a first step in addressing the challenges relating to non-normative models of transition in late life, diversity and the acquisition of impairment in late life.

Future directions

Two process-based directions emerge from the reconsideration of transition as it relates to late life. The first is that late-life transitions be reconsidered from a multidisciplinary perspective that takes account of experiences and process-based pathways throughout the lifecourse. As attempted in this research, such an endeavour would turn more closely to the accounts of older people in order to better understand the relationships between structures and lived experiences. It would take account of the turning points and trajectories that older people identify in their lives, contrasting these with the taken-for-granted stocks of knowledge that currently surround age- and stage-based transitions. This type of analysis involves considering experiences and identities that are deemed significant and can characterise, change or alter pathways. Further, it would focus on the typifications that exist, how such expectations are enacted in various forms of practice, and how older people position themselves or negotiate their experiences as a result. This includes direct attention to the subjective interpretations and the emotional processes that exist within and between the objective and standard expectations of age. In particular, the meanings that constructs have in the lives of older people, and inquiry into the rationale or motivations for choices and actions, including those of drawing on identity or adjustment. Linking the social, cultural, psychological and personal processes that occur in relation to continuity and change could inform policy and practice for ageing and late life. The challenge at this point is whether governments and policymakers are open to hearing such detailed accounts that may profoundly challenge professional and standard accepted understandings of transition in late life.

Second, while age remains an important aspect of experience, more detailed attention to how diverse social locations may alter the organisation or interpretation of experience across the lifecourse is required. Older people's accounts challenge the types of location that are considered to link or divide late-life experience. They raise questions about whether the taken-for-granted understandings of age are outdated, and whether they currently speak to contemporary experience or ever did so. The dominant approaches have overlooked fluidity, timing, development in late life and social locations. Taken together, the accounts in this book point to aspects of late life that have not been adequately addressed in contemporary research. As such, the insights of older people seriously challenge practices related to ageing and transition in late life. However, in pointing to fluidity, process and meaning across the lifecourse, they highlight that while commonalities do exist between dominant guidelines for ageing and late life, and older people's experiences, they may be organised differently than previously understood. Once again, the accounts draw attention to the margins and boundaries that exist between older people's experiences and policy discourses, and the varying ways these are negotiated through age, experience and multiple forms of difference. In particular, they point to the importance of asking questions about subjective interpretations and the meanings made in relation to cultural constructs, social relations and practices of age.

Emerging questions

By reconsidering transition and by examining the ways in which older people challenge models for growing old, this book has raised various issues for further deliberation. Some of the more pressing questions are as follows:

- Were they not organised around age, how might transitions and the study of late life be differentially approached?
- How might alternative forms of transition, such as those explored in Chapter Seven, be used to approach continuity and change across the lifecourse?
- How can transitions be understood in a context whereby ageing is accompanied by contradictory expectations of cumulative disadvantage, a paucity of social resources, and slow decline on one hand and healthy successful ageing on the other? Can a multidisciplinary perspective on transition redress this imbalance?
- Can existing theoretical models adequately address the contemporary issues and challenges raised in this analysis? Will linking the analysis of structure and experience more adequately address contemporary issues in ageing?

- What do older people's insights mean for social policy and practice? Can such understandings be used to reshape policy and practice in ways that better correspond with older people's experiences? How can this be achieved without denying or neglecting difficult issues of ageing such as impairment?
- How can diversity and social locations be integrated into understandings of transitions in late life? Furthermore, what approaches can be used to better understand the intersections between diversity, cumulative disadvantage and impairment in late life?

Conclusion

This book's reconsideration of transitions as they relate to ageing and late life reveals that the field of gerontology is becoming aware of the tensions and contradictions that exist between dominant and alternative interpretations of late life. A focus on ongoing debates in various contexts highlights the fact that the tools for unlocking taken-for-granted assumptions and practices already exist. The challenge is in finding the means to dislodge them from their deeply entrenched locations, in order to create the space for a complex analysis of policy, practice and experience. Focusing on the spaces in-between, including diversity, advanced age and cumulative disadvantage, may represent a new pathway into understanding transitions across the lifecourse. The ideas expressed in the critical perspectives of ageing and the lifecourse become important channels from which to challenge dominant age- and stage-based understandings of transition. An analysis of transitions in late life requires a perspective that views the lifecourse, policies, practices and experiences as constructed and interpreted in interwoven ways. That is, it requires a reconsideration of the binary tension that exists between the lifecourse as a whole and specific periods in late life, as well as an understanding of the relationship between the two. The major question to be addressed is how these experiences are mediated through social structures, socio-cultural practices and emotional experiences that take on significance in late life. Above all, a fresh approach such as this requires more detailed attention to the distinction that exists between typified constructions, expected models and older people's experiences of ageing and late life.

References

Achenbaum, A.W. (1995) *Crossing frontiers: Gerontology emerges as a science*, New York, NY: Cambridge University Press.

Agence de développement de réseau locaux de services de santé et de services sociaux (2004) *Portrait de la population: Centre de santé et de services sociaux de Réne-Cassin et NDG/Montreal-Ouest*, Montréal: Centre de santé et de services sociaux de René-Cassin et NDG Montréal-Ouest (CSSS)

Agence de la santé et des services sociaux de Montréal (2006) *Portrait socio-sanitaire de la population CSSS Cavendish: perte d'autonomie liée au vieillissement*, Montréal: Centre de santé et de services sociaux de René-Cassin et NDG Montréal-Ouest (CSSS).

Andersson, L. (2002) *Cultural gerontology*, Westport, CT: Auburn House.

Anthias, F. and Yuval-Davis, N. (1992) *Racialized boundaries: race, nation, gender, colour and class and the anti-racist struggle*, London: Routledge.

Antonnuci, T., Jackson, J.S. and Biggs, S. (2007) 'Intergenerational relations: theory, research and policy', *Journal of Social Issues*, vol 63, no 4, pp 679-93.

Antonucci, T., Sherman, A.M. and Akiyama, H. (1996) 'Social network, support, and integration', in J.E. Birren (ed) *Encyclopedia of gerontology: Age, aging and the aged*, San Diego, CA: Academic Press, pp 505-15.

Arber, S. and Evandrou, M. (eds) (1993) *Ageing, independence and the life course*, London: Jessica Kingsley.

Arber, S. and Ginn, J. (eds) (1995) *Connecting gender and ageing: A sociological approach*, Buckingham: Open University Press.

Ashcroft, B., Griffiths, G. and Tiffin, H. (2007) *Post-colonial studies: The key concepts*, New York, NY: Routledge, pp 117-18.

Atchley, R.C. (1989) 'A continuity theory of normal aging', *The Gerontologist*, vol 29, no 2, pp 183-90.

Atchley, R.C. (1999) *Continuity and adaptation in aging: Creating positive experiences*, Baltimore, MD: Johns Hopkins University Press.

Atchley, R.C. (2000) *Social forces and aging*, Belmont, CA: Wadsworth.

Baars, J. (1997) 'Concepts of time and narrative temporality in the study of aging', *Journal of Aging Studies*, vol 11, no 4, pp 283-95.

Baars, J. (2010) 'Time and aging: enduring and emerging issues', in D. Dannefer and C. Phillipson (eds) *International handbook of social gerontology*, New York, NY/London: Sage Publications.

Baars, J., Dannefer, D., Phillipson, C. and Walker, A. (eds) (2006) *Aging, globalization, and inequality: The new critical gerontology*, Amityville, NY: Baywood.

Baker, T.A. and Wang, C.C. (2006) 'Photovoice: use of a participatory action research method to explore the chronic pain experience in older adults', *Qualitative Health Research*, vol 16, no 10, pp 1405-13.

Bakhtin, M. (1978) *The formal method in literary scholarship: A critical introduction to sociological poetics*, Baltimore, MD: John Hopkins University Press.

Bal, M. (2004) *Introduction to the theory of narrative,* Toronto: University of Toronto Press.

Baltes, P. (1987a) 'Theoretical propositions of life-span developmental psychology: on the dynamics between growth and decline', *Developmental Psychology,* vol 23, pp 611-26.

Baltes, P. (1987b). 'Developmental psychology', in G.L. Maddox (ed) *The Encyclopedia of aging,* New York, NY: Springer, pp 170-5.

Baltes, P. (1997) 'On the incomplete architecture of human ontogeny: selection, optimization, and compensation as foundation of developmental theory', *American Psychologist,* vol 52, pp 366-80.

Baltes, P. (2003) 'On the incomplete architecture of human ontogeny: selection, optimization, and compensation as foundation of developmental theory', in U.M. Staudinger and U. Lindenberger (eds) *Understanding human development: Dialogues with lifespan psychology,* Boston, MA: Kluwer, pp 17-43.

Baltes, P. and Baltes, M.M. (1990) 'Psychological perspectives on successful aging: the model of selective optimization with compensation', in P.B. Baltes and M.M. Baltes (eds) *Successful aging: Perspectives from the behavioural sciences,* Cambridge: Cambridge University Press, pp 1-34.

Baltes, P. and Smith, J. (1999) 'Multilevel and systemic analyses of old age: theoretical and empirical evidence for a fourth age', in V.L. Bengston and K.W. Schaie (eds) *Handbook of theories of aging,* New York, NY: Springer, pp 153-73.

Baltes, P. and Smith, J. (2002) 'New frontiers in the future of aging: from successful aging of the young old to the dilemmas of the fourth age', Keynote lecture at the Valencia Forum, International Scientific Congress, Valencia, Spain, 1-4 April.

Baltes, P. and Smith, J. (2003) 'New frontiers in the future of aging: from successful aging of the young old to the dilemmas of the fourth age', *Gerontology,* vol 49, pp 123-35.

Baltes, P., Reese, H. and Lipsitt, L (1980) 'Lifespan developmental psychology', *Annual Review of Psychology,* vol 31, pp 65-110.

Baltes, P., Staudinger U.M. and Lindenberger, U. (1999) 'Lifespan psychology: theory and application to social functioning', *Annual Review of Psychology,* vol 50, pp 471-507.

Bateson, G. (1972) *Steps to an ecology of mind: A revolutionary approach to man's understanding of himself,* New York, NY: Ballantine Books.

Baumann, G. (1992) 'Ritual implicates "others": rereading Durkheim in a plural society', in D. de Coppet (ed) *Understanding rituals,* London: Routledge, pp 97-116.

Beck, U. (1992) *Risk society: Towards a new modernity,* London: Sage Publications.

Becker, E. (1973) *The denial of death,* New York, NY: Free Press.

Bell, C. (1992) *Ritual theory, ritual practice,* New York, NY: Oxford University Press.

Bengston, V. L., Burgess, E.O. and Parrott, T.M. (1997) 'Theory, explanation and a third generation of theoretical development in social gerontology', *Journals of Gerontology,* vol 52, no 2, pp S72-S88.

Bengtson, V.L. Cutler, N.E. Mangen, D.J. and Marshall, V.W. (1985) 'Generations, cohorts, and relations between age groups', in R. Binstock and E. Shanas (eds) *Handbook of aging and the social sciences* (2nd edn), New York, NY: Van Nostrand Reinhold, pp 304-38.

Ben-Shlomo, Y. and Kuh, D. (2002) 'A life course approach to chronic disease epidemiology: conceptual models, empirical challenges and interdisciplinary perspectives', *International Journal of Epidemiology*, vol 31, no 2, pp 285-93.

Berger, P. and Luckman, T. (1967) *The social construction of reality*, Garden City, NY: Doubleday.

Bergman, H., Ferrucci, L., Guralnik, J., Hogan, D.B., Hummel, S., Karunanthan, S. and Wolfson, C. (2007) 'Frailty: an emerging research and clinical paradigm – issues and controversies', *Journals of Gerontology Series A*, vol 62, no 7, pp 731-7.

Bernard, M. and Scharf, T. (2007) 'Critical perspectives on ageing societies', in M. Bernard and T. Scharf (eds) *Critical perspectives on ageing societies*, Bristol: The Policy Press, pp 3-12.

Bhabha, H. (1994) *The location of culture*, New York, NY: Routledge.

Biggs, S. (1997) 'Choosing not to be old? Masks, bodies and identity management in later life', *Ageing & Society*, vol 17, no 5, pp 553-70.

Biggs, S. (1999) *The mature imagination: Dynamics of identity in midlife and beyond*, Buckingham: Open University Press.

Biggs, S. (2001) 'Toward a critical narrativity: stories of aging in contemporary social policy', *Journal of Aging Studies*, vol 15, no 4, pp 303-16.

Biggs, S. (2004a) 'Age, gender, narratives, and masquerades', *Journal of Aging Studies*, vol 18, no 1, pp 45-58.

Biggs, S. (2004b) 'New ageism: age imperialism, personal experience and ageing policy', in S.O. Daatland and S. Biggs (eds) *Ageing and diversity: Multiple pathways and cultural migrations*, Bristol: The Policy Press, pp 95-106.

Biggs, S., Lowenstein, A. and Henricks, J. (2003) *The need for theory: Critical approaches to social gerontology*, Amityville, NY: Baywood.

Biggs, S., Phillipson, C., Leach, R. and Money, A. (2007) 'Baby boomers and adult ageing: issues for social and public policy', *Quality in Ageing: Policy, Practice and Research*, vol 8, no 3, pp 32-40.

Biggs, S., Phillipson, C., Money, A. and Leach, R. (2006) 'The age-shift: observations on social policy, ageism, and the dynamics of the adult life course', *Journal of Social Work Practice: Psychotherapeutic Approaches in Health, Welfare and the Community*, vol 20, no 3, pp 239-50.

Blaikie, A. (1999) *Ageing and popular culture*, Cambridge: Cambridge University Press.

Blair, T. and Minkler, M. (2009) 'Participatory action research with older adults: key principles in practice', *The Gerontologist*, vol 49, no 5, pp 651-62.

Blakemore, K. and Boneham, M. (1994) *Age, race and ethnicity: A comparative approach*, Buckingham: Open University Press.

Blau, D.M. and Riphahn, R.T. (1999) 'Labor force transitions of older married couples in Germany', *Labour Economics*, vol 6, no 2, pp 229-52.

Bollas, C. (1989) *Forces of destiny: Psychoanalysis and the human idiom*, London: Free Association Books.

Bollas, C. (1992) *Being a character*, London: Routledge.

Bornat, J. (1999) *Biographical interviews: The link between research and practice*, London: Centre for Policy on Ageing.

Bornat, J. (2001) 'Reminiscence and oral history: parallel universes or shared endeavour?' *Ageing & Society*, vol 21, no 2, pp 219-41.

Bornat, J. (2002) 'Doing life history research', in A. Jamieson and C. Victor (eds) *Researching ageing and later life*, Buckingham: Open University Press, pp 117-34.

Bortz, W. (1993) 'The physics of frailty', *Journal of the American Geriatrics Society*, vol 41, no 9, pp 1004-8.

Bortz, W. (1997) 'An examined life', *Journal of Applied Gerontology*, vol 16, no 3, pp 263-6.

Bortz, W. (2002) 'A conceptual framework of frailty: a review', *Journals of Gerontology Series A,* vol 57, no 5, pp M283-M288.

Bowsher, J., Bramlett, M., Burnside, I. and Gueldner, S.H. (1993) 'Methodological consideration in the study of frail elderly people', *Journal of Advanced Nursing*, vol 18, no 6, pp 873-9.

Boyd, C.M., Xue, Q.L., Simpson, C.F. Guralnik, J.M. and Fried, L.P. (2005) 'Frailty, hospitalization and progression of disability in a cohort of disabled older women', *The American Journal of Medicine*, vol 118, no 11, pp 1225-31.

Brotman, S. (2003) 'The limits of multiculturalism in elder care services', *Journal of Aging Studies*, vol 17, no 2, pp 209-29.

Brotman, S. and Levy, J.J. (eds) (2008) *Intersections: Cultures, sexualités et genres*, Quebec: Presses de l'Université du Québec.

Brotman, S., Ryan, B. and Cormier, R. (2003) 'The health and social service needs of gay and lesbian elders and their families in Canada', *The Gerontologist*, vol 43, no 2, pp 192-202.

Bruner, J. (1986) *Actual minds, possible worlds*, Cambridge, MA: Harvard University Press.

Bühler, C. and Burgental, J.F.T. (1968) *The course of human life: A study of goals in the humanistic perspective*, New York, NY: Springer.

Burgess, E.W. (1950) 'Personal and social adjustment in old age', in M. Derber (ed) *The aged and society*, Champaign, IL: Industrial Relation Research Association, pp 138-56.

Burgess, E.W. (1960) *Aging in Western societies*, Chicago, IL: University of Chicago Press.

Butler, J. (1990) *Gender trouble: Feminism and the subversion of identity*, New York, NY: Routledge.

Butler, R.N. (1963) 'The life review: an interpretation of reminiscence in the aged', *Psychiatry*, vol 26, pp 65-76.

Butler, R.N. (1969) 'Age-ism: another form of bigotry', *The Gerontologist*, vol 9, no 4, pp 243-6.

Butler, R.N. (1975) *Why survive? Being old in America*, San Francisco, CA: Harper and Row.

Butler, R.N. (1980) 'Ageism: a foreword', *Journal of Social Issues*, vol 36, no 2, pp 8-11.

Bytheway, B. (1994) *Ageism*, Buckingham: Open University Press.

Bytheway, B. (2005) 'Ageism', in M.L Johnson, V.L. Bengtson, P.G. Coleman and T.B.L. Kirkwood (eds) *The Cambridge handbook of age and ageing*, Cambridge: Cambridge University Press, pp 338-45.

Bytheway, B. (2009) 'Writing about age, birthdays and the passage of time', *Ageing & Society*, vol 29, no 6, pp 883-901.

Bytheway, B. and Johnson, J. (1990) 'On defining ageism', *Critical Social Policy*, vol 10, no 20, pp 27-39.

Cain, L. (1964) 'The life course and social structure', in R. Faris (ed) *Handbook of modern sociology*, Chicago, IL: Rand McNally, pp 272-309.

Cain, L. (1967) 'Age status and generational phenomena: the new old people in contemporary America', *The Gerontologist*, vol 7, no 2, pp 83-92.

Calasanti, T. (1996) 'Incorporating diversity: meaning, levels of research, and implications for theory', *The Gerontologist*, vol 36, no 2, pp 147-56.

Calasanti, T. (2009) 'Theorizing feminist gerontology and sexuality: an intersectional approach', in V. Bengtson, M. Silverstein, N. Putney and D. Gans (eds) *Handbook of theories of aging*, New York, NY: Springer, pp 471-86.

Calasanti, T. (2010) 'Gender relations and applied research on aging', *The Gerontologist*, vol 50, no 6, pp 720-34.

Calasanti, T.M.. and King, N. (2007) 'Beware of the estrogen assault: ideals of old manhood in anti-aging advertisements', *Journal of Aging Studies*, vol 21, no 4, pp 357-68.

Calasanti, T.M. and Slevin, K.F. (eds) (2001) *Gender, social inequalities and aging*, Walnut Creek, CA: AltaMira Press.

Campbell, A.J. and Buchner, D.M. (1997) 'Unstable disability and the fluctuations of frailty', *Age and Ageing*, vol 26, no 4, pp 315-18.

Carr, D. (1986) *Time narrative and history*, Bloomington, IN: Indiana University Press.

Carstensen, L. (1992) Social and emotional patterns in adulthood: support for socioeconomic selectivity theory, *Psychology and Aging*, vol 7, no 3, pp 331-8.

Cerulo, K.A. (1997) 'Identity construction: new issues, new directions', *Annual Review of Sociology*, vol 23, pp 385-409.

Chamberlayne, P., Bornat, J. and Wengraf, T. (2000) *The turn to biographical methods in social science: Comparative issues and examples*, London: Routledge.

Chambers, P. (1984) *Older widows and the life course: Multiple narratives of hidden lives*, Burlington, VT: Ashgate Publishing.

Chambers, P. (2000) 'Widowhood in later life', in M. Bernard et al (eds) *Women ageing: Changing identities, challenging myths*, London: Routledge.

Chambon, A.S. (1999) 'Foucault's approach: making the familiar visible', in A.S. Chambon, A. Irving and L. Epstein (eds) *Reading Foucault for social work*, New York, NY: Columbia University Press.

Chapman, S.A. (2005) 'Theorizing about aging well: constructing a narrative', *Canadian Journal on Aging*, vol 24, no 1, pp 9-18.

Charmaz, K. (1999) 'Stories of suffering: subjective tales and research narratives', *Qualitative Health Research*, vol 9, no 3, pp 362-82.

Clandinin, J.D. and Connelly, M.F. (2000) *Narrative inquiry: Experience and story in qualitative research*, San Francisco, CA: Jossey-Bass.

Clark, P.G. (1996) 'Communication between provider and patient: values, biography and empowerment in clinical practice', *Ageing & Society*, vol 16, no 6, pp 747-74.

Clarke, S., Hoggett, P. and Thompson, S. (eds) (2006) *Emotion, politics and society*, Basingstoke: Palgrave Macmillan.

Clausen, J. (1986) *The life course: A sociological perspective*, Englewood Cliffs, NJ: Prentice Hall.

Clausen, J.A. (1993) *American lives*, New York, NY: Free Press.

Clausen, J.S. (1991) 'Adolescent competence and the shaping of the life course', *American Journal of Sociology*, vol 96, no 4, pp 805-42.

Cohen, G. (1987) 'Introduction: the economy, the family and the lifecourse', in G. Cohen (ed) *Social change and the life course*, London: Tavistock Publications, pp 1-32.

Cohen, L. (1994) 'Old age: cultural and critical perspectives', *Annual Review of Anthropology*, vol 23, pp 137-58.

Cole, T. (1992) *The journey of life: A cultural history of aging in America*, New York, NY: Cambridge University Press.

Cole, T., Achenbaum, W.A., Jakobi, P.L. and Kastenbaum, R. (eds) (1993) *Voices and visions of aging: Toward a critical gerontology*, New York, NY: Springer.

Cole, T. and Gadow, S. (1986) *What does it mean to grow old? Reflections from the humanities*, Durham: Duke University Press.

Cook, T. (1983) 'Cataclysm and career rebirth: the imperial military elite', in D.W. Plath (ed) *Work and lifecourse in Japan*, Albany, NY: State University New York Press, pp 135-52.

Couillard, P. (2004) 'Careful consideration: decision making in the health care system', Keynote address to the Institute for Research on Public Policy Conference, Toronto, Ontario, www.irpp.org/events/archive/nov04/couillard.pdf, accessed 6 January 2007.

Coupland, J. (2000) *Small talk: Language in social life series*, Harlow: Longman.

Coupland, N. and Coupland, J. (1988). 'Reshaping lives: constitutive identity work in geriatric medical consultations', *Text*, vol 18, no 2, pp 159-89.

Crawford, M. (1973) 'Retirement: a rite de passage', *Sociological Review*, vol 21, no 3, pp 447-61.

Crenshaw, K., Gotanda, N., Peller, G. and Thomas, K. (eds) (1995) *Critical race theory: The key writings that formed the movement*, New York, NY: New Press.

Crossley, M.L. (2000) Narrative psychology, trauma and the study of self/identity, *Theory Psychology*, vol 10, no 4, pp 527-46.

Cumming, E. and Henry, W.E. (1961) *Growing old, the process of disengagement*, New York, NY: Basic Books.

Czarniawska, B. (2004) *Narrative in social science research*, London: Sage Publications.

Danish, S., Symer, M. and Nowak, C. (1980) 'Developmental intervention: enhancing life-event processes', in P. Baltes and O. Brim (eds) *Lifespan development and behavior*, New York, NY: Academic Press.

Dannefer, D. (1988) 'What's in a name? An account of the neglect of variability in the study of aging', in J.E. Birren and V. Bengston (eds) *Emergent theories of aging*, New York, NY: Springer, pp 356-84.

Dannefer, D. (1989) 'Human action and its place in theories of aging', *Journal of Aging Studies*, vol 3, pp 1-20.

Dannefer, D. (1996) 'The social organization of diversity and the normative organization of age', *The Gerontologist*, vol 36, no 2, pp 174-7.

Dannefer, D. (2003) 'Cumulative advantage/disadvantage and the life course: cross-fertilizing age and social science theory', *Journals of Gerontology Series B*, vol 58, no 6, pp S327-S337.

Dannefer, D. and Settersen, R.A. (2010) 'The study of the life course: implications for social gerontology', in D. Dannefer and C. Phillipson *The SAGE handbook of social gerontology*, London: Sage Publications, pp 3-19.

Davenhill, R. (2004) 'Old and new: Freud and others', in S. Evans and J. Garner (eds) *Taking over the years: A handbook of dynamic psychotherapy with older adults*, New York, NY: Brunner-Routledge, pp 3-18.

Davenhill, R. (ed) (2007) *Looking into later life: A psychoanalytic approach to depression and dementia in old age*, London: Karnac.

de Coppet, D. (1992) *Understanding rituals*, London: Routledge.

Delgado, R. and Stefancic, J. (2000) *Critical race theory: The cutting edge*, Philadelphia, PA: Temple University Press.

Diehl, M. (1999) 'Self-development in adulthood and aging: the role of critical life events', in C.D. Ryff and V.W. Marshall (eds) *The self and society in aging processes*, New York, NY: Springer, pp 150-86.

Diener, E. (2009) 'The science of well-being: the collected works of Ed Diener', *Social Indicators Research Series*, vol 37, New York, NY: Springer, pp 11-58.

Dittmann-Kohli, F. (1990). The construction of meaning in old age: possibilities and constraints, *Ageing & Society*, vol 10, no 3, pp 279-94.

DWP (Department for Work and Pensions) (2005) *Opportunity age: Meeting the challenges of ageing in the 21st century*, London: DWP.

Eakin, P.J. (1999). *How our lives become stories – making selves*, Ithaca, NY: Cornell University Press.

Edmondson, R. and von Kondratowitz, H.J. (eds) (2009) *Valuing older people: A humanist approach to ageing*, Bristol: The Policy Press.

Elder, G. (1974) *Children of the great depression*, Chicago, IL: University of Chicago Press.

Elder, G. (1975) 'Age differentiation and the life course', *Annual Review of Sociology*, vol 1, pp 165-90.

Elder, G. (1978) 'Family history and the life course', in T.K. Hareven (ed) *Transitions*, New York, NY: Academic Press, pp 17-64.

Elder, G. (1982) 'Historical experiences in the later years', in T. Hareven and K.J. Adams, *Aging and life course transitions: An interdisciplinary perspective*, New York, NY: The Guilford Press, pp 75-108.

Elder, G. (1985) *Life course dynamics: Trajectories and transitions*, Ithaca, NY: Cornell University Press.

Elder, G. (1994) 'Time, human agency, and social change: perspectives on the life course', *Social Psychology Quarterly*, vol 57, no 1, pp 4-15.

Elder, G. (1998) 'The life course as developmental theory', *Child Development*, vol 69, no 1, pp 1-12.

Elder, G. and Pellerin, L.A. (1998) 'Linking history and human lives, life course as developmental theory', in J.Z. Giele and G. Elder (eds) *Methods of life course research: Qualitative and quantitative approaches*, Thousand Oaks, CA: Sage Publications, pp 264-94.

Elder, G., Johnson, M.K. and Crosnoe, R. (2003) 'The emergence and development of life course theory', in J. Mortimer and M. Shanahan (eds) *Handbook of the life course*, New York, NY: Plenum, pp 3-19.

Elder, G., Pavalko, E.K. and Hastings, T.J. (1991) 'Talent, history and the fulfilment of promise', *Psychiatry*, vol 54, no 3, pp 251-67.

Elliot, J. (2005) *Using narrative in social research: Qualitative and quantitative approaches*, London: Sage Publications.

England, P. (2008) 'The separative self: androcentric bias in neoclassical assumptions', in N.W. Biggart (ed) *Readings in economic sociology*, Oxford: Blackwell.

Erikson, E.H. (1959). *Identity and the life cycle: Selected papers*, New York, NY: International Universities Press.

Erikson, E.H. (1963) *Childhood and society* (2nd edn), New York, NY: W.W. Norton.

Erikson, E.H. (1982) *The life cycle completed*, New York, NY: WW Norton.

Erikson, J.M. (1997) ' The ninth stage', in E.H. Erikson *The life cycle completed: Extended version*, New York, NY: W.W. Norton.

Erikson, E.H. and Erikson, J.M. (1998) *The life cycle completed: extended version*, New York, NY: WW Norton.

Estes, C.L. (1979) *The aging enterprise*, San Francisco, CA: Jossey-Bass.

Estes, C.L. (1991) 'The new political economy of aging: introduction and critique', in M. Minkler and C. Estes (eds) *Critical perspectives on aging: The political and moral economy of growing old*, New York, NY: Baywood, pp 19-36.

Estes, C.L. (1993) 'The aging enterprise revisited', *The Gerontologist*, vol 33, no 3, pp 292-8.

Estes, C.L. (2001) *Social policy and aging: A critical perspective*, Thousand Oaks, CA: Sage Publications.

Estes, C.L. (2005) 'Women, ageing and inequality: a feminist perspective', in M. Johnson (ed) *Cambridge handbook of age and ageing*, Cambridge: Cambridge University Press.

Estes, C.L. (2006) 'Critical feminist perspectives, aging and social policy', in J. Baars, D. Dannefer, C. Phillipson and A. Walker (eds) *Aging, globalization, and inequality: The new critical gerontology*, Amityville, NY: Baywood.

Estes, C.L. and Binney, E. (1989) 'The biomedicalization of aging: dangers and dilemmas', *The Gerontologist*, vol 29, no 5, pp 587-96.

Estes, C.L., Biggs, S. and Phillipson, C. (2003) *Social theory, social policy and ageing: A critical introduction*, Buckingham: Open University Press.

Evans, S. and Garner, J. (eds) (2004) *Talking over the years: A handbook of dynamic psychotherapy with older adults*, Hove: Brunner-Routledge.

Fanon, F. (1965) *The wretched of the earth*, New York, NY: Grove Press.

Fanon, F. (1967 [1952]) *Black skin, white masks* (trans. R. Philcox), New York, NY: Grove Press.

Featherstone, M. and Hepworth, M. (1989) 'Ageing and old age: reflections on the postmodern lifecourse', in B. Bytheway, T. Kiel, P. Allat and A. Bryman (eds) *Becoming and being old*, London: Sage Publications.

Featherstone, M. and Hepworth, M. (1991) 'The mask of ageing and the postmodern lifecourse', in M. Featherstone, M. Hepworth and A. Wernick (eds) *Images of ageing*, London: Routledge.

Featherstone, M., and Wernick, A. (eds) (1995) *Images of aging: Cultural representations of later life*, London: Routledge.

Ferraro, K. (1984) 'Widowhood and social participation in later life', *Research on Aging*, vol 6, no 4, pp 451-68.

Ferraro, K.L. and Johnson, J. (1983) 'How women experience battering: the process of victimization', *Social Problems*, vol 30, no 3, pp 325-38.

Ferraro, K. and Kelley-Moore, J.A. (2001) 'Self-rated health and mortality among black and white adults: examining the dynamic evaluation thesis', *Journal of Gerontology: Social Sciences*, vol 56B, no 4, pp S195-S205.

Ferraro, K. and Shippee, T. (2009) 'Aging and cumulative inequality: how does inequality get under the skin', *The Gerontologist*, vol 49, no 3, pp 333-43.

Fine, M. and Gordon, S.M. (1989) 'Feminist transformations of/despite psychology', in M. Crawford and M. Genty (eds) *Gender and thought: Psychological perspectives*, New York, NY: Springer, pp 161-74.

Fishman, J., Binstock, R. and Lambrix, M. (2008) 'Anti-aging science: the emergence, maintenance, and enhancement of a discipline', *Journal of Aging Studies*, vol 22, no 4, pp 295-303.

Foner, A. (1975) 'Age in society: structure and change', *American Behavioural Scientist*, vol 19, no 2, pp 144-65.

Foner, A. and Kertzer, D. (1978) 'Transitions over the life course: lessons from age-set societies', *American Journal of Sociology*, vol 83, no 5, pp 1081-104.

Foucault, M. (1972) *The archeology of knowledge* (trans. A.M. Sheridan-Smith), London: Tavistock.

Foucault, M. (1973) *The birth of the clinic: An archeology of medical perception* (trans. A.M. Sheridan-Smith), London: Tavistock.

Foucault, M. (1979 [1995]) *Discipline and punish* (trans. A. Sheridan), New York, NY: Vintage Books.

Foucault, M. (1980a) *The history of sexuality, volume 1* (trans. R. Hurley), New York, NY: Vintage Press.

Foucault, M. (1980b) 'Two lectures' in C. Gordon (ed) *Power/knowledge: Selected writings and other interviews 1972-1977*, New York, NY: Pantheon Books, pp 78-108.

Foucault, M. (1982) 'The subject and power', in H.L. Dreyfus and P. Rabinow (eds) *Michel Foucault: Beyond structuralism and hermeneutics* (2nd edn), Chicago, IL: University of Chicago Press, pp 208-26.

Foucault, M. (1994) *The order of things*, New York, NY: Vintage Books

Fox, N.J. (1993) *Postmodernism, sociology and health*, Buckingham: Open University Press.

Frank, A. (1991) *At the will of the body: Reflections on illness*, Boston, MA: Houghton Mifflin Harcourt.

Frank, A. (1995) *The wounded storyteller: Body, illness and ethics*, Chicago, IL: University of Chicago Press.

Fraser, N. (1987) 'Women, welfare and the politics of need interpretation', *Hypatia*, vol 2, no 1, pp 103-21.

Fraser, N. (1989) 'Talking about needs: interpretive contests as political conflicts in welfare-state societies', *Ethics*, vol 99, no 2, pp 219-313.

Fraser, N. (1997) *Justice interruptus: Critical reflections on the 'postsocialist' condition*, New York, NY: Routledge.

Fraser, N. and Gordon, L. (1994) 'A geneology of dependency: tracing a keyword of the U.S. welfare state', Signs: *Journal of Women in Culture and Society*, vol 19, no 2, pp 309-35.

Freud, S. (1910) 'The origin and development of psychoanalysis', *American Journal of Psychology*, vol 21, no 2, pp 181-218.

Fried, L. and Walston, J. (1999) 'Frailty and the failure to thrive', in W. Hazzard (ed) *Principles of geriatric medicine and gerontology*, New York, NY: McGraw Hill, pp 1387-402.

Fried, L., Tangen, C., Walston, J., Newman, A., Hirsch, C., Gottdiener, J., Seeman, T., Tracy, R., Kop, W., Burke, G. and McBurnie, M. (2001) 'Frailty in older adults: evidence for a phenotype', *Journals of Gerontology Series A*, vol 56, no 3, pp M146-M157.

Fries, J.F. (1980) 'Aging, natural death and the compression of morbidity', *New England Journal of Medicine*, vol 303, no 3, pp 130-5.

Fries, J.F. and Crapo, L.M. (1981) *Vitality and aging: Implications of the rectangular curve*, San Francisco, CA: W.H. Freeman.

Froggett, L., and Chamberlayne, P. (2004) 'Narratives of social enterprise: from biography to practice and policy critique', *Qualitative Social Work*, vol 3, no 1, pp 61-77.

Froggatt, K. (2001) 'Life and death in English nursing homes: sequestration or transition?', *Ageing & Society*, vol 21, no 3, pp 319-22.

Frosh, S. and Baraitser, L. (2008) 'Psychoanalysis and psychosocial studies', *Psychoanalysis, Culture & Society*, vol 13, no 4, pp 346-66.

Gadow, S. (1983) 'Frailty and strength: the dialectic in aging', *The Gerontologist*, vol 23, no 2, pp 144-7.

Gadow, S. (1991) 'Recovering the body in aging', in N. Jecker (ed) *Aging and ethics: Philosophical problems in gerontology*, Clifton, NJ: Humana Press, pp 113-20.

Gadow, S. (1996) 'Aging as death rehearsal: the oppressiveness of reason', *The Journal of Clinical Ethics*, vol 7, no 1, pp 35-40.

Gee, E.M. and Gutman, G.M. (2000) *The overselling of population aging: Apocalyptic demography, intergenerational challenges, and social policy*, New York, NY: Oxford University Press.

George, L.K. (1993) 'Sociological perspectives on life transitions', *Annual Review of Sociology*, vol 19, pp 353-73.

George, L.K. (1996) 'Missing links: the case for a social psychology of the life course', *The Gerontologist*, vol 36, no 2, pp 248-55.

George, L.K. (2005) 'Socioeconomic status and health across the life course: progress and prospects', *Journals of Gerontology Series B*, vol 60, (Special Issue 2), ppS135-S139.

Gilleard, C. (2004) 'Cohorts and generations in the study of social change', *Social Theory and Health*, vol 2, no 1, pp 106-19.

Gilleard, C. and Higgs, P. (2000) *Cultures of ageing: Self, citizen and the body*, New York, NY: Prentice Hall.

Gilleard, C. and Higgs, P. (2002) 'The third age: class, cohort or generation?', *Ageing & Society*, vol 22, no 3, pp 369-82.

Gilleard, C. and Higgs, P. (2005) *Contexts of ageing: Class, cohort and community*, Cambridge: Polity Press.

Gilleard, C. and Higgs, P. (2010) 'Aging without agency: theorizing the fourth age', *Aging and Mental Health*, vol 14, no 2, pp 121-8.

Ginn, J. (2003) *Gender, pensions and the life course*, Bristol: The Policy Press.

Glaser, B.G. and Strauss, A.L. (1967) *The discovery of grounded theory: Strategies for qualitative research*, Chicago, IL: Aldine.

Gluckman, P.D. and Hanson, M.A. (2006) *Mismatch: The lifestyle diseases timebomb*, New York, NY: Oxford University Press.

Goffman, E. (1974) *Frame analysis: An essay on the organization of experience*, Cambridge, MA: Harvard University Press.

Goffman, E. (1959) *The presentation of self in everyday life*, New York, NY: Doubleday.

Gouvernement du Québec (2005) *Ministère de la Famille et des Aînés: Une pleine participation des aînés au développement du Québec, Rapport de l'équipe de travail*. Québec: Gouvernement du Québec.

Gouvernement du Québec (2006) *Ministère de la Famille et des Aînés: Étude sur la participation des aînés au développement de la société et sur les politiques du vieillissement au sein de quelques administrations de l'OCDE*. Québec: Gouvernement du Québec.

Gouvernement du Québec (2009). *Ministère de la Famille et des Aînés: Plan stratégique 2008-2012*. Québec: Gouvernement du Québec.

Grenier, A. (2003) 'Diverse older women: narratives negotiating frailty', Unpublished doctoral dissertation, Montreal: McGill University/l'Université de Montréal.

Grenier, A. (2005) 'The contextual and social locations of older women's experiences of disability and decline', *Journal of Aging Studies*, vol 19, no 2, pp 131-46.

Grenier, A. (2006a) 'Recognizing and responding to loss and "rupture" in older women's accounts', *Journal of Social Work Practice: Psychotherapeutic Approaches in Health, Welfare and the Community*, vol 22, no 2, pp 195-209.

Grenier, A. (2006b) 'The distinction between being and feeling frail: exploring emotional experiences in health and social care', *Journal of Social Work Practice: Psychotherapeutic Approaches in Health, Welfare and the Community*, vol 20, no 3, pp 299-313.

Grenier, A. (2007a) 'Crossing age and generational boundaries: exploring intergenerational research encounters', *Journal of Social Issues*, vol 63, no 4, pp 713-27.

Grenier, A. (2007b) 'Constructions of frailty in the English language, care practice and the lived experience', *Ageing & Society*, vol 27, no 3, pp 425-45.

Grenier, A. (2009a) 'Critical perspectives on "frailty" in late life', Paper presented at the 19th International Association on Geriatrics and Gerontology World Congress of Gerontology and Geriatrics, Paris, 6 July.

Grenier, A. (2009b) 'Les femmes âgées et la fragilité : la résistance face aux pratiques de soins de santé et de services sociaux', in M. Charpentier and A. Quéniart (eds) *Femmes, vieillissement et société: regards pluridisciplinaires*, Montréal: Editions du remue-ménage, pp 249-70.

Grenier, A., Airton, L., Isenberg, S. and Ferrer, I. (2010) 'Older people in Black communities: the Black demographics project', Research report prepared for the Black Communities Demographics project, Montreal Consortium for Human Rights Advocacy Training and McGill Consortium for Ethnicity and Strategic Social Planning, funded by Heritage Canada.

Grenier, A. and Brotman, S. (2010) 'Les multiples viellissements et leurs representations', in M. Charpentier, N. Guberman, V. Billette, J.P. Lavoie, A. Grenier, and I. Olazabal (eds) *Viellir au pluriel: perspectives sociales*, Quebec: Presses de l'Université du Quebéc, pp 23-34.

Grenier, A. and Guberman, N. (2009) 'Creating and sustaining disadvantage: the relevance of a social exclusion framework', *Health & Social Care in the Community*, vol 17, no 2, pp 116-24.

Grenier, A. and Hanley, J. (2007) 'Older women and "frailty": aged, gendered and embodied resistance', *Current Sociology*, vol 55, no 2, pp 211-28.

Gruman, G.J. (2003) *A history of ideas about the prolongation of life*, New York, NY: Springer.

Gubrium, J.F. (1975) *Living and dying at Murray Manor*, New York, NY: St Martin's Press.

Gubrium, J.F. (2001) 'Narrative, experience, and aging', in G. Kenyon, P. Clark and D.B. De Vries (eds) *Narrative gerontology: Theory, research and practice*, New York, NY: Springer, pp 237-72.

Gubrium, J.F. (2005) 'Narrative environments and social problems', *Social Problems*, vol 52, no 4, pp 525-8.

Gubrium, J.F. and Holstein, J.A. (1994) 'Analyzing talk and interaction', in J. Gubrium and A. Sankar (eds) *Qualitative methods in aging research*, Thousand Oaks, CA: Sage Publications, pp 173-88.

Gubrium, J.F. and Holstein, J.A. (1998) 'Narrative practice and the coherence of personal stories', *The Sociological Quarterly*, vol 39, no 1, pp 163-87.

Gubrium, J. F. and Holstein, J.A. (1999) 'Constructionist perspective on aging', in V.L. Bengston and K. Warner Schaie (eds) *Handbook of theories of aging*, New York, NY: Springer, pp 287-305.

Gubrium, J.F. and Holstein, J.A. (2000) *The self we live by*, Oxford: Oxford University Press.

Gubrium, J.F. and Holstein, J.A. (eds) (2003) *Ways of aging*, Malden, MA: Blackwell.

Gubrium, J.F. and Holstein, J.A. (2009) *Analyzing narrative reality*, Thousand Oaks, CA: Sage Publications.

Guillemard, A.M. (1972) *La retraite, une mort sociale*, Paris: Mouton.

Guillemard, A.M. (1980) *La vieillesse de l'état*, Paris: Presses Universitaires de France.

Guillemard, A.M. (2002) 'De la retraite mort sociale à la retraite solidaire: la retraite une mort sociale (1972) revisitée trente ans après', *Gerontologie et Société*, vol 3, no 102, pp 53-66.

Gullette, M.M. (1997) *Declining to decline: Cultural combat and the politics of the midlife*, Charlottesville, VA: University of Virginia Press.

Gullette, M.M. (2004) *Aged by culture*, Chicago, IL: University of Chicago Press.

Hagestad, G.O. (1990) 'Social perspectives on the life course', in R. Binstock and L. George (eds) *Handbook of aging and the social sciences*, San Diego, CA: Academic Press, pp 151-68.

Hagestad, G.O. and Neugarten, B.L. (1985) 'Age and the life course', in R.H. Binstock and E. Shanas (eds) *Handbook of aging and the social sciences*, New York, NY: Van Nostrand Reinhold, pp 46-61.

Halberstam, J. (2005) *In a queer time and place: Transgender bodies, subcultural lives*, New York, NY: New York University Press.

Hall, C. (1998) *Social work as narrative: Storytelling and persuasion in professional texts*, Aldershot: Ashgate.

Hamerman, D. (1999) 'Medical writings: toward an understanding of frailty', *Annals of Internal Medicine*, vol 130, no 11, pp 945-50.

Hareven, T. (1978a) 'The last stage: historical adulthood and old age', in E. Erikson (ed) *Adulthood*, New York, NY: Norton, pp 201-16.

Hareven, T. (ed) (1978b) *Transitions: The family and the life course in historical perspective*, New York, NY: Academic Press.

Hareven, T. and Adams, K. (eds) (1982) *Aging and life course transitions: An interdisciplinary perspective*, New York, NY: Guildford Press.

Harré, R. and Moghaddam, F.M. (2003) *The self and others: Positioning individuals and groups in personal, political, and cultural contexts*, Westport, CT: Praeger.

Havingurst, R.J. (1963) 'Successful aging', in R.H. Williams, C. Tibbits and W. Donahue (eds) *Process of aging: Social and psychological perspectives, volume 1*, New York, NY: Atherton Press, pp 299-320.

Hazan, H. (2009a) 'Essentialized others: anthropology and the return of the old savage', *International Journal of Sociology and Social Policy*, vol 29, no 1/2, pp 60-72.

Hazan, H. (2009b) 'Beyond dialogue: entering the fourth space in old age', in R. Edmonson and H.J. von Kondratowitz (eds) *Valuing older people: A humanist approach to ageing*, Bristol: The Policy Press, pp 91-106.

Heaphy, B. (2007) 'Sexualities, gender and ageing: resources and social change', *Current Sociology*, vol 55, no 2, pp 193-210.

Hendricks, J. (2003) 'Structure and identity: mind the gap', in S. Biggs, A. Lowenstein and J. Hendricks (eds) *The need for theory: Critical approaches to social gerontology*, Amityville, NY: Baywood, pp 63-90.

Hendricks, J. (2004) 'Public policies and age identity', *Journal of Aging Studies*, vol 18, no 4, pp 1-16.

Hendricks, J. and Hendricks, C.D. (1977) *Aging in mass society: Myths and realities*, Cambridge, MA: Winthrop Publishers.

Hennessy, C.H. and Walker, A. (2004) *Growing older – quality of life in old age*, Buckingham: Open University Press.

Henretta, J.C., O'Rand, A.M. and Chan, C.G. (1993) 'Joint role investments and synchronization of retirement: a sequential approach to couples' retirement timing', *Social Forces*, vol 71, no 4, pp 981-1000.

Hertz, R. 1960 ([1907]) *Death and the right hand* (trans. C. Needham and R. Needham), London: Routledge.

Higgs, P. and Jones, I.R. (2008) *Medical sociology and old age: Towards a sociology of health in later life*, Oxford: Routledge.

Hitlin, S. and Elder, G.H. (2007) 'Time, self, and the curiously abstract concept of agency', *Sociological Theory*, vol 25, no 2, pp 170-91.

Hockey, J. and James, A. (2003) *Social identities across the lifecourse*, Basingstoke: Palgrave Macmillan.

Hoggett, P. (1998) 'Hatred of dependency: where are the people? Expertise and experience', Paper presented at Psychoanalysis and the Public Sphere 11th annual conference, University of East London, 30-31 January.

Hoggett, P. (2000) *Emotional life and the politics of welfare*, Basingstoke: Palgrave Macmillan.

Hoggett, P (2001) 'Agency, rationality and social policy', *Journal of Social Policy*, vol 30, no 1, pp 37-56.

Hoggett, P. (2006) 'Pity, compassion, solidarity', in S. Clarke, P. Hoggett and S. Thompson (eds) *Emotions, politics and society*, Basingstoke: Palgrave Macmillan.

Hoggett, P (2008) 'Relational thinking and welfare practice', in S. Clarke, H. Hahn and P. Hoggett (eds) *Object relations and social relations: The implications of the relational turn in psychoanalysis*, London: Karnac Books.

Holliday, R. (2004) 'The multiple and irreversible causes of aging', *Journals of Gerontology Series A*, vol 59, no 6, pp B568-B572.

Hollway, W. (2006) *The capacity to care: Gender and moral subjectivity*, New York, NY: Psychology Press, pp 100-19.

Holstein, J.A. and Gubrium, J.F. (2000) *Constructing the life course* (2nd edn), Lanham: General Hall

Holstein, M.B. and Minkler, M. (2003) 'Self, society, and the "new gerontology"', *The Gerontologist*, vol 43, no 6, pp 787-96.

Honzik, M.P. (1984) 'Life-span development', *Annual Review of Psychology*, vol 35, pp 309-31.

Hook, D. (2008) 'Articulating psychoanalysis and psychosocial studies: limitations and possibilities', *Psychoanalysis, Culture & Society*, vol 13, no 4, pp 397-406.

Huntington, R. and Metcalf, P. (1979) *Celebrations of death: The anthropology of mortuary ritual*, New York, NY: Cambridge University Press.

Hurd Clarke, L. (2002) 'Beauty in later life: older women's perceptions of physical attractiveness', *Canadian Journal on Aging*, vol 21, no 3, pp 429-42.

Hutchinson, D.L. (2002) 'Critical race studies – progressive race blindness? Individual identity, group politics and reform', *UCLA Law Review*, vol 49, no 5, p 1455.

Irwin, S. (1995) *Rights of passage: Social change and the transition from youth to adulthood*, London: UCL Press.

Jones, I.R., Hyde, M., Victor, C., Wiggins, R., Gilleard, C. and Higgs, P. (2008) *Ageing in a consumer society: From passive to active consumption in Britain*, Bristol: The Policy Press.

Jones, R. (2006) '"Older people" talking as if they were not older people: positioning theory as an explanation', *Journal of Aging Studies*, vol 20, no 1, pp 79-91.

Kahn, R.L. and Antonucci, T.C. (1980) 'Convoys over the life course: attachment, roles, and social support', in P. Baltes and O. Brim (eds) *Life-span development and behavior*, New York, NY: Academic Press.

Katz, S. (1995) 'Imagining the lifespan: from premodern miracles to postmodern fantasies', in M. Featherstone and A. Wernick (eds) *Images of ageing: Cultural representations of later life*, London: Routledge.

Katz, S. (1996) *Disciplining old age: The formation of gerontological knowledge*, Charlottesville, VA: University Press of Virginia.

Katz, S. (2000) 'Busy bodies: activity, aging, and the management of everyday life', *Journal of Aging Studies*, vol 14, no 2, pp 135-52.

Katz, S. (2003) 'Technology, life course and the post-industrial landscape', *Gerotechnology*, vol 2, no 3, pp 255-9.

Katz, S. (2005) *Cultural aging: Life course, lifestyle, and senior worlds*, Peterborough, ON: Broadview Press.

Katz, S. (2005) 'Busy bodies: activity, aging and the management of everyday life', in *Cultural aging*, Peterborough, ON: Broadview Press, pp 121–39.

Katz, S. and Green, B. (2002) 'The government of detail: the case of social policy on aging', *Aging and Identity*, vol 7, no 3, pp 149–63.

Kaufman, S. (1986) *The ageless self: Sources of meaning in late life*, Madison, WI: University of Wisconsin Press.

Kaufman, S.R. (1994) 'The social construction of frailty: an anthropological perspective', *Journal of Aging Studies*, vol 8, no 1, pp 45–58.

Kaufman, S. and Becker, G. (1996) 'Frailty, risk, and choice: cultural discourses and the question of responsibility', in M. Smyer, K. Schaie and M. Kapp (eds) *Older adults' decision-making and the law*, New York, NY: Springer, pp 48–71.

Keating, N. (ed) (2008) *Rural ageing: A good place to grow old*, Bristol: The Policy Press.

Kelly, M.P. and Dickinson, H. (1997) 'The narrative self in autobiographical accounts of illness', *The Sociological Review*, vol 45, no 2, pp 254–78.

Kenyon, G., Clark, P. and de Vries, B. (eds) (2001) *Narrative gerontology: Theory, research and practice*, New York, NY: Springer.

Kenyon, G. and Randall, W. (2001) 'Narrative gerontology: stories in theory, research, and practice', in G. Kenyon, P. Clark and B. de Vries (eds) *Narrative gerontology: Theory, research and practice*, New York, NY: Springer, pp 3–18.

Kerner Furman, F. (1997) *Facing the mirror: Older women and beauty shop culture*, New York, NY: Routledge.

Kertzer, D.I. and Keith, J. (1984) *Age and anthropological theory*, Ithaca, NY: Cornell University Press.

Kimball, S.T. (1960) 'Introduction', in A. van Gennep *Rites of passage*, Chicago, IL: University of Chicago Press, pp v–xxii.

Kirkwood, T.B.L. and Holliday, R. (1979) 'The evolution of ageing and longevity', *Proceedings of the Royal Society of London, Series B, Biological Sciences*, vol 205, no 1161, pp 531–46.

Kirkwood, T.B.L. (2002) 'Evolution of aging', *Mechanisms of Ageing and Development*, vol 123, no 7, pp 737–45.

Kleinman, A. (1988) *The illness narratives: Suffering, healing and the human condition*, New York, NY: Basic Books.

Kohli, M. (1986a) 'Social organization and subjective construction of the life course', in A. Sorensen, F.E. Weinert and L.R. Sherrod (eds) *Human development and the life course: Multidisciplinary perspectives*, Hillsdale, NJ: Lawrence Erlbaum.

Kohli, M. (1986b) 'The world we forgot: a historical review of the life course', in V.W. Marshall (ed) *Later life: The social psychology of aging*, Beverly Hills, CA: Sage Publications.

Kohli, M. (2007) 'The institutionalization of the life course: looking back to look ahead', *Research in Human Development*, vol 4, no 3, pp 253–71.

Kohli, M. and Meyer, J.W. (1986) 'Social structure and the social construction of life stages', *Human Development*, vol 29, no 3, pp 145–9.

Kokmen, E., Bossemeyer, R.W., Barney, J. and Williams, W.J. (1977) 'Neurological manifestations of aging', *Journal of Gerontology*, vol 32, no 4, pp 411–19.

Kreager, P. and Schroder-Butterfill, E. (2004) *Aging without children: European and Asian perspectives*, Oxford: Berghann Books.

Labov, W. and Waletzky, J. (1967) 'Narrative analysis: oral versions of personal experience', in J. Helm (ed) *Essays on the verbal and visual arts*, Seattle, WA: University of Washington Press, pp 12-14.

Lang, F.R. and Carstensen, L.L. (1998) 'Social relationships and adaptation in late life', in A.S. Bellack and M. Hersen (eds) *Comprehensive clinical psychology*, Oxford: Pergamon, pp 55-72.

Laslett, P. (1989) *A fresh map of life: The emergence of the third age*, Cambridge, MA: Harvard University Press.

Lawton, J (2000) *The dying process: Patients' experiences of palliative care*, London: Routledge.

Leonard, P. (1997) *Postmodern welfare: Reconstructing an emancipatory project*, London: Sage Publications.

Levinson, D.L. (1986) 'A conception of adult development source', *American Psychologist*, vol 41, no 1, pp 3-13.

Levinson, D.L. and Darrow, C.N. (1978) *The seasons of a man's life*, New York, NY: Ballantine Books.

Liebing, A. (2010) *Les technologies de l'espoir: la fabrique d'une histoire a accomplir*, Quebec: Presses de l'Université Laval.

Lloyd, L. (2004) 'Mortality and morality: ageing and the ethics of care', *Ageing & Society*, vol 24, no 2, pp 235-56.

Lloyd, L. (2006) A caring profession? The ethics of care and social work with older people. *British Journal of Social Work*, vol 36, no 7, pp 1171-1185.

Maines, D.R. (2005) 'Narrative's moment and sociology's phenomena: toward a narrative sociology', *Sociological Quarterly*, vol 34, no 1, pp 17-38.

Maioni, A. (2004) 'Roles and responsibilities in health care policy', in T. McIntosh, P.G. Forest and G.P. Marchildon (eds) *The governance of health care in Canada*, Toronto: University of Toronto Press, pp 169-98.

Martin-Mathews, A. (1991) *Widowhood in later life*, Toronto: Butterworth.

Mayer, K.U. (1986) 'Structural constraints in the life course', *Human Development*, vol 29, no 3, pp 163-70.

Mayer, K.U. (2000) 'Promises fulfilled? A review of twenty years of life course research', *Archives Européennes de Sociologie*, vol XLI, no 2, pp 259-82.

Mayer, K.U. (2002) 'The sociology of the life course and life span psychology – diverging or converging pathways?', in U. Staudinger and U. Lindenberger (eds) *Understanding human development: Lifespan psychology in exchange with other disciplines*, Dordecht: Kluwer Academic Publishers.

Mayer, K.U. (2004) 'Whose lives? How history, societies and institutions decline and shape life courses', *Research in Human Development*, vol 1, no 3, pp 161-87.

McAdams, D.P. (1993) *The stories we live by: Personal myths and the making of the self*, New York, NY: William Morrow.

McAdams, D.P. (2003) 'Identity and the life story', in R. Fivush and C. Haden (eds) *Autobiographical memory and the construction of a narrative self: Developmental and cultural perspectives*, Mahwah, NJ: Lawrence Erlbaum, pp 187-207.

McAdams, D.P. (2006) *The redemptive self: Stories Americans live by*, Oxford: Oxford University Press.

McIlvane, J.M. Ajrouch, K.J. and Antonucci, T.C. (2007) 'Generational structure and social resources in mid-life: influences on health and well-being', *Journal of Social Issues*, vol 63, no 4, pp 759-73.

McMullin, J.L. (2000) 'Diversity and the state of sociological aging theory', *The Gerontologist*, vol 40, no 5, pp 517-30.

McMullin, J.A. (2004) *Understanding inequality: Intersections of class, age, gender, ethnicity, and race in Canada*, Toronto: Oxford University Press.

McMullin, J. (2010) *Understanding inequality: Intersections of class, age, gender, ethnicity and race in Canada* (2nd edition), Toronto: Oxford University Press.

Mead, G.H. (1934) *Mind self and society from the standpoint of a social behaviorist*, Chicago, IL: University of Chicago Press.

Means, R., Richards, S. and Smith, R. (2003) *Community care: Policy and practice*, Basingstoke: Palgrave Macmillan.

Meyer, J. (1986) 'The self and the life course: institutionalization and its effects', in A.B. Sørensen, F.E. Weinert and L.R. Sherrod (eds) *Human development and the life course: Multidisciplinary perspectives*, Hillsdale, NJ: Lawrence Erlbaum Associates, pp 199-217.

Michel, D.J.P. (2001) 'La fragilité est-elle un critère utile?', Paper presented at the Conférences scientifiques en gériatrie 2001-2002, Montreal.

Midwinter, E. (1996) *Thriving people: The growth and prospects of the U3A in the UK*, London: Third Age Trust.

Midwinter, E. (2004) *500 beacons: The U3A story*, London: Third Age Press.

Midwinter, E. (2005) 'How many people are there in the third age?', *Ageing & Society*, vol 25, no 1, pp 9-18.

Milette, C. (1999) *Bien vivre avec son age: revue de literature sur la promotion de la santé des personnes agees*, Quebec: Ministère de la Santé et des Services Sociaux.

Mills, C.W. (1959) *The sociological imagination*, New York, NY: Oxford University Press.

Minkler, M. and Estes, C. (1997) *Critical gerontology: Perspectives from political and moral economy*, New York, NY: Baywood.

Mishler, E. (1986) *Research interviewing: Context and narrative*, Cambridge, MA: Harvard University Press, pp 66-116.

Mishler, E. (1999) *Storylines: Craftartists' narratives of identity*, Cambridge, MA: Harvard University Press.

Mitford, J. (1963) *The American way of death*, New York, NY: Simon and Schuster.

Moen, P., Kim, J.E. and Hofmeister, H. (2001) 'Couples' work/retirement transitions, gender, and marital quality', *Social Psychology Quarterly*, vol 64, pp 55-71.

Mohanty, S.P. (1993) 'The epistemic status of cultural identity: on "beloved" and the postcolonial condition', *Cultural Critique*, vol 24, pp 41-80.

Moody, H.R. (1988) 'Toward a critical gerontology: the contribution of the humanities to theories of aging', in J.E. Birren and V.L. Bengston (eds) *Emergent theories of aging*, New York, NY: Springer, pp 19-40.

Moody, H.R. (1992) 'Gerontology and critical theory', *The Gerontologist*, vol 32, no 3, pp 294-5.

Moody, H.R. (1993) 'What is critical gerontology and why is it important?', in T.R. Cole, W.A. Achenbaum, P. Jakobi and R. Kastenbaum (eds) *Voices and visions of aging: Towards a critical gerontology*, New York, NY: Springer, pp xv-xli.

Moody, H.R. (1995) 'Critical theory and critical gerontology', in R. Schulz (ed) *Encyclopedia of aging*, New York, NY: Springer, pp 272-4.

Moody, H.R. (2001) 'Productive aging and the ideology of old age', in N. Morrow-Howell, J. Hinterlong and M. Sherraden (eds) *Productive aging: Concepts and challenges*, Baltimore, MD: John Hopkins University Press, pp 175-96.

Morley, J.E., Perry, H.M. and Miller, D.K. (2002) 'Something about frailty', *Journals of Gerontology Series A*, vol 57, no 11, pp M698-M704.

Morris, J. (1991) *Pride against prejudice*, London: Women's Press.

Morrow-Howell, N., Hinterlong, J. and Sherraden, M. (2001) *Productive aging: Concepts and challenges*, Baltimore, MD: John Hopkins University Press.

Myerhoff, B. (1979) *Number our days*, New York, NY: Dutton.

Myerhoff, B. (1984) 'Rites and signs of ripening: the intertwining of ritual, time, and growing older', in D. Kertzer and J. Keith (eds) *Age and anthropological theory*, Ithaca, NY: Cornell University Press, pp 305-30.

Meyerhoff, B. (1992) *Remembered lives: The work of ritual, storytelling, and growing older*, Ann Arbor, MI: University of Michigan Press.

Myerhoff, B. (2000) 'A death in due time: conviction, order and continuity in ritual drama', in J.F. Gubrium and J.A. Holstein (eds) *Aging and everyday life*, Oxford: Blackwell.

Mykytyn, C.E. (2006) 'Anti-aging medicine: predictions, moral obligations, and biomedical intervention', *Anthropological Quarterly*, vol 79, no 1, pp 5-31.

National Urban League (1964) *Double jeopardy: The older Negro in America today*, New York, NY: National Urban League.

Nazroo, J., Bajekal, M., Blane, D. and Grewal, I. (2004) 'Ethnic inequalities', in A. Walker and C. Hagan Hennessy (eds) *Growing older: Quality of life in old age*, Maidenhead: Open University Press, pp 35-59.

Neugarten, B.L. (1968) 'Adult personality', in B.L. Neugarten (ed) *Middle age and aging*, Chicago, IL: University of Chicago Press, pp 137-47.

Neugarten, B.L. (1969) 'Continuities and discontinuities of psychological issues into adult life', *Human Development*, vol 12, no 2, pp 121-30.

Neugarten, B.L. (1976) 'Adaptation and the life cycle', *The Counseling Psychologist*, vol 6, no 1, pp 16-20.

Neugarten, B.L. (1979a) 'Time, age, and the life cycle', *American Journal of Psychiatry*, vol 136, no 7, pp 887-94.

Neugarten, B.L. (1979b) 'The young old and the age-irrelevant society', in D. Neugarten (ed) *The meanings of age: Selected papers of Bernice L. Neugarten*, Chicago, IL: University of Chicago Press.

Neugarten, B.L. and Datan, N. (1973) 'Sociological perspective in the life cycle', in P. Baltes and K.W. Schaie (eds) *Life-span developmental psychology: Personality and socialization*, New York, NY: Academic Press, pp 53-68.

Neugarten, B.L. and Hagestad, G.O. (1976) 'Age and the life course', in R.H. Binstock and E.Shanas (eds) *Handbook of aging and the social sciences*, New York, NY: Van Nostrand Reinhold.

Neugarten, B.L., Moore, J.W. and Lowe, J.C. (1965) 'Age norms, age constraints, and adult socialization', *American Journal of Sociology*, vol 70, no 6, pp 710-17.

Neysmith, S. (1995) 'Feminist methodologies: a consideration of principles and practice for research in gerontology', *Canadian Journal on Aging*, vol 14, no 1, pp 100-18.

Neysmith, S. (ed) (1999) *Critical issues for future social work practice with aging persons*, New York, NY: Columbia University Press.

Neysmith, S. (ed) (2000) *Restructuring caring labour: Discourse, state practice and everyday life*, Don Mills: Oxford University Press Canada.

Neysmith, S., Bezanson, K. and O'Connell, A. (2005) *Telling tales: Living the effects of public policy*, Black Point: Fernwood Publishing.

Öberg, P. (1996) 'The absent body: a social gerontological paradox', *Ageing & Society*, vol 16, no 6, pp 701-19.

Oldman, C. (2002) 'Later life and the social model of disability: a comfortable partnership?', *Ageing & Society*, vol 22, no 6, pp 791-806.

Oliver, M. (1990) *The politics of disablement*, Basingstoke: Palgrave Macmillan.

Oxford English Dictionary (1989) 'Transition'. OED Online, 2nd edn, http:// dictionary.oed.com, accessed August, 2006.

Parkin, D. (1992) 'Ritual as spatial direction and bodily division', in D. de Coppet (ed) *Understanding rituals*, London: Routledge, pp 11-25.

Parsons, T. (1951) *The social system*, Glencoe, IL: Free Press.

Parsons, T. (1960) *Structure and process in modern societies*, Glencoe, IL: Free Press.

Parsons, T. (1977) *Social systems and the evolution of action theory*, New York, NY: Free Press.

Parsons, T. (1978) *Action theory and the human condition*, New York, NY: Free Press.

Patton, M.Q. (2002) *Qualitative research and evaluation methods* (3rd edn), Thousand Oaks, CA: Sage Publications.

Pescosolido, B.A. (2006) 'Sociology of social networks', in C. D. Bryant, and D.L. Peck (eds) *21st century sociology: A reference handbook*, Thousand Oaks, CA: Sage Publications, pp 208-17.

Phillips, J. (2006) *Social work with older people*, Basingstoke: Palgrave Macmillan.

Phillips, J. (2007) *Care: Key concepts*, Cambridge: Polity Press.

Phillipson, C. (1982) *Capitalism and the construction of old age*, London: Macmillan.

Phillipson, C. (1998) *Reconstructing old age: New agendas in social theory and practice*, London: Sage Publications.

Phillipson, C. (2002) *Transitions from work to retirement: Developing a new social contract*, Bristol: The Policy Press.

Phillipson, C. (2004) 'Work and retirement transitions: changing sociological and social policy contexts', *Social Policy and Society*, vol 3, no 2, pp 155-62.

Phillipson, C. and Powell, J.L. (2004) 'Risk, social welfare and old age', in E. Tulle (ed) *Old age and human agency*, Hauppauge, NY: Nova Science Publishers, pp 17-26.

Phillipson, C. and Walker, A. (1987) 'The case for critical gerontology', in S. DiGregorio (ed) *Social gerontology: New directions*, New York, NY: Croom Helm, pp 1-18.

Phoenix, C. and Sparkes, A.C. (2006) 'Keeping it in the family: Narrative maps of ageing and young athletes' perceptions of their futures', *Ageing & Society*, vol 26, no 4, pp 631-48.

Piaget, J. (1952 [1936]) *The origins of intelligence in children*, New York, NY: International University Press.

Piaget, J. (1972 [1966]) *The psychology of the child*, New York, NY: Basic Books.

Piaget, J. (1990 [1929]) *The child's conception of the world*, New York, NY: Littlefield Adams.

Polkinghorne, D. (1988) *Narrative knowing and the human sciences*, New York, NY: State University of New York Press.

Polkinghorne, D. (1995) 'Narrative configuration in qualitative analysis', *International Journal of Qualitative Studies in Education*, vol 8, no 1, pp 5-23.

Powell, J. and Longino, C.F. (2001) 'Towards the postmodernization of aging: the body and social theory', *Journal of Aging and Identity*, vol 6, no 4, pp 199-207.

PRI (Policy Research Initiative) (2004) *Population aging and life-course flexibility: The pivotal role of increased choice in the retirement decision*, Ottawa: PRI.

Price, S.J., McKenry, P.C. and Murphy, M.J. (2000) *Families across time: A life course perspective*, Los Angeles, CA: Roxbury.

Radhakrishnan, R. (1993) 'Postcoloniality and the boundaries of identity', *Callaloo*, vol 16, no 4, pp 750-71.

Randall, W. L. and Kenyon, G.M. (2001) *Ordinary wisdom: Biographical aging and the journey of life*, Westport, CT: Praeger.

Randall, W.L. and Kenyon, G.M. (2004) 'Time, story, and wisdom: emerging themes in narrative gerontology', *Canadian Journal on Aging*, vol 23, no 4, pp 333-46.

Raphael, D., Cava, M., Brown, I., Renwick, R., Heathcote, K., Weir, N., Wright, K. and Kirwan, L. (1995) 'Frailty: a public health perspective', *Canadian Journal of Public Health/Revue Canadienne de Santé Publique*, vol 86, no 4, pp 224-7.

Ray, M. (2007) 'Redressing the balance? The participation of older people in research', in M. Bernard and T. Scharf (eds) *Critical perspectives on ageing societies*, Bristol: The Policy Press, pp 59-72.

Ray, R. (2000) *Beyond nostalgia: Aging and life story writing*, Charlottesville, VA: University Press of Virginia.

Ray, R. (2007) 'Narratives as agents of social change: a new direction for narrative gerontologists', in M. Bernard and T. Scharf (eds) *Critical perspectives on ageing societies*, Bristol: The Policy Press, pp 59-72.

Ricoeur, P. (1988) *Time and narrative*, Chicago, IL: University of Chicago Press.

Riddell, S. and Watson, N. (2003) *Disability, culture and identity*, Harlow: Pearson/Prentice Hall.

Riessman, C.K. (1993) *Narrative analysis*, London: Sage Publications.

Riessman, C.K. and Quinney, L. (2005) 'Narrative in social work: a critical review', *Qualitative Social Work*, vol 4, no 4, pp 391-412.

Riley, M.W. (1971) 'Social gerontology and the age stratification', *The Gerontologist*, vol 11, no 1, part 1, pp 79-87.

Riley, M.W. (1987) 'On the significance of age in sociology', *American Sociological Review*, vol 52, no 1, pp 1-14.

Riley, M.W. and Foner, A. (1968) *Ageing and society*, New York, NY: Russell Sage Foundation.

Riley, M.W., Johnson, M. and Foner, A. (1972) *Aging and society: A sociology of age stratification, volume 3*, New York, NY: Russell Sage Foundation.

Riley, M.W., Kahn, R.L. and Foner, A. (1994) *Age and structural lag: Society's failure to provide meaningful opportunities in work, family, and leisure*, New York, NY: Wiley.

Ritchie, J. and Lewis, J. (2003) *Qualitative research practice*, London: Sage Publications.

Roberts, B. (2002) *Biographical research*, Buckingham: Open University Press.

Robson, C. (2002) *Real world research: a resource for social scientists and practitioner-researchers* (2nd edn), Oxford: Blackwell.

Rockwood, K. (2005) 'What would make a definition of frailty successful?', *Age and Ageing*, vol 34, no 5, pp 432-4.

Rockwood, K., Fox, R.A., Stolee, P., Robertson, D. and Beattie, B.L. (1994). 'Frailty in elderly people: an evolving concept', *Canadian Medical Association Journal*, vol 150, no 4, pp 489-95.

Rockwood, K. and Mitnitski, A. (2007) 'Frailty in relation to the accumulation of deficits', *Journals of Gerontology Series A*, vol 62, no 7, pp 722-7.

Rockwood, K., Stolee, P. and McDowell, I. (1996) 'Factors associated with institutionalization of older people in Canada: testing a multifactorial definition of frailty', *Journal of the American Geriatrics Society*, vol 44, no 5, pp 578-82.

Rosenfeld, D. (1999) 'Identity work among lesbian and gay elderly', *Journal of Aging,* vol 13, no 2, pp 121-44.

Rossi, A.S. (1980) 'Life-span theories and women's lives', *Signs*, vol 6, no 1, pp 4-32.

Rowe, J.W. and Kahn, R.L. (1998) *Successful aging*, New York, NY: Pantheon Books.

Rowles, G.D. (1978) *Prisoners of space? Exploring the geographic experience of older people*, Boulder, CO: Westview Press.

Rowles, G.D. (2008) 'Making and remaking place in old age', Plenary address to the Annual Meeting of the British Society for Gerontology, Bristol, 6 September.

Rutter, M. and Rutter, M. (1992) *Developing minds: Challenge and continuity across the life span*, London: Penguin.

Ryder, N.B. (1965) 'The cohort as a concept in the study of social change', *American Sociological Review*, vol 30, no 6, pp 843-61.

Said, E.W. (1978) *Orientalism*, New York, NY: Pantheon Books.

Sarbin, T. (1986) *Narrative psychology: The storied nature of human conduct*, New York, NY: Praeger.

Savage, M. (2005) 'Working-class identities in the 1960s: revisiting the affluent worker studies', *Sociology*, vol 39, no 5, pp 929-46.

Savage, M., Devine, F., Crompton, R. and Scott, J. (eds) (2004) *Rethinking class, identities, cultures and lifestyles*, Basingstoke: Palgrave Macmillan.

Sayer, A. (2005) *The moral significance of class*, Cambridge: Cambridge University Press.

Scharf, T., Phillipson, C. and Smith, A.E. (2004) 'Poverty and social exclusion: growing older in deprived urban neighbourhoods', in A. Walker and C. Hagan Hennessy (eds) *Growing older: Quality of life in old age*, Maidenhead: Open University Press, pp 81-106.

Scharf, T., Phillipson, C. and Smith, A.E. (2007) 'Aging in a difficult place: assessing the impact of urban deprivation on older people', in H. W. Wahl, C. Tesch-Römer and A. Hoff (eds) *New dynamics in old age: Individual, environmental and societal perspectives*, Amityville, NY: Baywood, pp 153-73.

Schlossberg, N., Waters, E. and Goodman, J. (1995) *Counselling adults in transition: Linking practice with theory*, New York, NY: Springer.

Schmaltz, H.N., Fried, L.P., Xue, Q., Walston, J., Leng, S.X. and Semba, R.D. (2005) 'Chronic cytomegalovirus infection and inflammation are associated with prevalent frailty in community-dwelling older women', *Journal of the American Geriatrics Society*, vol 53, no 5, pp 747-54.

Schröder-Butterfill, E. (2004) 'Inter-generational family support provided by older people in Indonesia', *Ageing & Society*, vol 24, no 4, pp 497-530.

Schröder-Butterfill, E. (2005) 'The impact of kinship networks on old-age vulnerability in Indonesia', *Annales de Demographie Historique*, vol 2, no 110, pp 139-63.

Schutz, A. (1962) *Collected papers, volume I: The problem of social reality*, Leiden: Martinus Nijhoff.

Schutz, A. (1970) *On phenomenology and social relations*, Chicago, IL: University of Chicago Press.

Searle, J.R. (1995) *The construction of social reality*, New York, NY: Free Press.

Settersten, R.A. (2006) 'Aging and the life course', in R. H. Binstock and L. K. George (eds) *Handbook of aging and the social sciences*, Amsterdam: Elsevier, pp 3-19.

Settersen, R.A. and Hagestad, G.O. (1996) 'What's the latest? Cultural age deadlines for family transitions', *The Gerontologist*, vol 36, no 2, pp 178-88.

Settersen, R.A., Flatt, M.A. and Ponsaran, R. (2008) 'From the lab to the front line: how individual biogerontologists navigate their contested field', *Journal of Aging Studies*, vol 22, no 4, pp 304-12.

Sevenhuijsen, S. (1998) *Citizenship and the ethics of care: Feminist considerations on justice, morality, and politics*, London: Routledge.

Shakespeare, T. (1996) 'Disability, identity and difference', in C. Barnes and G. Mercer (eds) *Exploring the divide*, Leeds: Disability Press, pp 94–113.

Shanahan, M.J. (2000) 'Pathways to adulthood in changing societies: variability and mechanisms in life course perspective', *Annual Review of Sociology*, vol 26, pp 667–92.

Sheehy, G. (1974) *Passages: Predictable crisis of adult life*, New York, NY: E.P. Dutton.

Sheets, D., Bradley, D. and Hendricks, J. (eds) (2005) *Enduring questions in gerontology*, New York, NY: Springer.

Smith, D. (1984) 'Textually mediated social organization', *International Social Science Journal*, vol 36, no 1, pp 59–75.

Smith, J. (2000) 'The fourth age: a period of psychological mortality?', Unpublished paper of the Max Planck Institute for Human Development and the Research Group of Psychological Gerontology, Department of Psychiatry, Medical School, Berlin, www.demogr.mpg.de/Papers/workshops/010730_paper01.pdf, accessed 5 April 2003.

Smith, J. and Baltes, P.B. (1993) 'Differential psychological aging: profiles of the old and very old', *Ageing and Society*, vol 13, no 4, pp 551–87.

Spencer, P. (1990) *Anthropology and the riddle of the sphinx: Paradoxes of change in the life course*, London: Routledge.

Spivak, G.C. (1995) 'Subaltern studies: deconstructing historiography', in D. Landry and G. MacLean (eds) *The Spivak reader: Selected works of Gayatri Spivak*, New York, NY: Routledge.

Stokes, R.G. and Maddox, G.L. (1967) 'Some social factors on retirement adaptation', *Journal of Gerontology*, vol 22, no 3, p 329.

Strauss, A.L. and Corbin, J. (1998) *Basics of qualitative research: Grounded theory procedures and techniques* (2nd edn), Thousand Oaks, CA: Sage Publications.

Strawbridge, W.J., Shema, S.J., Balfour, J.L., Higby, H.R. and Kaplan, G.A. (1998) 'Antecedents of frailty over three decades in an older cohort', *Journals of Gerontology Series B*, vol 53, no 1, pp S9–S16.

Sugarman, L. (1986) *Life-span development: Cconcepts, theories and interventions*, New York, NY: Methuen.

Swain, J., French, S., Thomas, C. and Barnes, C. (2004) *Disabling barriers: Enabling environments* (2nd edn), London: Sage Publications.

Szinovacz, M.E. and Davey, A. (2007) 'Changes in adult child caregiver networks', *The Gerontologist*, vol 47, no 3, pp 280–95.

Tennant, M. & Pogson, P. (1995) *Learning and change in the adult years*, San Francisco, CA: Jossey-Bass.

Thomson, D. (1991). *Selfish generations? The ageing of New Zealand's welfare state*, Cambridge: White Horse Press.

Thompson, P. (1992) '"I don't feel old": subjective ageing and the search for meaning in later life', *Ageing & Society*, vol 12, no 1, pp 23–47.

Tornstam, L. (2005) *Gerotranscendence: A developmental theory of positive aging*, New York, NY: Springer.

Torres, S. (2006a) 'Culture, migration, inequality, and periphery in a globalized world: challenges for ethno and anthropogerontology', in J. Baars, D. Dannefer, C. Phillipson and A. Walker (eds) *Aging, globalization, and inequality: The new critical gerontology*, Amityville, NY: Baywood.

Torres, S. (2006b) 'Elderly immigrants in Sweden: otherness under construction', *Journal of Ethnic and Migration Studies*, vol 32, no 8, pp 1341-58.

Townsend, P. (1957) *The family life of old people: An inquiry in East London*, London: Routledge & Kegan Paul.

Townsend, P. (1981) 'The structured dependency of the elderly: a creation of social policy in the twentieth century', *Ageing & Society*, vol 1, no 1, pp 5-28.

Tronto, J.C. (1998) 'An ethic of care', *Generations*, vol 22, no 3, pp 15-20.

Tulle-Winton, E. (1999) 'Growing old and resistance: towards a new cultural economy of old age?', *Ageing & Society*, vol 19, no 3, pp 281-99.

Tulle-Winton, E. (2000) 'Old bodies', in P. Hancock, B. Hughes, E. Jagger, K. Paterson, R. Russell, E. Tulle-Winton and M. Tyler (eds) *The body, culture and society*, Buckingham: Open University Press.

Turner, B. (1989) 'Ageing, status politics and sociological theory', *British Journal of Sociology*, vol 40, no 4, pp 588-606.

Turner, V. (1967) *The forest of symbols: aspects of Ndembu ritual*, Manchester: Manchester University Press.

Turner, V. (1969) *The ritual process: Structure and anti-structure*, London: Routledge & Kegan Paul.

Turner, V. (1987) *The forest symbols*, Ithaca, NY: Cornell University Press.

Twigg, J. (2006) *The body in health and social care*, New York, NY: Palgrave Macmillan.

Twigg, J. (2007) 'Clothing, age and the body: a critical review', *Ageing & Society*, vol 27, no 2, pp 285-305.

Twigg, J. (2010) 'The embodiment of age', Keynote lecture, British Society of Gerontology 39th Annual Conference, 6-8 July 2000, Brunel University, London.

Unger, J. and Seeman, T.E. (1999) 'Successful ageing', in M.B. Goldman and M.C. Hatch (eds), *Women and health*, San Diego, CA: Academic Press, pp 1238-50.

UN (United Nations) (1982) *Report of the world assembly on ageing*, New York, NY: UN.

UN (2002a) *World population ageing, 1950-2050*, Department of Economic and Social Affairs Population Division, New York, NY: UN.

UN (2002b) *Report of the second world assembly on ageing*, New York, NY: UN.

van Gennep, A. (1960 [1909]) *The rites of passage*, Chicago, IL: University of Chicago Press.

Victor, C. (2005) *The social context of ageing*, London: Routledge.

Waite, L.M., Broe, G.A., Creasey, H., Grayson, D. Edelbrock, D. and O'Toole, B. (1996) 'Neurological signs, aging, and the neurodegenerative syndromes', *Archives of Neurology*, vol 53, no 6, pp 498-502.

Walker, A. (1980) 'The social creation of poverty and dependency in old age', *Journal of Social Policy*, vol 9, no 1, pp 49-75.

Walker, A. (1981) 'Towards a political economy of old age', *Ageing & Society*, vol 1, no 1, pp 73-94.

Walker, A. (1982) 'Dependency and old age', *Social Policy and Administration*, vol 16, no 2, pp 115-35.

Walker, A. (2005a) (ed) *Growing older in Europe*, Maidenhead: Open University Press/McGraw Hill.

Walker, A. (2005b) The emergence of age management in Europe, *International Journal of Organisational Behaviour*, vol 10, no 1, pp 685-97.

Walker, A. (2005c) 'Towards an international political economy of ageing', *Ageing & Society*, vol 25, no 6, pp 815-39.

Walker, A. (2006a) 'Re-examining the political economy of aging: understanding the structure/agency tension', in J. Baars, D. Dannefer, C. Phillipson and A. Walker (eds) *Aging, globalization, and inequality: The new critical gerontology*, Amityville, NY: Baywood, pp 59-80.

Walker, A. (2006b) (ed) *Understanding quality of life in old age*, Buckingham: Open University Press.

Walker, A. and Naegele, G. (1999) *The politics of old age in Europe*, Milton Keynes: Open University Press.

Walkerdine, V. (2008) 'Contextualizing debates about psychosocial studies', *Psychoanalysis, Culture & Society*, vol 13, no 4, pp 341-6.

Walkerdine, V., Lucey, H. and Melody, J. (2001) *Growing up girl: Psychosocial explorations of gender and class*, New York, NY: New York University Press.

Warde, A. (2002) 'Setting the scene: changing conceptions of consumption', in S. Miles, A. Anderson and K. Meethan (eds) *The changing consumer: Markets and meaning*, London: Routledge.

Weil, F.D. (1987) 'Cohorts, regimes, and the legitimation of democracy: West Germany since 1945', *American Sociological Review*, vol 52, no 3, pp 308-24.

Wendell, S. (1996) *The rejected body: Feminist philosophical reflections on disability*, New York, NY: Routledge.

White, J. and Tronto, J. (2004) 'Political practices of care: needs and rights', *Ratio Juris*, vol 17, no 4, pp 425-53.

Wiggins, R.D., Higgs, P., Hyde, M. and Blane, D.B. (2004) 'Quality of life in the third age: key predictors of the CASP-19 measure', *Ageing & Society*, vol 24, no 5, pp 693-708.

Wilkinson, S. (1988) 'The role of reflexivity in feminist psychology', *Women's Studies International Forum*, vol 11, no 5, pp 493-502.

Williams, S. J. (1996) 'The vicissitudes of embodiment across the chronic illness trajectory', *Body & Society*, vol 2, no 2, pp 23-47.

Woodward, K. (1991) *Aging and its discontents: Freud and other fictions*, Bloomington, IN: Indiana University Press.

Woodward, K. (1999) *Figuring age: women, bodies, generations*, Bloomington, IN: Indiana University Press.

Woodward, K. (2003) 'Against wisdom: the social politics of anger and aging', *Journal of Aging Studies*, vol 17, pp 55-67.

Wray, S. (2003) 'Women growing older: agency, ethnicity and culture', *Sociology*, vol 37, no 3, pp 511-27.

Young, M. (1988) *The metronomic society: Natural rhythms and human timetables*, London: Thames and Hudson.

Young, M. and Schuller, T. (1991) *Life after work: The arrival of the ageless society*, London: HarperCollins.

Yu, W.K. (2000) *Chinese older people*, Bristol: The Policy Press.

Yuval-Davis, N. (2006) 'Intersectionality and feminist politics', *European Journal of Women's Studies*, vol 13, no 3, pp 193-209.

Index

Note: The following abbreviations have been used: t = table; n = note